ADVENTURES IN UNFASHIONABLE PHILOSOPHY

ADVENTURES

IN

UNFASHIONABLE

PHILOSOPHY

JAMES W. FELT

University of Notre Dame Press

Notre Dame, Indiana

Library of Congress Cataloging-in-Publication Data

Felt, James W., 1926–
    Adventures in unfashionable philosophy / James W. Felt.
        p.   cm.
    Essays in this volume have originally been published.
    Includes bibliographical references and index.
    ISBN-13: 978-0-268-02902-9 (pbk. : alk. paper)
    ISBN-10: 0-268-02902-4 (pbk. : alk. paper)
    1. Metaphysics.   2. Philosophy, Modern.   3. Thomas, Aquinas, Saint,
1225?–1274.   4. Whitehead, Alfred North, 1861–1947.   I. Title.
    BD111.F273   2009
    191—dc22

                                                2009038123

Contents

Preface

(2009)

The following essays unashamedly pursue metaphysics in the classical but now rather unfashionable sense. During my four decades of challenging undergraduate students with philosophic problems, the essays emerged like mushrooms, unpredictably, and even now seem worth reading for those interested in the problems they address. One readily recognizes their resonance with the thought of Thomas Aquinas, Henri Bergson, Alfred North Whitehead, and some of the phenomenologists. In particular the following themes recur: (1) the concern to enrich Thomistic philosophy with more modern ways of thinking (especially essays 2 and 15, which led to two subsequent books); (2) a critique of Whitehead's philosophy (essays 3, 5, and 9); (3) considerations of metaphysical method and its effect on metaphysical conclusions (essays 7, 8, 12, and 16); (4) the relation of possibility to actuality (essays 5, 6, 11, and 13); (5) the relation of time to experience (essays 11, 12, and 16); and (6) epistemological realism (essays 5, 13, and 16).

I did consider arranging the essays topically along the above lines, but in the end found that too cumbersome and artificial, given that those topics tend to overlap one another. If the essays embody an evolution of thought they seemed best left in the order and essentially in the form in which they first appeared, and so you find them here. I have felt free, however, to make minor stylistic improvements and, in a few cases, even to omit inessential passages, including some that I now regret and am loathe to perpetuàte. I preface each with a brief indication of its genesis and aim, its degree of technicality, and whether I would today still stand by the position I then took.

I hereby thank the original publishers, all of whom gave permission to reprint the essays in this volume. I thank the readers of this press for their helpful suggestions, and I thank my teachers, colleagues, and fellow Jesuits for their inspiration and encouragement over these many years. I also owe much to Santa Clara University for its support and its humanistic environment. JWF

Un philosophe digne de ce nom n'a jamais dit qu'une seule chose.

—Henri Bergson,
"L'Intuition Philosophique"

ONE

On Being Yourself

(1968)

This slight essay appeared in America *magazine at a time when "Be yourself!" was a popular slogan. It reflects on what that slogan can mean, and already leans toward a process view of reality as well as toward an affirmation of human personal freedom.*

"Be yourself!" Psychologists urge this upon us. Philosophers stress it. We increasingly recognize that it is profoundly necessary. But just what does it *mean* to "be yourself"?

In a sense this is a large question, and so I want to focus on just one sense in which I think "Be yourself" is often *mis*understood. I attack such a misinterpretation, of course, on the basis of what I believe to be an essential ingredient in what it does mean to "be yourself."

If there is anything we do with relish and at almost every opportunity it is make *things* out of *events*. When there is flashing we make a thing out of it and call it "lightning." When we get a shock we say there is "electricity" in the wire. When everything has been shaking

Originally published as "How To Be Yourself," *America*, May 25, 1968, page 705. Reprinted with permission of America Press, Inc. All rights reserved.

we say, "That was an earthquake," just as we might, in another context, say, "That was an elephant." And this is natural for us, because things are not only easier to think about than events, they are also easier to talk about. Both the language and the logic we inherit from the Greeks put a premium on the fixed, on the changeless, on *things*.

And so both psychotherapists and their patients spontaneously talk of "discarding masks," of "peeling off layers," of "uncovering the real self," as one would uncover the body by disrobing it. The question is, what can this "real self" signify?

When I "discard a false self" I am obviously not throwing away some *thing* as I would a gum wrapper: I am ceasing to live my life in an unauthentic way. What right, then, do I have to suppose that there is a "true self," waiting to be found under these "masks," as I would expect to find my foot if I took off my sock? But suppose that there is such a "myself" that I am to "be." Suppose, in other words, to "be yourself" means to "live up to your true self (which is already latent within you)." Then what is the nature of that self? The unspoken assumption seems to be that this "true self" was given from eternity or at least from conception, that it has a definite character, that it is just waiting to be filled out, as the acorn is waiting to turn into the oak. My problem in this case is simply to discover, to uncover, my "true self" so that I can live up to it.

Such a view is not far from the Greek idea of fate. We find something like this, I think, in Hermann Hesse's famous novel *Demian*. Its appeal to youth surely lies in its "Be yourself" theme. Hesse himself places on the title page of his work the following lines from its text: "I wanted only to live in accord with the promptings which came from my true self. Why was that so very difficult?"

But at the same time this true self of Hesse's is the self of fate:

> At this point a sharp realization burned within me: each man has his "function" but none which he can choose himself, define, or perform as he pleases. . . . An enlightened man had but one duty—to seek the way to himself. . . . He might end up as poet or madman, as prophet or criminal—that was not his affair, ultimately it was of no concern. His task was to discover his own destiny—not an arbitrary one—and live it out wholly and resolutely within himself.[1]

The ideal that Hesse holds up for us is the man who "seeks nothing but his own fate," the man who "only seeks his destiny."

But if, on the contrary, "Be yourself" means simply "Live authentically," then what sort of self is the object of this exhortation? There is just plain old me, the product of all my past experiences, my physical and mental limitations, above all of my past decisions. But this me is never settled nor is it prefabricated. It is always on the way, always in the process of self-creation. At every moment I am creating the me that I choose to be: there is nothing fated here. Whatever my limitations, whatever my past, I hold this me in my hands at every moment, to fashion as I will. Bergson claims we have an immediate experience, if we would only recognize it, "of being creators of our intentions, of our decisions, of our acts, and by that, of our habits, our characters, ourselves."[2] To be myself, then, does not amount to uncovering the sort of me that I was born or fated to be. It means discovering my own true freedom to fashion myself as I can and as I will.

In that sense psychotherapy may often leave off where it should begin. To discover *how* I am the product of my past only fills in the details of the obvious generalization that of course I *am* the product of my past. What I need at this point is to realize that, notwithstanding these limitations of the past, to learn to be myself means precisely to discover that I am in fact free to create my ever-emerging self on my own and in my own way.

If, then, I understand "Be yourself" to mean, "Uncover and live up to that destined self latent within you," I either chain myself to whatever image I evoke of this self, or else I abandon all responsibility for my actions on the grounds that what I do spontaneously lives up automatically to the demands of this hidden true self. But if I am skeptical of the existence of such a prefabricated self, if I take "Be yourself" to mean "Live authentically, according to values as you yourself grasp them," then I am thrown onto my own responsibility about my life. My fate then consists precisely in the formation of that self that I myself create with every new decision of my freedom. It is I who at every moment decide what sort of person I shall be, and this is my human dignity. To be myself is to be free.

TWO

Invitation to a Philosophic Revolution

(1971)

This essay appeared in The New Scholasticism *and was written in the flush of early enthusiasm for Whitehead's "process philosophy." The essay in fact influenced several other more traditional philosophers to take a harder look at Whitehead's philosophy. I believe now, however, that whatever its merits, the essay is simplistic in its criticism of traditional thinking, especially that of St. Thomas Aquinas. It is, I think, too much influenced by Charles Hartshorne's remarkable book,* The Divine Relativity: A Social Conception of God.[1] *But whatever the flaws of that book, or still more of this essay, Hartshorne's powerful challenge to traditional scholastic thinking had to be taken seriously, with a consequent enriching of Thomistic thought itself. In the essay I invite fellow philosophers to attempt in their own way to meld what seem to be the better aspects of the thought of both Aquinas and Whitehead and thus to form a new and more contemporary metaphysical view. Though it was later always on my mind, I myself only began trying to respond to that implausible challenge in the year 2000 with*

Originally published as "Invitation to a Philosophic Revolution," *The New Scholasticism* 45, no. 1 (1971): 87–109. Reprinted with permission.

essay 15 in this volume and with two books, Coming To
Be: Toward a Thomistic-Whiteheadian Metaphysics
of Becoming *(2001) and* Aims: A Brief Metaphysics for
Today *(2007). I would today not write this essay, since I am
now sensible of its faults. Yet for all its simplemindedness
and exaggeration it does point to problems to be solved, so
that the basic invitation still stands. The essay assumes
some familiarity with scholastic philosophy and is only
mildly technical.*

---

*—The progress of philosophy does not primarily involve reactions of agreement
or dissent. It essentially consists in the enlargement of thought, whereby contra-
dictions and agreements are transformed into partial aspects of wider points of
view.*

—Alfred North Whitehead[2]

Just two small clouds, Lord Kelvin noted, marred the skies of Newto-
nian physics in 1900: the resistance of "black-body" radiation to
analysis, and the unexpected negative result of the Michelson-Morley
ether detection experiments.[3] These clouds, the first portents of quantum and relativity physics, were to grow into a storm that would over-
whelm classical physics and effect the greatest scientific revolution
since Galileo and Newton.

It can hardly be doubted that this conceptual revolution constituted scientific progress. Yet it proves surprisingly difficult to specify
exactly wherein scientific progress consists. Perhaps it is even harder to
define progress in philosophy. But since, as I believe, progress in science is analogous to that in philosophy, let us initially examine the
notion of progress in science. Afterwards we can draw a parallel for
philosophy, then assess in that light some aspects of the current philosophic situation. What I shall propose is that in philosophy we are at
present in a revolutionary situation.

1. SCIENTIFIC REVOLUTIONS

If we accept the quantum and relativistic revolutions as an advance, we must recognize that progress in physics consists not so much in the solution of ordinary problems within the currently accepted conceptual framework as in the transformation to a new framework better capable of interpreting scientific experience. Transition to this new framework—this new "paradigm," to use Kuhn's terminology[4]—is an advance because, let us tentatively say, it somehow makes sense out of more scientific experience than did the old.

Such a shift of scientific paradigms takes place in much the same way as a political revolution (Kuhn, chap. 9). It begins with increasing dissatisfaction over crucial problems arising within the system and with the growing realization that within that system these problems are not only intolerable but also unsolvable. The old political system is then replaced by a different one thought to be capable of coping with these problems. Similarly, some scientific problems, instead of yielding to the conventional methods of solution, gradually take the shape of genuine anomalies incapable of solution by the hitherto successful paradigm. The paradigm will not, however, be abandoned until the appearance of an alternative conceptual scheme equally capable of solving the old conventional problems and of resolving the new anomalies.

Within a single political or scientific structure there is "progress," it is true, insofar as an increasing number of problems are solved within that structure. But the sense of "progress" that most concerns us involves the shift from one system to another, as with the adoption of the Athenian or the American Constitutions, or the redefinition of physical problems in quantum and relativistic terms. Kuhn has convincingly shown that these shifts of paradigm preclude viewing scientific progress as a linear development. Science is not a wall to which each new theory adds its own row of bricks. Rather, under a new paradigm the whole body of scientific facts and principles undergoes a radical transformation. Some of the old problems simply cease to be problems, as when Aristotle's problem of accounting for uniform motion was dissolved by Galileo's and Newton's substitution of the problem of accounting for acceleration; some new problems arise; all are subtly transformed. The Aristotelian's problem of accounting for the behavior of a rock swinging on a string is just not the same problem as that of the Galilean looking at the same physical situation. Similarly, mass and distance are differently understood in relativistic physics than they were before.

What then is the logical relationship of a new paradigm to the old? Or are there a variety of possible relationships? And how does the shift to a new paradigm constitute progress?

The possible relationships between the old and the new paradigms appear to be the following: (1) simple replacement of one paradigm by the other; (2) conventionality, the adoption of an alternative but equivalent description; (3) some kind of enlargement of horizon. Clearly only the last is progressive, since the second is only a matter of redefinition, and the first could be called progress only by reference to a larger background by which the two paradigms are systematically related to one another—in other words by the third possibility, enlargement of horizon.

. . . One can think, for instance, of the complementarity of the Aristotelian and Augustinian-Platonic linguistic contexts within the language of Thomas Aquinas. Their synthesis into the language of Thomas can even be regarded as the outcome of a kind of Hegelian dialectic.

We are still left with the question why such a synthesis constitutes progress. Of course one cannot ignore the historical and social elements: that the broad community of physicists has accepted a new paradigm is surely significant. But they have not accepted it simply because it solves a larger number of scientific problems, since the problems themselves are transformed with the shift of paradigm. And if one points out, truly enough, that the community of scientists finds the new paradigm more intellectually satisfying than the old, one has still to say *why* it is more satisfying. The danger is that we shall reduce the notion of "progress" to a tautological expression for whatever shifts of paradigm historically eventuate.

Without pretending to resolve this complex and difficult problem I must agree with that vast majority of scientists who, as I believe, are persuaded that by the adoption of a new paradigm they are in some way getting closer to an understanding of Nature itself. (This as distinguished from a pure conventionalism in which scientific paradigms are merely inference-tickets, instructions leading from one set of data to another.) Yet scientists have long since abandoned the idea that scientific theories depict the structure of the real in the direct sort of way that a blueprint reveals the structure of a house. The abstractions of the conceptual scheme help us understand Nature only in an indirect way. Furthermore, there is doubtless a strong element of subjectivity even in the communal decision of scientists to adopt a new paradigm, and this reliance on a kind of scientific instinct for progress is inevitable in principle: the only non-subjective norm by which two theories could be compared would be that ultimate paradigm which is the goal, not the possession, of science at any given time. Speaking roughly, then, scientific progress chiefly consists in improving our understanding of Nature by transformation to wider conceptual schemes or paradigms, even though these paradigms never exactly depict for us the structure of the real and are chosen partly in virtue of the subjective but communal decision of scientists.

2. PHILOSOPHIC REVOLUTIONS

I propose that progress in philosophy, much like that in science, consists not so much in the solution of ordinary problems arising within a particular metaphysics as in making increasing sense out of our total experience through the framing of wider and more effective conceptual frameworks, with an ensuing enlargement of viewpoint.[5]

If this thesis appears uncontroversial, the view of metaphysics that it implies is not widely accepted, judging at least by philosophic practice. For a metaphysics, like a scientific paradigm, is an abstractive scheme that sheds light on experience but is not to be mistaken for an exact dissection of that experience. Yet we naturally tend to commit what Whitehead called the Fallacy of Misplaced Concreteness, to mistake the abstract for the concrete. It is easy, at least unconsciously, to get to regard such metaphysical abstractions as substance, accident, matter, form, cogitative sense, imagination, or will as if they consti-

tuted the real in much the same way that bread, butter, and jelly constitute a sandwich.[6] But I shall rather assume with Whitehead that a
metaphysics is not so much a direct dissection of the real as a way of
understanding it. It attempts, it is true, to illuminate experience in
terms of its own deepest underlying principles. But these principles as
universalized are abstractions, and in any case we never attain to a clear
or comprehensive understanding of them. No metaphysics can be
regarded as final. Experience always bursts the conceptual nets we lay
for it, and every metaphysics appeals to a leap of imaginative insight
transcending it.[7]

I suggest therefore that important progress in philosophy takes
place in much the same way as it does in science. The metaphysical
scheme gradually displays itself as powerless to render intelligible certain elements in experience.[8] As the explication of these facts of experience appears increasingly impossible, it may happen—I do not here
inquire how—that a new outlook suggests itself, a new conceptual
framework able to deal with these problems in a more satisfactory manner. From this new point of view the difficulties become not merely
problems unsolved by the old system but counterinstances that tell
against it. The old system is not thereby refuted, logically speaking,
but is simply abandoned in favor of the new metaphysics, which yields
a more intelligible account of experience. Furthermore the accompanying transformation of thought enlarges the philosopher's outlook by
emphasizing the final importance of living experience itself, the explication of which is the goal of any metaphysics.

What is needed, then, for philosophic progress is constant reference to the fullness of concrete experience, coupled with a search for
newer and better ways of understanding it. Otherwise we become
bewitched by the inevitable shortcomings of our own conceptual formulae.[9] A value is realized, therefore, by the very discordance of con-
flicting philosophic schemes. It jogs us out of stereotyped ways of
thinking and helps us keep in mind the inevitable limitations of any
metaphysics. Whitehead writes:

> We cannot produce that final adjustment of well-defined gener-
> alities which constitute a complete metaphysics. But we can

produce a variety of partial systems of limited generality. The concordance of ideas within any one such system shows the scope and virility of the basic notions of that scheme of thought. Also the discordance of system with system, and success of each system as a partial mode of illumination, warns us of the limitations within which our intuitions are hedged. These undiscovered limitations are the topics for philosophic research.[10]

When we examine the present situation in philosophy we are struck by a certain polar discordance between the various schools of thought: the methodic discordance between analysis and phenomenology, or the discordance of ontic assertions between substance and process philosophies, to name only two. Philosophers, it seems, find themselves in a position similar to that of physicists at the beginning of the quantum mechanical revolution One inevitably wonders whether these divergent philosophic views might not be found complementary rather than antithetical within some wider viewpoint. The discovery and adoption of such a viewpoint would amount to a philosophic revolution.

It is not feasible within the space of this essay to examine carefully more than one potential case of complementarity. I propose to consider the discordance of interpretation between modern Thomism and the metaphysics of Alfred North Whitehead. The particular anomalies within Thomism that, as I think, most unfavorably contrast with a Whiteheadian viewpoint concern the philosophic description of our relationship with God. I shall not contend that Whitehead's philosophy, as it stands, constitutes that wider viewpoint of which we are in search, since from the Christian standpoint Whitehead's system proves, in my opinion, inadequate. Both Thomas and Whitehead say much that rings true, and I do not see how their viewpoints can be reconciled as they now stand. I suggest therefore that we are in need of a wider viewpoint under which they may be found mutually complementary. This is the philosophic revolution to which this essay is an invitation.

The first step toward such a revolution is dissatisfaction with the present state of affairs, and since I take it that many readers of this journal [*The New Scholasticism*] are in some sense Thomists, I wish to examine some of those problems within Thomism that, in my opinion, are genuine anomalies or counterinstances against it.[11]

3. ANOMALIES WITHIN THOMISM

God *knows* me with perfect knowledge. No one else knows me with such intimacy. But all our experience attests that knowledge relates the knower to the known: the more intimate the knowledge, the closer the relationship. The sea urchin relates itself to the sea washing over it more closely than does the rock to which it clings. The deer, taut in listening and scenting, relates itself even more intimately to surrounding nature. Man, whose mind reaches past the stars, thereby relates himself in a superior way to the whole universe. Knowledge, simply speaking, makes a difference to the knower; to the extent that I know, I relate myself to that which I know, and it is just this self-relation that constitutes my superiority to the stone that has no comparable knowledge. One would suppose, therefore—and revelation apparently confirms this—that by the perfection of His knowledge God would relate himself most perfectly and intimately to His creation.

Shall we not say the same with regard to *love*? What more evident than that love relates the lover to the beloved? It was Romeo, not the balcony, who was intimately self-related to Juliet. The balcony was related little because it loved not at all, neither did it understand. Yet if there is any message that stands out clearly in revelation it is the depth of God's love for us. But since knowledge and love, as we experience them, are constitutive of knower and lover, should we not expect that the utter perfection of God's love would relate Him to us most completely? The quasi-dependence that this relationship entails would in fact be the hallmark of love's self-giving and superiority. Love is love precisely insofar as it gives itself away.

Another aspect of God's revelation of Himself is his concern for us. He seriously wills the salvation of all men and women. He was so concerned about our salvation that He accomplished the Incarnation and Redemption.[12] What more striking depictions of this concern than the parables of the lost sheep and of the prodigal son? What can these mean if not that our welfare *makes a difference to God*? If He is truly concerned about us, if He has deliberately become our friend and companion as well as our lord, must He not share our happiness and our sorrows? "Compassion" sums it up in a single word. "Jesus wept" (John 11:36).

Now traditional Thomism cannot, I submit, give a satisfactory philosophic account of these facts. It is instead compelled in effect to deny them philosophically while admitting them theologically. For according to the usual interpretation God cannot be related to creatures in any way that makes a difference to God.[13] Thus, God can be related only by a relation of reason to His creatures, and that without any foundation in God for that relation.[14] For if God were related to creatures by a "real" relation, He would, as so related, not be identical with God as not so related. This would imply at the very least that God the Creator is intrinsically distinct from God apart from, or "antecedent" to, His free decision to create. Furthermore, such a real relationship would, in the view of Thomas, set up a certain dependence of God upon the creature, since the creature is essential to the existence of the relation.

But such a relation of God to creatures is impossible, according to Thomas, for the following correlative reasons: it would violate the traditional notion of God's perfection and immutability; it also would amount to denying that God is pure actuality, with no limitation of potentiality. God's perfection, as usually understood, entails His immutability, and both are entailed by His nature as pure act. Thus God can in no way be dependent upon creatures; in no way can God change.

How then are we to understand the facts of revelation sketched above? First, Thomas acknowledges that knowledge relates the knower to the known with a real relation (*Summa Theol.*, I, 13, 7), and does so hierarchically: the fuller the knowledge, the closer the relationship. The fuller, that is, until we get to God whose knowledge is perfect. At this point Thomas is compelled to deny any such relationship to God.[15] The same astonishing conclusion follows with respect to God's infinite love. It alone, of all loves, fails to relate the lover to the beloved.

A similar conclusion must evidently be reached with regard to God's concern for His creatures. This concern cannot be such as to involve the least change or dependence in God, regardless of the fate of the creature. Whether we rejoice or sorrow, are saved or are damned, *it must literally be all the same to God*. In that case it is difficult to understand what is left of "concern."[16]

. . .

Possibly the most telling instance of the failure of the traditional scholastic viewpoint concerns God's compassion for His creatures. Here is how St. Anselm, for instance, addresses God:

> But how art thou compassionate, and, at the same time, passionless? For, if thou art passionless, thou dost not feel sympathy, and if thou dost not feel sympathy, thy heart is not wretched from sympathy for the wretched; but this it is to be compassionate . . . how, then, art thou compassionate and not compassionate, O Lord, unless because thou art compassionate in terms of our experience, and not compassionate in terms of thy being. Truly, thou art so in terms of our experience, but thou art not so in terms of thine own. For, when thou beholdest us in our wretchedness, we experience the effect of compassion, but thou dost not experience the feeling. Therefore, thou art both compassionate, because thou dost save the wretched, and spare those who sin against thee; and not compassionate, because thou art affected by no sympathy for wretchedness.[17]

To this, Hartshorne replies:

> Anselm's God can give us everything, everything except the right to believe that there is one who, with infinitely subtle and appropriate sensitivity, rejoices in all our joys and sorrows in all our sorrows. But this benefit which Anselm will not allow God to bestow upon us is the supreme benefit which God and only God could give us. . . . To say, "all the effects of compassion, only not the compassion itself," is to mock us.[18]

There is another crucial anomaly to which I would draw your attention. Reverting to the question of God's knowledge of creatures, we note that according to the traditional Thomistic doctrine God does not know creatures in themselves but only in Himself.[19] The key to the sense of this distinction is that God, unlike creatures, must in His knowing in no way depend upon or be conditioned by what He knows. Thus, it is held, God does not know creatures because they are present to Him in their finite existence; rather, they exist because He knows them. He recognizes within His own essence all the possibilities for existence; and He also, by the same act, is aware of His own creative decrees. This is conjectured since God's creative participation of existence, His knowing, and His willing, are all thought identical with His own existing. God thus knows actual, contingent events, as distinguished from pure possibles, entirely by being aware of His own nature, including His creative decisions.

This solution, I am persuaded, is ingenious, systematically logical, and hard to believe. One is reminded of Koko's explanation to the Mikado of why he signed Nanki-Poo's death certificate even though Nanki-Poo had not in fact been executed. For it was the Mikado's command that someone be executed, and since when the Mikado gives an order it is as good as done, why not say so? "Nothing," said the Mikado, "could possibly be more satisfactory" than this explanation. Yet what Thomas seems to offer me is the assurance that God does not know this contingent "me" in my factual existence, but only "me" as a possibility that He has decreed should be fulfilled. George Washington never really slept here; he just liked the blueprints and ordered the house built.[20]

Doubtless Thomas is correct as usual in deducing this conclusion from his metaphysical premises. Rutherford was right, too, in deducing from Thomson's atomic model a certain behavior of alpha particles. When the particles failed to behave as expected, Rutherford revised the model. Perhaps it is time to revise our traditional metaphysics.

Consider one final peculiarity of Thomas' theory. How on this account are we to reconcile the contingency of creatures with the necessity and immutability of God? It is traditionally maintained that although God was free to create or not to create, His nature as Creator-God is no different than if He had chosen not to create; the only difference is to be found in the creation itself. Also, God's *knowledge* of His creation is held to be similarly immutable and therefore absolute. Thus, God has immutably known "from all eternity" that He would create. Similarly, He has eternally known all contingent events that are to take place in time, but without being in any way conditioned by this knowledge.

But there is this difficulty. Knowledge of a fact cannot be the same as knowledge of its contradictory. How can God-knowing-His-will-to-create be identical with God-knowing-His-will-*not*-to-create? It is unreasonable to maintain that Creator-God could be intrinsically identical

with non-Creator-God. How then can it be held both that God was free
in His eternal decision to create, and that His nature is in every respect
absolute and immutable?[21]

. . .

What finally are we to conclude? We may recall Bergson's remark
about the power of negation proper to the dominating intuition of a
philosophy. "Faced," he says, "with currently-accepted ideas, theses
which seemed evident, affirmations which had up to that time passed
as scientific, it whispers into the philosopher's ear the word: *Impossible!*"[22] Impossible, it would seem, that the traditional Thomistic
account is adequate to the facts—facts it should explain, not explain
away. Here we apparently have genuine anomalies, crucial issues that
traditional Thomism must deny rather than illuminate. We may particularly notice that the principles underlying the philosophic system
responsible for such conclusions are essentially Greek and do not form
a privileged matrix for interpreting the Judaeo-Christian revelation.
The Greek notion of perfection involved the idea of absolute immutability, of the eternal changelessness of a necessary being. But the
Hebrew saw God not as immutable but as steadfast. And if the Greek
notions of act and potency stand in the way of admitting that God
relates Himself to us in knowledge, love, and compassion, then should
we not look for more adequate metaphysical principles? Is it not time
for a metaphysical revolution?

4. THE WHITEHEADIAN ALTERNATIVE

I do not claim, as I have said, that Whitehead's philosophy satisfactorily supersedes Thomism, since it has, as I believe, deficiencies of its
own. It can, however, philosophically interpret the above-mentioned
facts of revelation in a more satisfying way. But for the two systems to
appear as potentially complementary within some larger viewpoint
they must both be seen as enjoying a certain validity of outlook. Though
we cannot here review Whitehead's complex metaphysics, we can remove some of the psychological obstacles that may stand in the way of

recognizing its advantages.[23] We can also note some of the ways in which Whitehead's process philosophy more easily seems to handle the problems discussed above.

What, first of all, may we reasonably expect from a metaphysics? That it should analyze and illuminate *experience*. We would expect it, then, to describe God only insofar as He enters into our experience, not as He is in Himself. Metaphysics therefore cannot describe God as totally absolute since this would amount to describing Him as totally other, totally outside human experience.

Thomas himself granted that one cannot prove by reason alone that the universe had a beginning in time. Consequently one would not expect that a metaphysics founded on reason alone would provide for a creation, as it is usually understood. For whatever "creation" may mean in the Christian context, it seems necessarily to involve reference to God as He is in Himself, "antecedent to," or at any rate apart from, His creative act or His creature. One cannot expect that, apart from revelation, a metaphysics would describe a being which in itself stands absolute with no relationship to anything else.

On the other hand, a metaphysics should not *preclude* integration with divine revelation, even if this is done by way of enlargement of the scope of that metaphysics. For the Thomist may fairly point out that divine revelation is included within the experience that the Christian metaphysician seeks to illuminate. St. Thomas thought he was doing just that when he put so much weight on the Scriptural statement, "*Ego sum, qui sum*." The Christian, then, may object that Whitehead's "God" does not enter freely into his relationship with other entities.[24] Neither is there in Whitehead's system adequate provision for personal immortality, so that Whitehead's description of the "kingdom of heaven" is far from the Christian vision of the final fulfillment in Christ. Is, then, Whitehead's metaphysics foreclosed as a living option for the convinced Christian?

What Whitehead attempted to describe is how the world given in our ordinary experience is intelligible. As a result of this analysis, based on his best insights into the general principles underlying experience, Whitehead found that at every turn he had to acknowledge the presence and efficacy of a unique, infinite entity, to whom he gave the name "God." I do not see why his whole system could not be regarded as an analysis of the metaphysical implications of the Judaeo-Christian God's creative decree, for what Whitehead's metaphysics attempts to describe is the structure of the given world, including the relations that obtain among all actual entities, infinite as well as finite. From the Christian point of view, in other words, Whiteheadian philosophy can be regarded as describing the factual embodiment of God's creative decision. I think Whitehead's system is entirely neutral with regard to a description of God apart from His involvement with the world as Creator.

So much by way of forestalling the Christian philosopher's possible objections against giving serious consideration to Whitehead's philosophy in the first place. Let us now turn back to the anomalies discussed earlier. In most of these cases a supposed lack of relationship of God to creatures led to conclusions antithetical to the facts of revelation: neither God's knowledge nor His love could be admitted to relate Him to creatures with a "real" relation (roughly, a relation that makes a difference to God); God is neither concerned about us with a personal concern, nor is He interiorly compassionate. Furthermore, the knowledge He has of us appears to be more a knowledge of His *idea* of us. In all these cases the conclusions are reached fundamentally on the grounds that God is pure act with no potentiality, but also through consideration of God's infinite perfection by reason of which, it is held, He cannot acquire anything or change in any way. Similarly, God is regarded as in Himself absolute and in no way contingent—hence the problem of reconciling the absoluteness of God's knowledge with the contingency of events. Finally, tacit assumptions about God's omnipotence grounded Thomas's acceptance of divine reprobation.

I wish for the moment to postpone consideration of the relation of the act-potency doctrine to the above conclusions. Let us consider instead some general notions about perfection, relativity, immutability, and omnipotence.

Because we inherit our notion of perfection largely from the Greeks, and because of the scholastic tradition, we are accustomed to regard God as "perfect" in the sense that He could not possibly acquire any advantage He did not have before, nor realize any enhancement of value. Now if this be true it is at once apparent that we cannot really "do anything for God"; our service is only a service to ourselves. Does it not seem unfortunate that God is the one person to whom we are in principle unable to bring a gift, even the gift of our own love? A gift is scarcely a gift unless it has value for the one receiving it. But why, after all, should we cling to this artificial notion of perfection in the teeth of our instincts and of God's self-revelation? For again we are contradicting our clear insights. No lover in human experience, however altruistic and unselfish his love, is indifferent to a return of that love. We realize this profoundly, yet find ourselves forced by our traditional metaphysics to say that God is—let us admit it—indifferent to our return of love; otherwise our love, which only we can give, would be of some value to God! It is not our insights that are at fault here but our inherited notions about God's perfection.

"Let us define perfection," says Hartshorne, "as an excellence such that rivalry or superiority on the part of other individuals is impossible, but self-superiority is not impossible. Or again, let us say that the perfect is the 'self-surpassing surpasser of all'" (DR 20). God's perfection would still be unique to God; nor would God at any moment fall short of the greatest perfection realizable by Him in the situation, the "situation" being His interrelatedness with His creation at that moment. Admittedly this places us in a process framework in which God Himself is in certain respects (not, it should be noticed, in *every* respect)[25] in a self-creative process, in conjunction with the universe, by reason of which He enjoys the values being realized throughout it.[26] Whatever of value that has taken place in the world is enjoyed by God, and in such a way as to preserve that value everlastingly in its freshness; what is evil or valueless is dismissed into oblivion.

What can be said about God as relative or absolute? There is no question here of suggesting that God is in every respect relative; on the contrary, both Whitehead and Hartshorne maintain that there are two aspects to God, one of which is indeed absolute and independent of relationship to other entities. But must we say that God is in no respect relative?

If so we are again contradicting the direct deliverances of our experience. Thomas himself allows that the pillar is on the right of the animal because of the animal's relation to the pillar, not because the pillar is related to the animal (*Summa Theol,* I, 13, 7). Furthermore, as Hartshorne points out, it is precisely the animal's superiority to the pillar that renders the animal relative (DR 7). Now as was illustrated earlier, in our experience, the greater the love and the knowledge, the closer the relationship to that which is known and loved. Can we abruptly deny this of the highest love and the highest knowledge, that of God Himself?[27] If we do, we must seriously ask ourselves whether we are using language responsibly. Can *love-without-relation* be *love* at all? If, as far as we can discover, self-relatedness is essential to love, then by what right do we use the same word to designate a complete lack of self-relatedness? Should we not simply confess that we cannot philosophically allow that God loves us?

Again, what is our hesitation to posit a self-relatedness of God through love and knowledge if the world we are describing is, as we hold, precisely the working out of God's free creative decision? Is it not to be expected that we would then be describing a relationship into which God has freely placed Himself as Creator?

Finally, would not a complete lack of relativity on God's part deprive me of my own creative freedom as an agent? For if I do not by my own creative decisions decide the content of God's knowledge of me (for instance, that I decide to sit rather than stand)—thereby rendering God in some way relative, at least in His know edge—then they are not *my* decisions but parts of a scenario pre-written in and by God.

From what has been said it is also clear that God cannot be thought to be immutable in every respect, nor would there be any advantage in such a supposition. Aristotle's First Mover was immutable in his ceaseless contemplation of himself—not, it should be noted, of the world of other beings. The living God, on the other hand, who knows the free creative decisions of His creatures and who is personally concerned for them, cannot be in every respect immutable precisely because of His perfection as a personal being.

What, finally, of divine omnipotence? Are we to suppose with Thomas that God's omnipotence is to be defined as the power to do everything that can be done absolutely (*Summa Theol.,* I, 25, 3)? This seems difficult to maintain, since clearly God cannot make up my mind for me or even walk down the street for me. In any case, why should we suppose that God's providence requires that He be capable of arranging all events? For then we immediately encounter unsolvable problems concerning the existence of evil in the world. Is it not enough to say simply that God's power is adequate and unique? It consists especially in this, that God alone is intimately present to all other entities, and in such a way as always to be luring them to the best possible enhancement of value in their particular situation. Whitehead's criticism of some of the traditional philosophic doctrine is trenchant:

> When the Western world accepted Christianity, Caesar conquered; and the received text of Western theology was edited by his lawyers. The code of Justinian and the theology of Justinian are two volumes expressing one movement of the human spirit. The brief Galilean vision of humility flickered throughout the ages, uncertainly. In the official formulation of religion it has assumed the trivial form of the mere attribution to the Jews that they cherished a misconception about their Messiah. But the deeper idolatry, of the fashioning of God in the image of the Egyptian, Persian, and Roman imperial rulers, was retained. The Church gave unto God the attributes which belonged exclusively to Caesar.[28]

Over against this view Whitehead posits one more consonant, as he believes, with the true spirit of Christianity. There is, he says, a strain in the Galilean origin of Christianity that "does not emphasize the ruling Caesar, or the ruthless moralist, or the unmoved mover. It dwells upon the tender elements in the world, which slowly and in quietness operate by love; and it finds purpose in the present immediacy of a kingdom not of this world" (PR 343). In virtue of his metaphysics Whitehead is able to describe a God much more like the God of revelation, I think, than the God of Pure Act described by Thomas. Whitehead describes a God concerned with the world in such a way as to be constantly responding to each novel situation. God feels and values each succeeding phase of the growth of the universe according to the eternal (and absolute) hierarchy of values for which He alone is responsible. For each actual entity He envisions and feels the value of the best possible issue from its given situation. Since God, precisely with this vision and these feelings, enters into the constitution of the entity in question, He lures it by this presence to greater good. In this notion of providence God invites us to what is good; He does not nor is He able to coerce us.[29]

Here is how Whitehead describes this response of God to the world:

> The perfected actuality passes back into the temporal world, and qualifies this world so that each temporal actuality includes it as an immediate fact of relevant experience. For the kingdom of heaven is with us today. The action of [this] . . . phase is the love of God for the world. It is the particular providence for particular occasions. What is done in the world is transformed into a reality in heaven, and the reality in heaven passes back into the world. By reason of this reciprocal relation, the love in the world passes into the love in heaven, and floods back again into the world. In this sense, God is the great companion—the fellow-sufferer who understands (PR 351).

5. CONCLUSION

However plausible the above considerations may be, we must face at last the fundamental reason underlying Thomas's conclusions on the above issues: his description of God as Pure Act. Here we are thrown back onto a central thesis of this essay: that metaphysical conceptions are not direct revelations of the structure of the real. If then it is impossible to reconcile necessary conclusions of Thomas's system with known facts of experience, let us have the courage to replace that system with another more consonant with experience. This is just what we might expect Thomas himself to do if he were with us today.

It is high time for a philosophic revolution among new scholastics. If Whitehead's philosophy cannot without alteration be fitted into a Christian setting, let us develop a wider viewpoint under which the fruitful conceptualizations of both Thomas and Whitehead may be found complementary rather than antithetical. This philosophic revolution is an adventure of ideas to which I think the present situation challenges all of us.

THREE

The Temporality of Divine Freedom

(1974)

This essay was inspired by a need to complement a major essay by Lewis S. Ford, "The Non-Temporality of Whitehead's God."[1] Without disagreeing with anything Ford wrote, I was convinced that there was another side of the story that must be worked out if the Whiteheadian viewpoint is to square with revelation and our deepest religious convictions. Ford had admirably described the sense in which, in the Whiteheadian framework, God can be said to be nontemporal. What seemed missing was the sense in which, granted the above, God's influence in the world can be thought of as freely tailored to God's love for individual, particular entities rather than simply preprogrammed by his nontemporal, universal matrix of value. The essay, therefore, is written entirely within the Whiteheadian scheme of metaphysics and is necessarily quite technical. Readers unacquainted with the intricacies of that metaphysics may wish to pass to the next essay.

Originally published as "The Temporality of Divine Freedom," *Process Studies* 4, no. 4 (1974): 252–62. Reprinted with permission.

—I will love them freely, for my anger has turned from them.

—Hosea 14:4

A chief attraction of process philosophy for Christian thinkers has been its ability to formulate in a new way the relationship of God to the world. By contrast, traditional philosophy tends to emasculate biblical texts like the above, construing them as mere anthropomorphisms, since obviously God cannot be described in emotional and temporal terms—or so the doctrine goes, despite massive evidence of religious experience to the contrary.

Even in process philosophy, however, skies are not all blue when it comes to talking about God. There is a deep cleavage between those who agree with Whitehead in describing God as a single actual entity, nontemporal in his primordial nature and everlasting in his consequent nature (the "entitative" view), and those who prefer with Charles Hartshorne to regard God as a personally ordered temporal society of successive occasions (the "societal" view). Though I shall speak in terms of the entitative view, toward which I incline, what I have to say has nothing to do with debating the above issue since it will apply equally well to the societal view. I wish rather to call attention to a peculiar aspect of one of the arguments used to support the latter view, since I think it betrays an inadequacy in all current Whiteheadian views that has not been appreciated.

Delwin Brown, supporting the societal view, writes: "On the entitative view, God is free but once (even if, as we shall consider later, 'once' is to be construed in some unique nontemporal sense). This single evaluative adjustment of possibility permanently fixes the character of God's consequent commerce with the world."[2] He then proceeds to argue that God's primordial nature, thus understood, is like a computer that once-for-all programs all God's decisions in history. It follows that even in his freedom God cannot be faithful, since "faithfulness" entails adhering freely through time to one's previous commitment, and on this view God is "free but once," not temporally free.

Lewis S. Ford reviews the same general objection even more sharply:

If God acts solely in terms of his primordial nature, is not everything simply cut and dried, following inexorably from the implications of that conceptual unity? This is an ancient problem:
how does Leibniz' God, programmed to choose the best of all
possible worlds, or even Aquinas' God, whose will is assimilated
to his reason, differ from a computer? ("Non-Temporality," 355)

Ford retorts, however, that the objection fails to notice that God's
primordial decision was not made at some time in the dim, dark past.
Rather, it is not made in time at all. It is nontemporal, hence unrepeat-
able, but emerges in time insofar as it gradually acquires its definition
with respect to the world. What we find in the temporal world is a bur-
geoning of God's timeless free decision as seen from our temporal perspective. Only if God's primordial decision lay in time (in the past),
would Whitehead's position be faced with the Leibnizian difficulties.

Now although Ford's finely nuanced exposition may answer the
objection as Brown posed it, Whitehead's position (and Ford's and
Brown's, for that matter) is vulnerable to a more fundamental objection
latent beneath Brown's argument. For even if we grant that God's free
decision is temporally emergent though intrinsically nontemporal,
Whitehead seems to grant, and Ford and Brown clearly do, that God's
freedom is solely the freedom of his primordial envisagement. Brown
writes: "On either view [entitative or the societal], . . . God's freedom
lies in his primordial evaluation of possibility" (PS 145). I propose to
show that insofar as Whitehead holds this view, even implicitly, he
reverts to a Leibnizian position that fails to do justice to religious experience.[3] I shall also suggest a way in which we *can* speak significantly
of a temporality of God's freedom.

I

I have said that Whitehead appears to hold that God's freedom is solely
the freedom of his primordial envisagement. This may seem a hard saying, since in the final chapter of *Process and Reality* he terms the action
of the consequent nature "judgment," "tenderness," and "patience,"
and that of the superjective nature "love."[4] Nevertheless he also writes:

"The perfection of God's superjective aim, derived from the completeness of his primordial nature, issues into the character of his consequent nature" (PR 345). He even describes God's patience as "the overpowering rationality of his conceptual harmonization" (PR 346). And he had already asserted that "the initial phase of the 'subjective aim' [of an actual occasion] . . . is a direct derivate from God's primordial nature" (PR 67). Indeed, it seems clear that in *Process and Reality* Whitehead considered initial aims to be derived directly from the pure valuations of divine conceptual feeling. But even if we accept with Cobb[5] the systematic extension of Whitehead's position, whereby initial aims mirror divine *propositional* feelings, thus involving also the consequent nature, it remains true that the character (predicate) of God's propositional feelings toward a concrescing actual occasion is just the emergent manifestation of the relevant aspects of his nontemporal primordial nature. Indeed it cannot differ from it, given that God's subjective aim is supreme and that the primordial nature constitutes the optimal adjustment of possibilities for value. It is therefore inevitable that the form of God's propositional feelings should exactly mirror the conceptual valuations of his primordial nature. Hence only in the constitution of his primordial nature is God significantly free.

In Ford's analysis of Whitehead this point is quite explicit: "God's decision can only be nontemporal. . . . Further, it is only as nontemporally actual that God can be prehended" ("Non-Temporality," 369). Ford speaks, it is true, of a divine "temporal freedom," but this freedom wholly derives from the divine nontemporal decision and thus amounts only to the temporal emergence of a nontemporal freedom: "God's temporal freedom is exercised in his integrative and propositional activity, where he *fits* to each actual world that gradation of pure possibilities *best suited* to contribute to the *maximum* intensity and harmony of his consequent physical experience" (376; my emphasis). All the decisions of the consequent nature flow from the primordial nature, and though the former does not fit the present actual occasions into a ready-made pattern of the *temporal past* (as Ford carefully points out, "Non-Temporality," 356), yet for Whitehead, "the weaving of God's physical feelings upon his primordial concepts" (PR 345) amounts to the emergence into time, as predicates of God's propositional feelings, of the very valuations of his nontemporal decision.

The upshot of all this, and the trouble with it, is, first, that it equates the concrete with the abstract, identifying God's decisions for concrete particulars with his decisions for pure possibilities. Facts are graded entirely according to their correspondence with a primordial ordering among pure possibilities (even though the ordering be nontemporal and the possibilities only potentially distinct from one another as nontemporal). This implies that the concrete particular can be exhaustively evaluated in terms of its forms of definiteness, although Whitehead himself affirms that "each fact is more than its forms" (PR 20). Second, it identifies God's self-creative subjectivity solely with the constitution of his primordial nature, as Ford argues at length in "Non-Temporality." Third, it implies that God does not love particulars as such, but only the universal patterns ingredient within them. As Whitehead wrote late in his life: "If you are enjoying a meal, and are conscious of pleasure derived from apple-tart, it is the sort of taste that you enjoy."[6] I submit, rather, that it is the tart that you enjoy, although the tart with that sort of taste. And religious experience testifies that it is individuals whom God loves, and that when he loves a person he is not just loving that person's characteristics.

To return to the first and central difficulty, God's primordial nature is clearly a valuation of pure possibilities:

> God's "primordial nature" is abstracted from his commerce with "particulars," and is therefore devoid of those "impure" intellectual cogitations which involve propositions. . . . It is God in abstraction, alone with himself. (PR 34)

> He, in his primordial nature, is unmoved by love for this particular, or that particular; for in this foundational process of creativity, there are no preconstructed particulars. (PR 105)

> His unity of conceptual operations is a free creative act, untrammeled by reference to any particular course of things. It is deflected neither by love, nor by hatred, for what in fact comes to pass. The *particularities* of the actual world presuppose *it;* while *it* merely presupposes the *general* metaphysical character of cre-

ative advance, of which it is the primordial exemplification. (PR 344; Whitehead's emphasis)

Furthermore, the primordial nature—or rather, God considered only in his primordial nature—is unconscious (PR 345). It is, then, these unconscious valuations of pure conceptual possibilities that rise to consciousness in God's propositional feelings about the world. It is necessary that this be so, for "God's conceptual realization is nonsense if thought of under the guise of a barren, eternal hypothesis. It is God's conceptual realization performing an efficacious role in multiple unifications of the universe" (PR 349). The predicates of God's intellectual feelings for real possibility simply reflect the pure conceptual valuations of his primordial nature. As Ford explains it: "God's own inner subjective contribution to this temporal activity is wholly derived from his nontemporal activity. His conscious, temporal decisions are all *temporalizations of a single, unified, underlying unconscious temporal decision*" ("Non-Temporality," 368; my emphasis). As with the apple-tart, then, God's love for this particular occasion is really his love for this *sort* of occasion inasmuch as the occasion instantiates one of the abstract patterns valuated in the primordial nature.

Now this is Leibnizian, and the source of the trouble is that no provision has been made for a dimension of divine freedom directed toward concrete individuals as such, a dimension of freedom that lies *within the "weaving" itself* of God's feelings for actual occasions. Ford is correct in maintaining that on the occasion of God's dealing with particulars the appropriate aspects of his purely conceptual, nontemporal decision come into being in time as the character of his propositional feelings, but that cannot be the whole story of divine freedom. It is not by reason of a nontemporal, unconscious adjustment of pure conceptual valuations that God exclaims through a prophet: "How can I give you up, O Ephraim! How can I hand you over, O Israel! . . . My heart recoils within me, my compassion grows warm and tender" (Hosea 11:8).

Furthermore, the almost exclusive emphasis that Whitehead normally lays on the primordial nature seems doubtfully consistent with passages that reflect his deepest insights. In the lyrical final chapter of *Process and Reality,* a chapter he is said to have thought the best thing he ever wrote, he says that it is "the perfected actuality [which he has just identified not with the primordial but with the consequent nature] that passes back into the temporal world and qualifies it" (PR 351). Similarly, in the last section of *Adventures of Ideas*,[7] having spoken throughout of the primordial nature of God (in terms of the supreme "Eros" of the Universe), Whitehead adds that the feeling of Transcendence

> requires for its understanding that we supplement the notion of the Eros by including it in the concept of an Adventure in the Universe as One. This adventure embraces all particular occasions but as an actual fact stands beyond any one of them. . . . [It] includes among its components all individual realities, each with the importance of the personal or social fact to which it belongs. Such individual importance in the components belongs to the essence of Beauty. . . . [It] requires the real occasions of the advancing world each claiming its due share of attention. (AI 380–81)

II

How then can we coherently ascribe a temporality to God's freedom, beyond the nontemporal constitution of his primordial nature, so as to make concrete entities, as such, the objects of God's free response?

The most obvious solution might seem to lie in adopting the societal view of God, as Brown in fact recommends. Yet whatever other reasons we may have for adopting that view, *this* cannot be a reason! For in this respect the societal view is in the same predicament as the entitative. True, on Brown's view God continually and freely reconstitutes his primordial nature in each successive divine occasion, but he always reconstitutes it the same way. He could hardly do otherwise and still be God, as Ford has pointed out ("Non-Temporality," 374). More importantly, for the societal view as well as for the entitative, the primordial nature is an adjustment of pure conceptual possibilities, so that although in the former view there is a temporality to its successive reconstitution, there is no temporality in its valuation. On neither view is the primordial nature a divine decision regarding temporal particulars, and in neither view is there allowance for a freedom of the divine decision with regard to these particulars. Consequently, adopting the societal view does nothing to solve our present problem.

If then we need to look elsewhere in order to find room for temporality in divine freedom, the temptation is strong to furnish it by the simple expedient of transferring a few responsibilities from the primordial to the consequent nature. (We inevitably do this if we think of divine temporal freedom as consisting in the same sort of valuations as those of the primordial nature.) But how do we adjust this division of labor—where do we draw the line? Vagueness can be avoided, of course, if we go to the logical extreme of such a move, which would lie in attributing to the consequent nature *all* valuations, reserving to the primordial nature only the constitution of metaphysical possibility and the subjective aim toward value realization in general. Then God's temporal decisions for particulars would in their everlastingness (on the entitative view; in their objective immortality, on the societal view) constitute the value norm for all subsequent time.

Such a view would not be quite so absurd as might at first appear: the divine temporal evaluations would seem to be no more arbitrary than those of the constitution of the primordial nature in Whitehead's view; and the divine subjective aim toward the maximum of value intensity, together with the property of everlastingness and the Categoreal Obligations (constituted by the primordial nature) of Subjective Unity and Subjective Harmony, would seem sufficient to insure the mutual coherence of the growing series of divine temporal evaluations. Yet the idea must be rejected as radically inconsistent with the heart of Whitehead's metaphysical insight, the identification of actuality with "something that matters."[8] There is no way of removing valuations from the primordial nature, no way of divorcing sheer possibility from possibility-for-value-realization. Similarly, it would make no sense to think of a subjective aim at value realization in complete abstraction from a hierarchy of valued possibilities.

We take a more promising tack, however, if we consider that there is necessarily a certain incommensurability between an actual entity and any description of it in terms of eternal objects. That is, an actual entity is not identified with its own forms of definiteness. Whitehead writes:

Each fact is more than its forms, and each form "participates" throughout the world of facts. The definiteness of fact is due to its forms; but the individual fact is a creature, and creativity is the ultimate behind all forms, inexplicable by forms, and conditioned by its creatures. (PR 20)

An actual entity cannot be described, even inadequately, by universals. (PR 48)

This is true both of the actual occasion that is the object of God's love and of God himself in his love toward it.

Further, the free act, precisely as such, is not describable in terms of forms. Bergson was the eloquent defender of this thesis in modern times,[9] and Whitehead accepts it when he agrees that creativity is "inexplicable by forms." The free act is not wholly describable antecedently, in view of its conditions, nor consequently, as the inevitable outcome of its conditions. It is itself the sole ultimate reason for its own decision. This is in fact another way of putting Whitehead's ontological principle, granted that every actual entity exercises at least some degree of freedom.

But then it must follow that God's particular affective response, his yearning for value fulfillment for the world at any moment, is somehow more than the realization within time of some limited aspect of his primordial, nontemporal valuation. We need to describe a freedom precisely in God's response to particulars as such. This response embodies the abstract value relations of the primordial nature, but cannot simply be defined in terms of them.

"Freedom," Bergson writes, "is the relation of the concrete self to the act which it performs. This relation is indefinable, just because we are free. For we can analyze a thing, but not a process; we can break up extensity, but not duration" (TFW 219). To attempt to define freedom, to conceptualize it, would be (in modern terms) to commit a category mistake. Yet though it cannot be defined, the free temporal act of God's particular satisfaction toward a particular can be *described* in terms of its *intensity*. According to Whitehead: "A subjective form has two factors, its qualitative pattern and its pattern of *intensive quantity*. But these two factors of pattern cannot wholly be considered in abstraction from each other" (PR 233; my emphasis). Elsewhere Whitehead speaks of "quantitative feeling," and of "quantitative emotional intensity" (PR 116). Bergson would be unhappy with this quantification of subjective states (TFW 70–74), and Whitehead's expressions may go too far, but this issue is not critical for our present purposes. Bergson notwithstanding, it obviously makes some kind of sense to speak of one emotional state as "more" or "less" intense than another, even if this "more" be not strictly quantitative.

In a passage worth pondering, Whitehead explains that the self-creative contribution of the freedom of each actual entity consists precisely in the subjective emphasis it lays upon the factors that are given it, including its own purposes and subjective aim:

> The doctrine of the philosophy of organism is that, however far the sphere of efficient causation be pushed in the determination of components of a concrescence—its data, its emotions, its appreciations, its purposes, its phases of subjective aim—*beyond the determination of these components there always remains the final reaction* of the self-creative unity of the universe. This final reaction *completes the self-creative act by putting the decisive stamp of creative emphasis upon the determinations of efficient cause.* Each occasion exhibits its measure of creative emphasis in proportion to its measure of subjective intensity. The absolute standard of such intensity is that of the primordial nature of God, which is neither great nor small because it arises out of no actual world. (PR 47; my emphasis)

I take it that the "self-creative unity of the universe" refers to the actual entity insofar as it is a particular instance of creativity. I am less clear on the sense of the last sentence but one, but I believe that Whitehead means that the quantitative emotional intensity of the entity's satisfaction must of course be related to the intensity of its drive toward value as furnished by its subjective aim. And the absolute standard of such a drive toward value is the primordial nature of God.

Whitehead's immediate reference to the primordial nature should not distract us from applying the above description to the consequent nature. Granted that the primordial nature constitutes God's "free" (though unconscious), nontemporal decision, yet as an actual entity he is completed by the conscious, temporal, self-creative propositional feelings he bears toward particular occasions. Why should they too not be characterized as "putting the decisive stamp of creative emphasis upon the determinations" received from the occasions of the actual world?

This is not to assert that in his consequent nature God adds any *formal* determination to the valuations of the primordial nature, still less that he in any way contradicts them. The contribution of his temporal freedom does not lie in forms of definiteness but in emotional intensity. This emotional intensity stands related to but is not determined by the qualitative pattern established by the primordial nature.

What I mean is this, and this is the heart of the matter. In the entitative view we can accept Ford's analysis wherein, of God's nontemporal valuation of all pure possibility, those particular aspects that relate to concrete particulars first come into being and are essentially time-related, from our temporal point of view, in the propositional feelings of the consequent nature. But this temporal coming into being of an aspect of God's nontemporal adjustment of possibility is itself clothed with emotion, with greater or less intensity of feeling on God's part. This intensity of feeling lies precisely in the act itself whereby God loves particular actual occasions. This act is free in the sense that there is a certain *incommensurability,* hence absence of determination, between the act itself in its emotional intensity and the conceptual adjustment of possibilities that it includes. This is another way of affirming with Bergson that the free act, as such, is both intrinsically unforeseeable and, even in retrospect, conceptually indefinable. Granted, therefore, that God's infinite conceptual valuation of pure possibility may justly be termed "free" since it is "limited by no actuality which it presupposes" (PR 345), yet the temporal, integrative activity of his consequent nature, whereby he loves particular occasions of the actual world, may also be called "free," though in a somewhat different sense.

To affirm therefore a temporality of divine freedom is not to multiply divine acts beyond those already described in Ford's analysis, but merely to notice an overlooked dimension of freedom in the concrete divine act wherein there also emerges the relevant aspect of God's nontemporal, free adjustment of pure value possibility. This dimension of freedom consists in the spontaneous intensity of emotion by which God's propositional feelings toward particulars are clothed. Since this view introduces no new divine acts, it furnishes no new argument in favor of adopting the societal view of God. On the other hand, *mutatis mutandis* it also fits the societal view, since, as we have seen, that view too must allow for an aspect of the divine decision regarding particulars that goes beyond pure conceptual valuation.

If we use the above proposal to interpret religious experience we are able to make sense of saying that although God loves only what is lovable, the intensity of his love for this or that particular thing or person is a matter of his free temporal activity. God took a people to himself and loved them, not only because they had lovable qualities (and perhaps unlovable ones as well), but because he chose to. That is, his heart in fact went out to them, he loved them with a special intensity for which no reason can be assigned other than the act itself whereby he loved them. And in different temporal circumstances the intensity of God's feelings may vary: "I will love them freely, for my anger has turned from them."

Further, if we integrate this interpretation of divine temporal freedom with God's *providence* for the world, we notice a remarkable result. In Whitehead's view God acts in the world by loving it:

> For the perfected actuality passes back into the temporal world, and qualifies this world so that each temporal actuality includes it as an immediate fact of relevant experience. . . . The action of the fourth phase is the love of God for the world. It is the particular providence for particular occasions. (PR 351)

In more technical terms, this "inclusion as an immediate fact of relevant experience" by each temporal actuality is the feeling by each concrescing occasion of its own initial aim. The hybrid prehension of God, not only in his primordial but in his consequent nature, "in his particular providence for particular things," *constitutes* the occasion's feeling of its initial aim.

But the actual occasion does not feel God purely in terms of universals—that is, solely in terms of the forms of definiteness (hence the primordial valuations) ingredient within God's propositional feelings. Whitehead's remark is applicable: "Owing to the disastrous confusion, more especially by Hume, of conceptual feelings with perceptual feelings, the truism that we can only *conceive* in terms of universals has been stretched to mean that we can only *feel* in terms of universals. This is untrue" (PR 230; Whitehead's emphasis). Furthermore, Whitehead's famous assertion that "in the real world it is more important that a proposition be interesting than that it be true" (PR 259) applies exactly here. The interest, the effective impact, that the divine propositional feelings make on an actual occasion in constituting its initial aim does not so much lie in their correspondence to the abstract conceptual valuations of the primordial nature *as in the emotional intensity with which they are felt in God's consequent nature.*

On God's own part, the function of his primordial valuations, when they become real possibilities applicable to concrete occasions, is to evoke emotional intensity within God's own consequent nature:

> It is evident . . . that the primary function of theories is as a lure for feeling, thereby providing immediacy of enjoyment and purpose. Unfortunately theories, under their name of "propositions," have been handed over to logicians, who have countenanced the doctrine that their one function is to be judged as to their truth or falsehood. (PR 184)

And again: "The main function of intellectual feelings is neither belief, nor disbelief, nor even suspension of judgment. The main function of these feelings is to heighten the emotional intensity accompanying the valuations in the conceptual feelings involved" (PR 272).

God is effective in the world through the love that he pours back into it, which is his "particular providence for particular occasions" (PR 351); the "'superjective' nature of God is the character of the pragmatic value of his specific satisfaction qualifying the transcendent creativity in the various temporal instances" (PR 135). Also, what Whitehead says about "physical purposes" seems quite applicable to this "pragmatic value of his specific satisfaction":

The valuation according to the physical feeling endows the transcendent creativity with the character of adversion, or of aversion. The character of adversion secures the reproduction of the physical feeling, as one element in the objectification of the subject beyond itself. . . . [A] physical feeling, whose valuation produces adversion, is thereby an element with some force of persistence into the future beyond its own subject. (PR 276)

III

In sum, then, the penalty for neglecting to allow for a divine temporal freedom beyond that of God's primordial nature is to be required to grant, in effect, that the timeless and the abstract adequately describe the temporal and the concrete, even the concrete acts of divine love for individuals.[10] Such a view does not agree with the deliverances of religious experience. God's freedom is temporal as well—that is, insofar as God relates himself freely to the things of the temporal world precisely in their individuality. It lies in the spontaneous intensity of God's affection for the particulars of the temporal world. To God's freely constituted, pure conceptual valuations there is coupled, as it were in another dimension, his free emotional response, his love for individuals. Cod's freedom is thus also temporal, not in the sense that his free acts take time, but that they are directed toward temporal occasions as such and cannot be adequately described solely in terms of the primordial nature. God's propositional feelings toward particulars require the nontemporal conceptual valuations of his primordial nature, but their emotional intensity is not a matter of forms of definiteness or qualities. Further, it is this intensity of the divine propositional feelings that most contributes to their effectiveness in achieving the divine purpose in the world. *All* relevant possibilities as conceptually felt in the primordial nature are ingredient within God's complex propositional feeling toward a particular occasion, but only that will be most influential on the occasion that is felt by God with the greatest emotional intensity. And that intensity is not determined by either the primordial nature or the actual world.

Charles Hartshorne once remarked that it is characteristic of Whitehead's God that he lands on both sides of all antitheses. Ford has convincingly argued the importance of the nontemporal freedom of God's primordial nature. I wish to add that God's freedom is also temporal as well as nontemporal, and that his influence on the world, beyond his free, nontemporal valuation of pure possibilities, lies in the emotional intensity with which he freely loves the particulars of the world both for what they are and for what they can become.

FOUR

Philosophic Understanding and the Continuity of Becoming

(1978)

This moderately technical essay arose, as I now imagine, out of puzzlement over how central philosophic interpretations of Bergson and of Whitehead concerning the nature of becoming, especially the becoming that is human experiencing, could both be correct. The arguments for both views seemed quite persuasive yet mutually contradictory. Experiencing for Bergson was regarded as continuous, but for Whitehead as successive or "epochal." What was wrong here? I thought at the time, and still do, that the relationship I here propose between the two views illustrates in fact two different modes of philosophic thinking, so that the diverse conclusions can be regarded as complementary rather than antithetical to each other. The extent to which the proposed conclusion may be original, I do not know, but it has stayed with me for more than thirty years and finds further expression in essays 10 and 16 of this volume. Note 10 of this essay, however, points to a possible shift of my present position regarding time and the act of deciding.

Originally published as "Philosophic Understanding and the Continuity of Becoming," *International Philosophical Quarterly* 18, no. 4 (1978): 375–93. Reprinted with permission.

"Instinct," wrote Bertrand Russell, "is seen at its best in ants, bees, and Bergson."[1] Russell's mistrust of Bergson's philosophic method is not at all exceptional. Whitehead, for instance, while indebted to Bergson, was concerned to rescue his thought (and that of James and Dewey) from the charge of anti-intellectualism.[2] He aimed to achieve this precisely by providing an intellectual description of what Bergson described only in the metaphorical terms of intuition.

The results of these two different ways of understanding, intuition and intellection, differ markedly, and in their analysis of becoming seem outright antithetical. For Bergson the passage of the universe, which we recognize in its purest state within the immediacy of our own reflective experience, is a flow that is continuous. The past penetrates the present in such a way as to preclude our marking a division between the two, or even in fact calling them "two" rather than simply a qualitative diversity within an ever-expanding unity. But Whitehead concluded that process is in fact (though not in potentiality) "epochal," "atomic," discontinuous in the sense of constituting definite temporal quanta of becoming.

Within the usual context of discussion these two positions are demonstrably irreconcilable, but the irreconcilability stems, I think, from failing to attend to the way in which the two modes of understanding are related to one another. When intellectual understanding is viewed as ancillary to the intuitive, the respective conclusions, I shall argue, are not antithetical but complementary.

At stake here is not so much the resolution of an intramural dispute between two philosophers; it is the whole question of the validity of intuitive understanding. If, as I think, intuitive understanding cannot be denied without thereby implicitly being affirmed, reasons are nonetheless easy to find for its meretricious reputation. Not the least is Bergson's own habit of laying more stress on the distinction between these two ways of understanding than on their interrelation. Another is our natural tendency, as Bergson was fond of emphasizing, to trust ourselves to the security of intellectual understanding, with its timeless concepts and its practical utility, rather than to the ever-changing flow of introspective awareness. Nevertheless Bergson claimed that intuitive understanding lies at the heart of metaphysics, and I think he is right. But even if he is right, we must still ask whether we are prepared to accept the consequences. This will be possible only if the two ways of understanding can be seen in their mutual interrelationship.

Watching Bergson and Whitehead draw diverse conclusions about the continuity of becoming provides a singularly illuminating example of two ways of understanding brought more or less separately to bear on a single problem. In the ultimate reconciliation of their views we can see, I think, not only what Bergson and Whitehead stand to gain from one another, but also how we can enrich our own understanding of philosophic understanding.

I. TWO VIEWS ON BECOMING

Bergson's Insistence on the Continuity of Becoming

Bergson always insisted that continuity belongs to the essence of *"duration"* (*durée*), that inner process of becoming that is both the core of all our experience and our primary analog for world-process and time. This internal duration is a "succession which is not juxtaposition, a growth from within, the uninterrupted prolongation of the past into a present which is already blending into the future."[3] And if we sometimes think of our inner states as if they were a multiplicity of items placed end to end, this stems in part from the diverse psychological acts by which we take note of the character of our inner life. "The apparent discontinuity of the psychical life is then due to our attention being fixed on it by a series of separate acts: actually there is only a gentle slope."[4]

Another reason we tend to think of our experience in terms of discrete successive states is the normal tendency to view it through the prism of quantity. Time, as we naturally think of it, has practically all the characteristics of space: we speak of long and short times; we measure it by a one-to-one correspondence with the marks on the face of a clock or the position of the earth; most significantly, we tacitly suppose that past, present, and future share a simultaneity or togetherness in essentially the same way as the different parts of a quantified whole. This tacit spatialization of time underlies the common supposition that statements about the future are either true or false. Most persons will grant that the statement, "There will be a collision at this intersection tonight before midnight," must be either true or false, even though prior to midnight no one may be in a position to know which. Compare this with the statement, "There is a boulder on the highway around the next bend." It must be granted, I think, that this statement must either be true or, if not true, false, even though one does not know which until one gets around the bend. But if it is in fact true, it is the boulder on the road that makes it true; if it is false, it is the absence of a boulder. Similarly, to suppose that the first statement must either be true or be false, regardless of our own state of knowledge, is to suppose that it in fact corresponds to, or fails to correspond to, the factual situation that it describes. But that is to suppose that a definitive future already shares a simultaneity with the present, that it is in a sense already "now." It is to suppose that the future is "together" with the present in essentially the same way as quantified parts are together with one another. This in effect reduces time to space, for it belongs to space to interrelate a multiplicity of parts within a unity. To think of time in this way is to destroy just what is unique about it, namely that its "parts" flow successively and can *never* be "together." Time thought of as a highway along which we travel leaves room for neither novelty nor freedom; in such a time we do not fashion our future, we only arrive at it.

Bergson claims that it is inappropriate—a category mistake, if you will—to describe the immediacy of our experience in terms of this space-like conception of time. One proof of this, he thinks, lies in our immediate experience of freedom. Looked at through the lenses of spatialized time, human experience allows of no freedom since its passage from moment to moment must be described in terms of determinate causal connections between the present and the immediate past. Yet, he contends, there is no fact clearer than the fact of freedom:

> Every demand for explanation in regard to freedom comes back, without our suspecting it, to the following question: "Can time be adequately represented by space?" To which we answer: Yes, if you are dealing with time flown; No, if you speak of time flowing. Now, the free act takes place in time which is flowing and not in time which has already flown. Freedom is therefore a fact,

and among the facts which we observe there is none clearer. All the difficulties of the problem, and the problem itself, arise from the desire to endow duration with the same attributes as extensity, to interpret a succession by a simultaneity, and to express the idea of freedom in a language into which it is obviously untranslatable.[5]

We know we are free because we feel it, Bergson claims, and the time of our freedom is not spatial but a more fundamental time, duration, the time of immediate lived experience.

Duration is the very becoming of inner experience in the qualitative (not quantitative) multiplicity of its succeeding states. It is "a qualitative multiplicity, with no likeness to number; an organic evolution which is yet not an increasing quantity; a pure heterogeneity within which there are no distinct qualities. In a word, the moments of inner duration are not external to one another" (TFW 226).

Since duration is a process rather than a thing it cannot adequately be captured by the conceptual terms of a definition. Hence Bergson repeatedly appeals to images and analogies by which to point to duration rather than attempt to define it. His most impressive analogy is that of a melody. A melody is not a discrete collection of successive notes but a single *Gestalt* in which the earlier notes remain present in the later ones. Duration is thus the "indivisible and indestructible continuity of a melody where the past enters into the present and forms with it an undivided whole which remains undivided and even indivisible in spite of what is added at every instant, or rather, thanks to what is added" (CM 83). Thus understood, duration is time flowing, not flown; it is the time of agency, freedom, and creative novelty. It is the time of subjectivity as such.

It is essential to notice that this dynamic continuity of process or duration is quite different from the static continuity of space. The latter is homogeneous, the former heterogeneous. The latter permits juxtaposition of parts, hence measurement, the former does not. There is no way to get one lived moment to hold still long enough to be compared with another. As Whitehead himself once remarked, "You can't catch a moment by the scruff of the neck—*it's gone,* you know."[6] The continuity that Bergson attributes to duration is thus a dynamic continuity of qualitative heterogeneity, not a spatial continuity of homogeneity. Because of the persistent temptation to understand the former as if it were the latter, Milič Čapek recommends that, with Whitehead, we speak of the "becoming of continuity" rather than the "continuity of becoming."[7]

Whitehead's View of Becoming as Epochal

"If we admit that 'something becomes,'" wrote Whitehead, "it is easy, by employing Zeno's method, to prove that there can be no continuity of becoming" (PR 35). He agreed with William James that our experience comes in "drops," not instants, and he claims that the only way to make rational sense out of becoming is to hold that instances of becoming succeed one another in time and are temporally "thick," yet not themselves temporally divisible.

Whitehead's contention that becoming is atomic is most convincingly seen in the context of trying to make intellectual sense out of freedom.[8] John B. Cobb has developed this argument with exceptional clarity.[9] It takes for granted that each event or occurrence (and every aspect of it) is either caused or uncaused. If uncaused, then it simply happens, for no reason, hence cannot be an act of moral agency. Human acts must be caused if we are to make sense of their ethical dimension. Further, they must be caused from within, for if they are caused by outside agents they are once again deprived of the ethical dimension of responsibility. The concern therefore centers neither on indetermination, nor on determination from without, but on self-determination.

But even self-determination is not compatible with freedom so long as we retain the usual assumption that the cause must temporally precede its effect. For on that assumption self-determination reduces to a succession of inner states and we are faced once again with the same dilemma as before: if each state is caused by a preceding state there is no *locus* for a free state; if on the other hand the determination or decision in question is simply *un*caused, we are in the arena of chance not freedom. Clearly the kind of "causation" that takes place in free self-determination must be such that the "cause" (the agent or agency) is somehow simultaneous with its "effect" (the decision), not antecedent to it.

Now this moment of deciding must either be instantaneous or occupy some finite interval of time. But it cannot be the former, for no action can occur in a timeless instant.[10] But neither can it be the latter so long as we continue to view process as continuous! We could not then justify supposing that the free act occurs during an extended temporal interval. For if we continue to suppose that becoming is continuous, not only is the length of the assumed interval essentially arbitrary, its unity becomes ultimately illusory. Just as the temporal flow is infinitely divisible, so also is the act of deciding. Zeno's arguments shiver the act into an infinite succession of instantaneous states, in which, as we remarked, there can be no process.

Only two routes of escape seem to lie open. One route is to suppose that although freedom makes no sense within the causal fabric of human experience, it yet makes intelligible sense within a realm transcending that experience. This is the route taken by Kant. The other is to suppose that process or becoming is *dis*continuous; that although acts of becoming succeed one another in such a way as to "take time," they are not themselves temporally divisible but are in some sense all-at-once, thus forming atomic yet temporally thick units of becoming. This is the position taken by Whitehead. He wrote:

> The conclusion is that in every act of becoming there is the becoming of something with temporal extension; but that the act itself is not extensive, in the sense that it is divisible into earlier and later acts of becoming which correspond to the extensive divisibility of what has become. (PR 69)

And, in another place:

> Temporalisation is not another continuous process. It is an atomic succession. Thus time is atomic (i.e. epochal), though what is temporalised is divisible.[11]

But what is divisible is not yet divided. Thus Whitehead places continuity on the side of potentiality, whereas the actual is "incurably atomic" (PR 61, 67).

It is essential to notice two other aspects of Whitehead's position. The first is that the continuity he attributes to potentiality is just that quantitative homogeneity that Bergson insisted on denying to concrete becoming. But this quantitative homogeneity of extensiveness has also what Whitehead called a "separative" character (SMW 64). By its very nature extensiveness sets apart as well as joins together. But—and this is the second point to be noticed—when Whitehead asserts that actual becoming is epochal or atomic, the distinctness he thereby sets up between diverse individual actual occasions is exactly not the distinctness of part from part in an extensive whole. He has explicitly maintained that the characteristics of quantitative homogeneity belong to potentiality rather than to actuality. Furthermore, in quantitative homogeneity the parts are not related together internally, but only externally by juxtaposition, whereas it is essential to Whitehead's actual entities that they be internally related. Thus his view that becoming is epochal does not at all imply that successive actual entities are discretely juxtaposed in time like notes on a staff or sections of railroad track. That mistaken (and perhaps not uncommon) view is unfortunately encouraged by the use of time-cone diagrams for displaying the relationship of an actual occasion to its actual world.

But if it is incorrect to think of Whitehead's epochal occasions as related to one another in the same way as extensive parts, it nevertheless seems clear that they cannot be thought of as forming that "uninterrupted prolongation of the past into a present" (CE 5) that is already blending into a future that Bergson attributes to duration. They are, rather, to use Whitehead's own word, "arrests" in becoming (SMW 125). The two positions are, on the face of it, antithetical.

Problems and a Challenge

Before considering a challenge to this last statement, I wish to call attention to two aspects of Whitehead's epochal view that have proved awkward if not downright embarrassing to Whitehead and his intellectual descendants. We shall have to take another look at these difficulties later on.

First, there is the perplexity already mentioned as to how various phases of the concrescence of an actual occasion can be referred to as

"earlier" and "later" with respect to one another if the process of concrescence itself cannot be thought of as temporally divided. We have
already noted the wide diversity of views as to how this makes sense,
and this testifies to more than a trivial problem. The second difficulty
lies in Whitehead's theory of personal identity through time. His
epochal theory of becoming forces him to define the enduring person as
"the historic route of living occasions which are severally dominant in
the body as successive instants" (PR 119). I am not alone in being dissatisfied with this. Professor Cobb writes:

> This lack of absolute self-identity through time does indeed
> pose problems for any doctrine of life after death. It poses many
> other problems as well Our ordinary moral and legal practice
> presupposes personal identity. If there is no such personal iden-
> tity, all justification for rewards and punishments seems to van-
> ish. It would seem that there is no particular necessity to accept
> responsibility for our past acts, since they were performed by a
> numerically different entity. Gratitude would seem to be misdi-
> rected when expressed after the moment of the beneficent act.
> Past promises would not bind. The list of consequences is end-
> less and disastrous.
>   Whitehead himself was troubled by the apparent conflict of
> his doctrine and the universal intuition and practice of mankind.
> He shared the intuition, and again and again he returned to the
> topic, seeking to shed light upon it.[12]

Sometimes Whitehead seems to suggest that personal identity consists in the retention of a "primary character" throughout successive
changes.[13] To this Cobb remarks: "It is a perplexing fact, and perhaps
an indication of some desperation on Whitehead's part, that he fell into
the trap of describing personal identity in terms that refer to a common
character" (CNT 74). On the other hand, Whitehead had also said:
"We—as enduring objects with personal order—objectify the occasions
of our own past with peculiar completeness in our immediate present"
(PR 161). Cobb enlarges on this phrase, "peculiar completeness," in
terms of memory, and in a way strikingly reminiscent of Bergson (CNT
75–76). In the end, however, he is not entirely satisfied with the theory,

nor am I content with any of the Whiteheadian interpretations of personal identity.[14] Despite what I take to be Cobb's legitimate appeal to memory as an essential ingredient, personal identity as revealed in inner experience seems incompatible with Whitehead's strict ontological diversity of the actual occasions within the personally ordered historical strand.[15] I think it is just not possible within Whitehead's view to say, "I did it!" taking the "I" in the sense that seems to be demanded by the experience of personal identity, namely, an "I" that shares not only a common character and even the memory of inheritance, but also an ontological identity with the "I" that did it in the past. I intend to propose, however, that this need not force us either to live with this discomfort or to abandon the Whiteheadian view altogether.

As to the wider views of Bergson and Whitehead on the continuity of becoming, have I perhaps exaggerated their incompatibility? In "Henri Bergson and the Epochal Theory of Time" David A. Sipfle has argued with considerable justice that Bergson's *durée* is less continuous, and Whitehead's "epochs" more so, than usually supposed.[16] He points out that the continuity of duration is one of qualitative heterogeneity, so that becoming itself requires a qualitative growth, hence in some sense a succession of qualitatively diverse phases. This aspect of qualitative diversity, even multiplicity, of states comes to the fore more fully in *Matter and Memory* and *Creative Evolution* than in the earlier *Time and Free Will*. Sipfle also stresses the internal relatedness of Whitehead's actual entities to one another. "Here," he says, "we have an 'interpenetration' of events which is surely as radical as Bergson's" (282).

Sipfle's article challenges a previous study[17] involving Whitehead's epochal theory of time, so the reader is warranted to suppose that he is using "epochal" in Whitehead's sense unless he declares otherwise. He does declare otherwise, but just once. Early in the article he suggests that his thesis will be "that Bergson holds something *very much like* an epochal theory of time" (281; my emphasis). That qualification, which renders the thesis defensible, gets rather forgotten in the sequel. He later asserts: "Bergson describes our experience of time as a multiplicity of *discrete* extended moments; our thesis is established. . . . Time, for Bergson, as for Whitehead, consists of radically continuous, but genuinely *discrete,* epochs" (287; my emphasis).

Even with the help of Sipfle's corroborating references I confess I have failed to find Bergson using the word "discrete" in connection with the qualitatively heterogeneous moments of duration. Sipfle says that in *Matter and Memory*,[18] as contrasted with *Time and Free Will*,[19] "time becomes more discrete" (283). I do not grasp how anything can literally be "more" (or "less") discrete. But even if the expression is only suggestive, I cannot find Bergson using it. In Sipfle's article, and perhaps in his thought, "heterogeneity" seems to have metamorphosed into "discreteness." When, for instance, Sipfle speaks of William James's "specious present," he states that "it occupies a finite temporal duration" (284). Apparently this suggests to him a discrete state. But a "finite" duration is not necessarily "definite," even though language inclines us to speak as if it were. So also, when Bergson says that a perception "always occupies a certain duration," (MM 25; Sipfle 286), he has not said a definite one, and only definite durations, I should think, can be discrete.

Again, Sipfle writes: "Bergson is not concerned to deny a multiplicity of temporal elements, but only to deny that they can be counted" (280). I submit that they cannot be counted precisely because they do not form a discrete multiplicity. To use an analogy that limps in every respect but one, the colors of the spectrum cannot, strictly speaking, be counted (except arbitrarily) precisely because they do not present a discrete multiplicity for the counting. And if as Bergson points out we count discrete psychical states, that is not because they are themselves discrete but because they correspond to distinct stages of our psychological attention:

> The transition is continuous. But, just because we close our eyes to the unceasing variation of every psychical state, we are obliged, when the change has become so considerable as to force itself on our attention, to speak as if a new state were placed alongside the previous one. . . . States thus defined cannot be regarded as distinct elements. They continue each other in an endless flow. (CE 4–5; and see 170, 179)

This later description of an "endless flow" is perfectly consistent with the earlier Bergson of *Time and Free Will:*

We should therefore distinguish two forms of multiplicity, two very different ways of regarding duration, two aspects of conscious life. Below homogeneous duration, which is the extensive symbol of true duration, a close psychological analysis distinguishes a duration whose heterogeneous moments permeate one another; below the numerical multiplicity of conscious slates, a qualitative multiplicity; below the self with well-defined states, a self in which *succeeding each other* means *melting into one another* and forming an organic whole. (TFW 128; Bergson's emphasis)

I take it that the latter passage implies that the qualitative multiplicity is not "numerical," hence countable, *precisely because* its moments "permeate" and "melt into" one another—that is, because they are not discrete from one another. We may compare this with a parallel passage from *Matter and Memory:*

The duration *wherein we see ourselves acting,* and in which it is useful that we should see ourselves, is a duration whose elements are dissociated and juxtaposed. The duration *wherein we act* is a duration wherein our states melt into each other. It is within this that we should try to replace ourselves by thought, in the exceptional and unique case when we speculate on the intimate nature of action, that is to say, when we are discussing human freedom. (MM 243–44; Bergson's emphasis)

I cannot believe that duration for Bergson consists of discrete epochs. Yet it indisputably does for Whitehead. In an essay that is a sort of preliminary sketch for *Process and Reality* Whitehead wrote:

Supersession is not a continuous process of becoming. If we try to combine the notions of supersession and continuity we are at once entangled in a vicious infinite regress.

. . . Supersession cannot be regarded as the continuous unfolding of a continuum. I express this conclusion by the statement that time is "epochal." The occasion B which acquires concretion so as to supersede A embodies a definite *quantum* of time which I call the "epochal character" of the concrescence.[20]

This divergence of views between Bergson and Whitehead appears to be fundamental and too deep to be glossed over. On the face of it it seems that we must side with either the one or the other.

II. A SUGGESTED RECONCILIATION

Bergson's Distinction between Intelligence and Intuition

At this point, in fact, we seem to find ourselves in the shadow of Kant's Third Antinomy. Striving to render freedom intelligible Bergson concludes that fundamental becoming must be continuous; Whitehead, with like cogency, that it must be discontinuous; Kant would advise us that such speculation is therefore pointless.

I believe, on the contrary, that we can find our way out of this fly bottle precisely by exploiting Bergson's well-known though not so well-esteemed distinction between *intelligence* and *intuition*. I say "exploiting" because although I shall build on Bergson's ideas I am not concerned to claim that the position I develop is perfectly Bergsonian. The distinction between intelligence and intuition is operative in the last two passages from Bergson quoted at the end of Section I. In the first, from *Time and Free Will,* Bergson speaks of "two very different ways of regarding duration, two aspects of conscious life." These two ways of regarding duration are correlative to two different versions of duration: the first, homogeneous and extensive, displays a numerical multiplicity of conscious states; the second, an organic whole, is a qualitative multiplicity in which the states are not well defined but melt into one another. The former version is grasped by intelligence, the latter by intuition. Similarly, in the passage from *Matter and Memory,* there is a duration in which we *see ourselves* acting, "a duration whose elements are dissociated and juxtaposed"; but there is also a duration in which we *act,* "a duration wherein our states melt into one another." Bergson maintains that if we wish to discuss human freedom, we have to replace ourselves by thought within this immediate duration in which we act. Such a deliberate mental effort reflectively to understand the act from within rather than from without is exactly what Bergson means by "intuition."

Intelligence, on the other hand, is at home in space and its function is largely practical; Bergson sets *homo faber* on a level with *homo sapiens* (CE 153). The practicality of intelligence consists mainly in its ability to view the rush of experience in terms of stable patterns mirrored in concepts. It takes snapshots of mobility (CE 306). These intellectual snapshots (concepts) help us understand and manipulate experience much as stroboscopic photographs of a bird's wing in flight help us understand the dynamics of flying. But no matter how finely such photographs are multiplied, what they systematically leave out is the flying itself. Analogously, intelligence alone is powerless to comprehend the becoming of experience that is duration: "The intellect is not made to think *evolution,* in the proper sense of the word—that is to say, the continuity of a change that is pure mobility. . . . [It] represents *becoming* as a series of *states,* each of which is homogeneous with itself and consequently does not change" (CE 179; Bergson's emphasis). By means of intelligence, "instead of attaching ourselves to the inner becoming of things, we place ourselves outside them in order to recompose their becoming artificially. We take snapshots, as it were, of the passing reality" (CE 332).

Intuition, by contrast, is a deliberate and effortful reflective attention to duration in its flowing, without interrupting it:

> The intuition we refer to then bears above all upon internal duration. It grasps a succession which is not juxtaposition, a growth from within, the uninterrupted prolongation of the past into a present which is already blending into the future. It is the direct vision of the mind by the mind—nothing intervening, no refraction through the prism, one of whose facets is space and another, language. Instead of states contiguous to states, which become words in juxtaposition to words, we have here the indivisible and therefore substantial continuity of the flow of the inner life. (CM 35)

Intuition is not *mere* instinct or feeling as Russell implies in the passage from which our initial quotation is taken. It is rather "instinct that has become disinterested, self-conscious, capable of reflecting upon its object and of enlarging it indefinitely" (CE 194). It is a reflection that requires attention and concentration; it is arduous and cannot be prolonged beyond short intervals (CM 103, 39). It is, thinks Bergson, the proper method of metaphysics, the science that claims to dispense with symbols.[21]

Intuition is perhaps best seen in contrast with intelligence. Bergson writes:

> To think intuitively is to think in duration. Intelligence starts ordinarily from the immobile and reconstructs movement as best it can with immobilities in juxtaposition. Intuition starts from movement, posits it, or rather perceives it as reality itself, and sees in immobility only an abstract moment, a snapshot taken by our mind, of a mobility. Intelligence ordinarily concerns itself with things, meaning by that, with the static, and makes of change an accident which is supposedly superadded. For intuition the essential is change: as for the thing, as intelligence understands it, it is a cutting which has been made out of the becoming and set up by our mind as a substitute for the whole. (CM 38–39)

Interrelation of Intelligence and Intuition: "Ancillarity"

Bergson makes plainer, I think, how intelligence and intuition differ than he does how they interrelate. This poses the danger of taking them as autonomous, insulated functions, whereas pure intuition and pure intelligence seem rather to be abstract limits in terms of which actual mental activity, a fusion of both, can be understood.[22] Intuition requires intelligence in the first place if it is to be communicated. "Intuition . . . is more than idea; nevertheless in order to be transmitted, it will have to use ideas as a conveyance. It will prefer, however, to have recourse to the most concrete ideas, but those which still retain an outer fringe of images. Comparisons and metaphors will here suggest what cannot be expressed" (CM 48). Furthermore, intelligence and intuition operate simultaneously though on diverse objects. Intelligence, says Bergson, is "the attention that mind gives to matter," whereas intuition is "the attention that the mind gives to itself, over and above, while it is fixed upon matter, its object" (CM 92).[23]

I propose that for metaphysics intelligence stands to intuition primarily in a relation that might fittingly be called *ancillarity*. It is true that Bergson says he values scientific (intellectual) knowledge as much as intuitive vision (CM 99). It is also true that although intuition transcends intelligence, it is from intelligence that has come the push which has made instinct rise to the level of intuition (CE 195). Nevertheless, for philosophical reflection intelligence stands mainly at the service of intuition. The method of metaphysics, Bergson says, is "mainly intuition" (CM 42). Intuition provides a corrective to the natural tendency to overrate intelligence:

> In default of knowledge properly so called, reserved to pure intelligence, intuition may enable us to grasp what it is that intelligence fails to give us, and indicate the means of supplementing it. On the one hand, it will utilize the mechanism of intelligence itself to show how intellectual molds cease to be strictly applicable; and on the other hand, by its own work, it will suggest to us the vague feeling, if nothing more, of what must take the place of intellectual molds. (CE 195)[24]

And if intelligence is indispensably instrumental in the rise of instinct to the level of intuition, it is intuition that inspires and guides intellectual construction. "As the diver feels out the wreck on the sea floor that the aviator has pointed out from the air, so the intellect immersed in the conceptual environment verifies from point to point, by contact, analytically, what had been the object of a synthetic and super-intellectual vision" (CM 74).

Against Kant, Bergson asserts the existence of supra- as well as infra-intellectual intuition and denies that intellect covers the whole ground of experience (CE 391).[25] If we are to achieve that precision that is the ideal and goal of philosophy, whereby our philosophy will "fit tightly" the reality it attempts to understand (CM 9), we must give up exclusive reliance on the method of construction and on intellectual molds, and emphasize rather an intuitive return to experience (CE 394).

Bergson's distinction between intuition and intelligence can, I think, advantageously be thought of in terms of the *perspectives* that the two functions afford on concrete process.[26] Through intuition we regard duration or process from within, whereas by intelligence we view it as it were from without. Bergson makes the same distinction in different words, and prior to his use of the word "intuition," in the first paragraph of his famous essay "Introduction to Metaphysics":

> Despite apparent discrepancies, . . . philosophers agree in making a deep distinction between two ways of knowing a thing. The first implies going all around it, the second entering into it. The first depends on the viewpoint chosen and the symbols employed, while the second is taken from no viewpoint and rests on no symbol. Of the first kind of knowledge, we shall say that it stops at the *relative;* of the second that, wherever possible, it attains the *absolute*. (CM 187; Bergson's emphasis)

Concepts—abstract, universal, timeless—take a certain measure of lived duration but they cannot duplicate it. If, for example, by intuition we enter directly but reflectively into the pure duration of our immediate experience, we find ourselves free; but if by intelligence we attempt to define this freedom in conceptual terms, we find that it has run through our fingers.

Now how does Bergson's distinction between intelligence and intuition apply to Whitehead's philosophic method? "The true method of philosophical construction," Whitehead writes, "is to frame a scheme of ideas, the best that one can, and unflinchingly to explore the interpretation of experience in terms of that scheme" (PR xiv). One's "best," in fact, flows from immediate inspection of experience. Thus we see Whitehead justifying his Category of the Ultimate solely by appeal to intuition (PR 21). Philosophy grows out of immediate experience; it also must return to it for corroboration. "The true method of discovery is like the flight of an aeroplane. It starts from the ground of particular observation; it makes a flight in the thin air of imaginative generalization; and it again lands for renewed observation rendered acute by rational interpretation" (PR 5).

Although Whitehead did not, I think, accurately understand what Bergson meant by "intuition,"[27] the "years of meditation" out of which his scheme developed (PR xiv) were certainly years of intuitive reflection as well as of intellectual construction. This is patent, for example, in his insistence that causal derivation is immediately given in experience. For Whitehead, "causal efficacy" names an experience as well as an intellectual concept explicative of it.

Nevertheless I think it has to be granted that his efforts toward a new structured metaphysics are entirely intellectual in Bergson's sense. The Categoreal Scheme resides exactly in the thin air of abstract imaginative generalization. What is more significant, however, is that the renewed observation of immediate experience, rendered acute by the rational interpretation afforded by the scheme, is more often than not made by Whiteheadian philosophers from a perspective outside that experience. For example, a discussion of human personal identity in terms of an historical route of epochal occasions is, as I hope to show, only intellectual, viewing experience from the outside rather than from within. Yet this is almost always the context of discussion both for Whitehead and for those who follow him. Again, analysis of an actual instance of experience in terms of distinct phases of concrescence is, as Whitehead himself acknowledged and perhaps with Bergson's vocabulary in mind, "only intellectual" (PR 227). At the same time it must be admitted that when Whitehead recognizes that experience naturally discloses itself in the threefold scheme, "The Whole," "That Other," and "This-My-Self," or when he maintains that it is of the essence of experience that it is *value* experience, he is operating on an intuitive level.[28]

What I have said about perspectives is illuminated by an obvious difficulty, or rather a pseudo-difficulty, that confronts Whitehead's epochal view of personal identity. It may appear that Whitehead's epochal theory of becoming does not stand the test of experience, since we do not in fact experience this theorized succession of ontically distinct occasions, but rather a continuity. Or if we psychologically notice a succession of fairly discrete psychical states, we do not at least experience the rapid successiveness that, on Whitehead's theory, would be present even within any single such psychical state. Now it seems obvious, yet is pointless, to reply that the succession is simply too rapid to be noticed, as in a well-made motion picture. For that reply swallows a contradiction contained within the difficulty itself. The only way to notice the successiveness of a series is to view it from the outside, as one views notes on a staff or cars on a passing train. This, however, is the usual standpoint for Whiteheadian analyses of personal identity. Yet at the same time the objection urges that the successiveness is not immediately experienced. But immediate experience views the series from within; in Whiteheadian terms, immediate experience pertains to the subjective immediacy of an actual occasion. The objection therefore is intrinsically inconsistent in demanding that we stand both within and without the series at the same time.

It does, however, suggest how the views of Bergson and Whitehead can be seen as *mutually complementary* rather than antithetical.[29] Why is it not possible to grant that becoming is both continuous and discontinuous, though in different senses correlative to diverse perspectives? With Whitehead and Cobb we may conclude to the (quantitative, homogeneous) discontinuity of becoming, while remembering that we are throughout arguing from an intellectual, not an intuitive, perspective; we are analyzing experience from without rather than from within. But we may at the same time accept Bergson's intuitive conviction, from his habitual perspective within experience, that experience as we live it is dynamically (that is qualitatively, heterogeneously) continuous.

To return to the above objection: becoming, when analyzed intellectually, discloses itself (if Whitehead is right) as epochal, successive. But from the intuitive perspective of immediate experience it shows itself (if Bergson is right) as continuous (with the non-spatial, dynamic continuity of qualitative heterogeneity). The experiencer, as such, is never in the Whiteheadian initial or final ("satisfaction") states, but always as it were in between; the experiencer, as such, does not leap from one discrete state to another, for the discreteness of the states is only intellectual.

What happens if we apply this notion of complementarity—or better, of the ancillarity of the intellectual to the intuitive—to the problem of personal identity about which Whitehead was himself uneasy?

Intellectual analysis had forced him by way of Zeno's arguments to conclude that becoming is epochal, yet he felt within his immediate experience, and saw within the experience of mankind, a deep conviction of the continuity of personal identity. Why can we not accept both these conclusions, realizing that they are the results of two different modes of analysis, two different perspectives? In this light the difficulties about reward and punishment, as well as the Whiteheadian problem about being able to say, "I did it!" simply vanish. Ontological identity is required only within the immediacy of experience. Within that experience, the now-I is often luminously identical with the then-I of "I did it!" As a consequence, the now-I feels the guilt or the elation of its identity with the then-I. The problems heretofore urged against the epochal theory in the name of personal identity disappear as soon as it is recognized that they are drawn from an intuitive perspective, from within experience, whereas Whitehead's analysis operates from an intellectual perspective, from without it.

This last statement holds even for Whitehead's analysis of subjectivity, though his *descriptions* of it are often intuitive. Consequently his distinction between microscopic and macroscopic (probably better called microcosmic and macrocosmic) analysis does not correspond to Bergson's distinction between intuition and intelligence. If microscopic analysis examines precisely subjectivity, it does so nonetheless in terms of abstract concepts, looking at it as a pathologist examines a body. It is a case, as Wordsworth would say, of dissecting an experience and thereby murdering it. But Whitehead knows what he is doing: he dissects in order to make his experience more vivid as well as wiser:

> The concrete reality is the starting-point of the process of individual experience, and it is the goal in the rationalization of consciousness. The prize at the goal is the enhancement of experience by consciousness and rationality. (MT 125)

> If you like to phrase it so, philosophy is mystical. For mysticism is direct insight into depths as yet unspoken. But the purpose of philosophy is to rationalize mysticism: not by explaining it away,

but by the introduction of novel verbal characterizations, rationally coordinated. (MT 174)

It is worth noticing how the interplay and the distinction between intuition and intelligence relate to two issues mentioned earlier. The first is the apparent awkwardness of speaking of the phases of concrescence as earlier or later with respect to one another, yet as not temporally analyzable. If Bergson is right, primordial time is duration, the flow of immediate experience itself. This duration is continuous, but with the dynamic continuity of becoming, not the static continuity of quantity. By intuition we place ourselves precisely within this duration; by intelligence we transform duration into a time that has all the essential characteristics of space, including quantitative continuity. This is the time, within the Whiteheadian analysis, in terms of which an actual occasion is temporally thick, not temporally divided (as concrescence), but temporally divisible (in potentiality, as concretum). Inevitably we think intellectually of the actual occasion as if it enjoyed quantitative continuity in its temporality. This distortion of time, natural though it is, gives rise to the perplexities about the phases of concrescence precisely by bestowing on these phases the wrong kind of continuity (as well as the wrong kind of distinctness). On the other hand, from an intuitive point of view there is no difficulty about understanding phases of our experiences as earlier or later, and as "melting into one another," within the dynamic continuity that is duration.

We may draw a parallel conclusion concerning the second issue, that of the general form of Whitehead's arguments for the epochal nature of becoming. It is now clear that they enjoy only a limited validity. For when Whitehead says, "there is no continuity of becoming," or when Cobb asserts, "if process is continuous, then freedom is unintelligible," the continuity referred to is the homogeneous continuity of quantity, and they are quite correct. There always remains, however, the awkwardness of asserting, within this context, that the resulting moments of becoming are temporally thick though not temporally anayzable. But this tells only half the story. Zeno's arguments should force us not only into an epochal theory of time, when viewed intellectually, they should also suggest to us that they need to be transcended if we are to achieve an integral view of what it is to become. From an intuitive viewpoint we have to abandon the tacit presupposition of the quantitative homogeneity of time in favor of the qualitative heterogeneity of duration.

III. CONCLUSION

I conclude, then, that Bergson and Whitehead are both right, Bergson in insisting that becoming is continuous, Whitehead in maintaining that it is epochal or discontinuous, for they argue from different perspectives and refer to different kinds of continuity. To see their positions as complementary rather than antithetical amounts to accepting the consequences of Bergson's contention that intuitive knowing is a distinct way of knowing: it operates in a different manner from intelligence—from a different perspective, if you will—and yields a different sort of result. Bergsonian intuition is more than instinct; it is reflective and judgmental. Hence Bergson's very conviction that, although intelligence is indispensable to the development of intuition, it is also, in its philosophical service, itself an intuitive judgment.

It is moreover an intuitive judgment shared by Whitehead. Whitehead recognized that however much the constructural elements of a scheme appear to acquire a certain unquestionability, "they remain metaphors mutely appealing for an imaginative leap." It is only by a "flash of insight" that philosophical first principles are captured (PR 4).

If with this distinction in mind between intuition and intelligence we reflect on the actual philosophical work of Bergson and Whitehead and of their followers, we may conclude, I think, that the viewpoint of each stands to gain something from that of the other.

What Bergson seems to need from Whitehead is precisely the kind of intellectual articulation of experience provided by the Categoreal Scheme.

Bergson is wrong, I think, in asserting that intellect "does not admit the unforeseeable," that it "rejects all creation" (CE 180). Whitehead's scheme exactly admits creation, and places it within the subjective immediacy of a highly complex organic unity of becoming. This does not dissipate the inherent mystery of self-creation but situates it within an abstract conceptual scheme. Furthermore, by his essential relegation of intellectual analysis to science rather than to philosophy Bergson renders himself vulnerable to the charge of subjectivism. He himself raises this difficulty: "if metaphysics is to proceed by intuition, . . . are we not going to shut the philosopher up in exclusive self-contemplation? Will not philosophy consist simply in watching oneself live, 'as a dozing shepherd watches the running water?'" (CM 217). I am not entirely satisfied with his reply; recognizing "the essentially active character of metaphysical intuition" is not enough. One must also recognize that if intuition has indeed a "character," then that character should be in some way accessible to intelligence. This criticism falls along nearly the same lines as that of Ingarden and Čapek. Čapek writes:

> (Ingarden) correctly points out that Bergson's criticism of the idea of absolute disorder . . . requires that even the dynamic processes, that is, duration itself, have a certain "order," a certain "structure," a certain recognizable, universal *whatness,* the correct grasping of which is one of the main goals of Bergson's epistemology. This implication of his own thought was overlooked by Bergson.[30]

To use the simplest but most profound instance: it is not a philosophical waste of time for Whitehead to analyze the basic character of becoming in terms of creativity, many, and one. Yet Whitehead himself would be the first to grant, along with Bergson, that "intuition may bring the intellect to recognize that life does not quite go into the category of the many nor yet into that of the one" (CE 195). As with all the other paraphernalia of Whitehead's conceptual scheme, creativity, many, and one are, as he said, metaphors mutely appealing for an imaginative leap.

What Whitehead, or at any rate, Whiteheadians, seem to need from Bergson is more attention to returning from abstraction to the immediacy of experience. Philosophy is sometimes less like the flight of an airplane than that of a balloon, which need not in principle come back down again. To confine discussion of personal identity, for instance, to the level of intellectual abstraction rather than that of intuitive immediacy is not, I am afraid, to return to that concrete experience in which philosophical wonder began. We need not suppose that accepting an intuited ontological identity of the "I" through time (at least as far as direct memory reaches) contradicts Whitehead's intellectual theory of inherited successive multiplicity. It is merely to tell the other side of the story. It is to let Bergson land the plane.

FIVE

Transmutation and Whitehead's Elephant

(1981)

This friendly criticism of two aspects of Whitehead's theory of sense perception was written for delivery at the First International Whitehead-Symposium held in Bonn, Germany, in 1981. The essay raises a problem internal to Whitehead's philosophy, a problem that did and still does bother me. It also adumbrates a criticism that Whitehead's philosophy seems to invite from the outside, a criticism of a possible incoherence between his intended epistemological realism and the epistemology implied in his theory of transmutation. I enlarge on what I consider to be a better notion of epistemological realism some years later (essay 13). Though transmutation is a technical notion in Whitehead's philosophy, the essay may yet be of some interest even to readers unacquainted with Whitehead's thought.

Originally published as "Transmutation and Whitehead's Elephant," in *Whitehead und der Prozeßbegriff; Whitehead and The Idea of Process,* Proceedings of the First International Whitehead-Symposium, eds. Harald Holz and Ernest Wolf-Gazo, 179–84 (Freiburg: Karl Alber, 1984). Reprinted with permission.

It has become almost axiomatic in science that the most fruitful experiment is often the one that fails. For if the experiment is rightly conceived and properly executed, its failure to yield the expected results must point to an inadequacy in the underlying theory. It shows that something has been left out, and it may suggest just those elements of the theory that need to be creatively recast. Lord Kelvin's two small clouds, which alone seemed to darken the skies of physics at the advent of the twentieth century, are a celebrated example of this kind of scientific adventure. The failure of theory to account for the behavior of radiating bodies and for the unexpected negative results of the Michelson-Morley ether detection experiments led ineluctably to the development of quantum mechanics on the one hand and of relativity theory on the other.

I wish here to propose a perplexity—or several entwined perplexities, both ontological and epistemological—that I find with Whitehead's theory of transmutation. I wish further to ask: May there not be here the equivalent of a negative experiment, a possibly fruitful failure calling for creative metaphysical reconstruction of Whitehead's system?

"We habitually observe by the method of difference," wrote Whitehead. "Sometimes we see an elephant, and sometimes we do not. The result is that an elephant, when present, is noticed."[1] Whitehead was right: when I was recently in the presence of an elephant, I noticed it. I now ask myself how, according to Whitehead's metaphysics, I am to explain my experience of noticing that elephant. No, let me simplify. I wish only to account for my *perceiving* the elephant. More simply still, I do not inquire how in perceiving it I recognize it as an elephant rather than, say, a water buffalo. I shall not even ask (though it needs to be asked) how I recognize it as an animal, as some kind of self-governing unity whose possibly capricious behavior I must allow for if I am in its proximity. Furthermore, I shall (perhaps mercifully) waive all the other senses and concentrate on vision alone, aware as I do so of Whitehead's telling criticism of the tendency to treat all sense perception in the exotic terms of sight.

Let me then begin simply by asking how, according to Whitehead, I perceive a large brown body that, for reasons we may for the present lay aside, I recognize as an elephant.

Well, says Whitehead, the actual occasions that make up the elephant's hide exhibit uniformly, in their physical, consequently also in their conceptual, feelings, the same or closely the same ingredient eternal object "brown." In prehending these multiple occasions the actual occasions of my visual organs themselves feel the brown feelings of the constituent occasions of the elephant's hide. It is in this way that eternal objects perform a two-way function: they qualify the subjective experience of the individual occasions, and they also serve as the link whereby one occasion becomes objectified in another. As Whitehead said, "We enjoy the green foliage of the spring greenly."[2] I was thus enjoying the brown of the elephant brownly. Finally, in some occasion of adequate complexity in my visual apparatus—if nowhere else at least in the dominant occasion of my perceiving—"transmutation" takes place. Since the same conceptual feeling of brown is indifferently felt in all my feelings of the constituent actual occasions of the elephant's hide, it is transmuted so as to be felt as characterizing the nexus itself that is the complexity of occasions—the corpuscular society—making up the hide. This may be summarized in Whitehead's own words: "We have to account for substitution of the one nexus in place of its component actual entities. This is Leibniz's problem that arises in his Monadology. He solves the problem by an unanalysed doctrine of 'confusion.' Some category is required to provide a physical feeling of a nexus as one entity with its own categoreal type of existence. This one physical feeling in the final subject is derived by transmutation from the various analogous conceptual feelings (with these various members as subjects) originated from these physical feelings . . . *The analogy of the physical feelings consists in the fact that their definite character exhibits the same ingredient eternal object.*"[3]

Before getting to my central difficulties I must confess that I have to strain to avoid thinking of experience, so explained, as illusory. For in Whitehead's theory brown does not belong to the nexus as such but to its individual constituent occasions. Transmutation takes place, after all, within the perceiver and does not constitute some additional unity ontologically cementing together the actual occasions perceived in the nexus. The elephant's hide, on the usual interpretation of Whitehead's theory, is really a nexus of countless microscopic actual occasions whose physical and conceptual feelings uniformly exhibit the ingredient eternal object "brown," but these individual brown feelings are blurred by the perceiver into brown belonging to a macroscopic elephant. Even if Whitehead has given an account of how a Leibnizian doctrine of "confusion" of experience can be analyzed, the resulting experience seems nonetheless to remain confused.

A more unsettling objection, however, is that Whitehead's theory of transmutation depends on projecting the felt-brown of individual actual occasions onto the nexus as a whole, *yet it is quite impossible that the individual actual occasions be felt as brown!* For on what might be called the orthodox interpretation, Whitehead's actual occasions, which are the ultimate constituents of the nexūs, the corpuscular societies that are physical bodies such as elephants, are truly microscopic both in space and in time, as small as or probably smaller than atoms or even electrons. Now it is a commonplace in modern physics that an atom cannot be thought of, let alone perceived, as colored. Color can be attributed only to the macroscopic bodies of ordinary experience, not to microentities. Yet Whitehead's fundamental actual occasions are of the atomic or even the subatomic order of magnitude. Thus the visual experience of a brown macroscopic object cannot possibly arise in the way Whitehead has described.

Brown cannot be prehended first in the constituent actual occasions of the elephant and then be transmuted so as to be felt as belonging to the elephant as a whole. Brown can only enter the picture as ingredient in some entity larger than Whitehead's actual occasions.

A second, related difficulty is that in this doctrine of transmutation Whitehead's epistemology seems to exemplify a kind of naive realism. For on his theory the eternal object "brown" is first ingredient in the conceptual feelings of the entities making up the elephant's hide, then is prehended by the perceiver. That is, brown is already in the elephant prior to its being perceived, and that same brown is what shows up in the perception.

But this kind of objectivism simply will not do. Both Galileo and Newton long ago pointed out, in effect, that the brown that I see in the elephant can by no means be *simply in* the elephant out there.[4] It can only be found in the seeing of the elephant.[5]

It does not, of course, thereby follow that the brown is wholly subjective, *solely* in the perceiver, as Galileo and Newton, followed by Descartes, Locke, and Hume proceeded most disastrously to assume in their representational epistemologies. There is a third possibility: brown is neither simply in the physical elephant, the elephant-as-it-is-in-itself, nor purely in the eye of the beholder. Brown is in the seen-elephant, the elephant-in-relation-to-the-seer, and that of course involves the seer as well as the elephant. In other words, color in the most proper and concrete sense is neither a simple objective ingredient of a macroscopic object, nor is it an interior fantasy (however provoked) in the viewer. It is rather a characteristic of the object precisely and only in its relationship to the seer within the very act of seeing.[6] The seen-elephant, which in fact is brown, is the real elephant but not the *Elefant-an-sich*. Yet I do not see how Whitehead's theory of transmutation, as it stands, is capable of incorporating this necessary kind of critical realism.

It is with special trepidation that I thus accuse Whitehead of relapsing into some kind of naive realism. For first of all, he was aware of the danger and wanted to avoid it. He wrote: "from the seventeenth century onwards the notion of the simple inherence of the colour in the stone has had to be given up" (PR 78). Furthermore, in her recent book Elizabeth Kraus has interpreted Whitehead's epistemology more benignly than I. She writes: "In an Indo-European language, 'blue' invariably ends up qualifying a noun (the 'name of a person, place or thing'); in Whitehead's conception, it is the subjective form of a relational activity: a vector feeling-tone, not a bare passive quality, an adverb not an adjective. 'Blue' cannot be abstracted from the eye's functioning in response to an environmental stimulus; it has *no* meaning apart from an eye."[7]

I agree that Whitehead *ought* to have thought of "blue" in the way Kraus describes in that last sentence. But I seriously doubt that in fact he did, or that if he did, he did it consistently with the rest of his metaphysics. How else are we to understand the following account he explicitly gives of transmutation and eternal objects of the subjective species?

In the first stage of B's physical feeling, the subjective form of B's feeling is conformed to the subjective form of A's feeling. Thus this eternal object in B's experience will have a two way mode of functioning. It will be among the determinants of A for B, and it will be among the determinants of B's way of sympathy with A.

For example, "redness" may first be the definiteness of an emotion which is a subjective form in the experience of A; it then becomes an agent whereby A is objectified for B, so that A is objectified in respect to its prehension with this emotion. But A may be only one occasion of a nexus, such that each of its members is objectified for B by a prehension with an analogous subjective form. Then by the operation of the Category of Transmutation, the nexus is objectified for B as illustrated by the characteristic "redness." (PR 291–92)

And in *Adventures of Ideas* he writes: "The point to be decided is whether the green meadow in spring-time, as it appears to us, in any direct way conforms to the happenings, within the region of the meadow, and more particularly within the regions of the blades of grass. Have we any grounds for the belief that in some way things really are in those regions as our senses perceive those regions?" (AI 322). From the context and the succeeding chapters it is clear that Whitehead thinks we have such grounds.

Related to the other difficulties I have mentioned is Whitehead's failure explicitly to incorporate into his theory of transmutation the dimension of time. Is this not curious? For color involves wave length, and wave length involves a time span. As Bergson wrote, "[T]here is no perception which is not full of memories."[8] Indeed, Bergson's theory of "contraction" may be an attractive alternative: that "the 'subjectivity' of sensible qualities consists above all else in a kind of contraction of the real, effected by our memory." And again: "In one sense, my perception is indeed truly within me, since it contracts into a single moment of my duration that which, taken in itself, spreads over an incalculable number of moments."[9] The sensory quality "brown" arises within the perceiving subject by reason of the contraction of the multiple vibrations of the light into the unity of perceptual experience.

If the above difficulties be genuine, one must ask how much weight to give them. Might we, like Hume with his missing shade of blue, simply write them off as not important enough to call for a major overhaul of Whitehead's metaphysics? Perhaps their import can be better assessed if we relate them to another familiar complaint.

Whitehead's theory of transmutation is essentially linked to his atomistic view of reality. Ivor Leclerc writes: "[T]hough Whitehead avoids Leibniz's phenomenalism, nevertheless for him a society or body must be an 'aggregate' in the same fundamental sense as it is for Leibniz, namely that it is does not constitute a real unitary entity, the 'unity' of the society being a feature within each of the component actual entities individually."[10] Finding this inadequate, Leclerc proposes an alternative theory of "compound substances." Analogously, Edward Pols maintains that the originative act of a macroscopic agent transcends the linear time of an event-ontology.[11] So also, Paul Weiss has urged the recognition of "natural individuals," complex wholes that can more believably be thought to be the seat of action and responsibility than the skeletal societies of microentities in terms of which Whitehead has to describe the person.[12] In fact this orthodox Whiteheadian view of the person appears so contrary to common sense and to some of his own statements that it has even been argued that Whitehead did not himself hold it![13]

I cannot believe this last claim, but I agree with the criticisms. Furthermore I must ask: Do the additional difficulties about transmutation perhaps constitute the straw that finally breaks the back, as it were, of the Whiteheadian corpuscular elephant? What can metaphysically be done to preserve the ontological and epistemological integrity of the elephant that I encountered?

SIX

Coming Around Again in Philosophy

(1982)

This is the presidential address I gave before the Jesuit Philosophical Association of America in 1982 in Houston. It reflects back on my natural attraction to Bergson's and Whitehead's philosophies, particularly as expressed in "Invitation to a Philosophical Revolution" ten years earlier (essay 2), but from the more critical view that the intervening years furnished.

In reviewing this address now I notice, with some surprise, that the viewpoint I here expressed is more closely aligned to that of Henri Bergson than to that of Whitehead. Here also may be my first enunciations of what I call the "Principle of Creative Synthesis" as well as of my polemic against "possible worlds," along with allusions to problems about time, human freedom, and teleological metaphysics, which occupy much of my later essays or books. I trust that the reader will forgive the unusually personal nature of these reflections, given my audience of fellow Jesuits, most of whom were old friends.

Originally published as "Coming Around Again in Philosophy," *Proceedings of the Jesuit Philosophical Association* for 1982. Reprinted with permission.

If your life is like mine, it has a curious way of coming full circle. I cannot help but be struck, for example, that as a twelve-year-old Boy Scout from Hollywood, and once again two years later, I overnighted with the troop in the very building at Santa Clara University in which I now reside, the present Jesuit residence.

Furthermore, I find that this kind of recurrence obtains not only in trivial circumstances but also in substantive philosophic issues. Even my boyhood illuminations and perplexities have a way of haunting my philosophic middle age. For instance, the very first intellectual thrill I can recall occurred when I was about four years old. It accompanied the sudden realization, without anyone having posed the question to me, that the toothpaste in the tube is not all curled up inside but just gets that way when it comes out. I remember how euphoric I felt at achieving this insight on my own, and, as you will see, I find that that same basic insight plays a central role in my philosophic thinking today. Another insight, or rather perplexity, which spontaneously occurred to me at about the age of fourteen and which in a sense perplexes me still, turns out, on educated reflection, to have been a legitimate and powerful variant of Zeno's paradoxes. I spare you the details, but report that when I tried to explain the difficulty to my grandfather he thought I had taken leave of my sanity. Perhaps he was right.

Now as I said, both of these boyhood experiences instantiate philosophic problems or viewpoints that are crucial in my thinking today. Furthermore there is another way in which I find I have come around again in philosophy. In the spring of 1971 I once before addressed this body, delivering myself of an invited paper, which I called, "Invitation to a Philosophic Revolution." That paper was deliberately written to be controversial, to stimulate discussion. It was a punching bag paper and I certainly got what I invited! One Jesuit in particular reacted exactly as my grandfather had done and pretty clearly insinuated that I had gone completely crackers! For in that paper I compared Thomistic philosophy in many ways unfavorably with the philosophy of Whitehead, and called for some kind of original synthesis that would embody the better central insights of both views. The paper, I am sorry to say, was not very scholarly in its critique of Thomas's philosophy, and it leaned heavily on the writings of Charles Hartshorne, who, though an original philosopher in his own right, was a principal proponent of Whitehead's basic thinking. Hartshorne, I fear, did not well understood St. Thomas, yet for all that his criticisms had to be taken seriously.

In the eleven years that have passed, my own enthusiasm for Whitehead's philosophy has altered considerably, so that I am moved here to engage in a kind of Augustinian *retractatio*—not necessarily a retraction but a reconsideration or rethinking of the issues. With Fagan in *Oliver* I am "reviewing the situation." In short, having for better or for worse pleaded before you on that former occasion on behalf of Whitehead's philosophy, and indeed, having by the publication of the same paper practically brought several Christian thinkers into the process fold (as they subsequently informed me), I come tonight neither to bury Whitehead nor to praise him, but carefully and briefly to assess what I now take to be the chief philosophic values and inadequacies of his metaphysical viewpoint. And since, of course, I can only do this from my present standpoint, this also amounts to a kind of philosophic confession.

First, then, the principal virtues of Whitehead's metaphysics. It lends itself more readily than does traditional Christian philosophy to a philosophic description of the scriptural account of the relation between God and creatures—that is to say, of a divine involvement with finite entities precisely in their temporality. In the traditional view, as you well know, God could not unequivocally be said to be really related to the world, but only the world related to God. Whereas knowledge and love normally relate the knower and the lover to the known and the beloved, it long seemed, oddly enough, that in the case of eminent or infinite knowledge and infinite love, God the knower and God the lover, instead of being preeminently related to what he knows and what he loves, was altogether unrelated. Our colleague Father Norris Clarke, feeling the weight of this criticism, has already gone a long way toward reconciling a neo-Thomist position with human and scriptural language in this regard. For Hartshorne's complaint about the God described by St. Anselm cannot, I think, lightly be disregarded. Anselm had inquired of God, you will remember, how it is that God could be compassionate, since he cannot suffer. In answer Anselm wrote, "Truly, thou art [compassionate] in terms of *our* experience, but thou art not so in terms of thine own. For, when thou beholdest us in our wretchedness, we experience the effect of compassion, but thou doest not experience the feeling."[1] To this, Hartshorne tellingly replies: "To say, 'all the effects of compassion, only not the compassion itself,' is to mock us."[2]

Furthermore, Whitehead's thought prohibits one from thinking of God as a kind of divine playwright, who either has inexorably dictated all the events in world history, or who, in the manner of Leibniz's God, has at least hypothetically examined the fully detailed concept of such a history and then, in effect, said, "Yes, let that world be." Whitehead-ian thought thinks rather of a kind of divine creative adaptation, with infinite conceptual resources, continuously adjusted according to the responses of the creature. In this view God is less like a playwright than like the chess player mentioned by William James. If Bobby Fisher plays chess with me he will most certainly win the game and win it according to a particular strategy of his own choosing; yet he will not be able to predict ahead of time every one of his own moves, for he must constantly adjust his moves to mine. In the process view it is not possible to suppose that God, as it were, knew what the course of historic events *would* be *if* he should decide to create the world and *apart* from his deciding to create it, and then so to speak went ahead and created it anyway. For, as I argue in a forthcoming publication (essay 8 of this volume) apart from the actual decisions of real agents there is just no such determinateness to be known, not even by God. The alternative is for God to appropriate to himself all determining activity in the world, thus depriving you and me of our freedom and responsibility.

Secondly, Whitehead's philosophy hinges on what I shall call a "Principle of Creative Synthesis," a metaphysical articulation of the ongoing process both in the world and in the immediacy of human experience. It regards this process as a kind of self-creative evolution that is through and through teleological and value-laden. It calls you to think of the immediacy of your human experience in terms of a creative synthesizing of the world as it affects you, a present synthesis of the past with a view toward the future. It thus regards human experience as mirroring the more general structure of cosmic evolution on the whole. This is an exciting viewpoint, stressing the adventure and the responsi-bility of everyday decisions. For given a certain width of possibility dictated by the fabric of present and past events, the synthetic activity of present process alone produces the definiteness of actuality, an exact configuration of the universe, a configuration that, prior to its getting determined by this activity of real agents, *had* no specification save perhaps in the actual conceptual projections of real agents.[3]

So you see, my earliest boyhood illumination was nothing other than a primitive version of the Principle of Creative Synthesis to which I now strongly adhere. The toothpaste is indeed not curled up inside the tube; it only gets its present dimensions *when* it comes out and by the *act* of coming out, which is in effect the activity of a real agent squeezing the tube. I therefore am convinced that Bergson was right in claiming that possibility—in the sense of determinate configuration—does not precede actuality. That is, temporally prior to the activities of real agents there was no determinate form in the present structure of actuality. Mozart's *Forty-First Symphony* cannot be said to have been possible before Mozart conceived it and thereby gave it its definiteness, for prior to that conception there just was no *it* to be called possible or impossible. You cannot legitimately ask, for instance, whether Mozart's *Forty-Second Symphony* was possible before Mozart died (I am assuming he wrote only forty-one). Had he written still another symphony it would presumably have been listed as the "forty-second," but there just *is* no determinate form, *not even in the realm of possibility,* which is that of Mozart's *possible Forty-Second Symphony* for the very good reason that there never was an *actual Forty-Second Symphony.*

At least two of the consequences of this view make a real difference in how I regard my life and the world. The first is that Whitehead's view, like Bergson's, takes time seriously in the sense of denying that the future lies out there waiting for us, even though we have not yet arrived at it. Such a conception destroys time and freedom just as surely as it destroys the function of present process. For example: we have all been urged in retreats to put ourselves on our own deathbeds, to contemplate our future deaths, and we have speculated whether we shall in fact die in bed or on the highway, and so forth, with all the particular attendant circumstances. According to the process view there is for us, here in time, just no such thing as your death or mine. I shall indeed die, but "my death," with the implied determinateness of that notion, simply is *not a reality* for me, and I therefore cannot realistically

speculate on it as if it were for me a fact. For me as a time-bound creature, there is just *no such thing* as "my death." If there were, the future
would be fated and nothing free.

I am not thereby denying a divine transcendent knowledge of all
temporal events; I am only granting, with Boethius, that such divine
knowledge is possible only because it is not *fore*knowledge at all.

The second consequence, to which I have already alluded, concerns
possible worlds and divine providence. For to hold with Leibniz, and
perhaps with St. Thomas, that God can promote a possible world (a
hypothetical, determinate, and complete cosmic history) to an actual
world, and that in fact He has once done so, seems to me intolerably to
aggravate the problem of evil in the world and of the possibility of
human freedom and responsibility. With process thinkers generally I
think it is just not metaphysically possible that God has available a
kind of metaphysical supermarket of possible worlds from which He
can select one or more for *realization*. There is nothing to prevent God
from conjecturing hypothetical world histories, but there *is* something
to prevent Him from promoting them to actuality, namely, his own
intention not to preclude human freedom by appropriating to Himself
all determining process. In this sense it follows from the process viewpoint—and I think it is correct—that there are simply *no* possible worlds
for God to choose from in creating an *actual* world. This also implies
that God Himself cannot know what *would* determinately happen in a
hypothetical world *if* He should decide to create it (but *apart* from that
decision). Here, of course, I am disagreeing with Molina; but then I
have always disagreed with Molina, from my childhood tube of toothpaste and through my theological studies. I think that his conception of
conditional futures, or "futuribles," is metaphysically untenable.

On another issue, I give credit to Whitehead for recognizing the
value dimension in immediate experience. This roughly corresponds to
the medieval association of *bonum* with *ens*. Whitehead writes:

> Our enjoyment of actuality is a realization of worth, good or
> bad. It is a value experience. Its basic expression is—Have a care,
> here is something that matters! Yes—that is the best phrase—the
> primary glimmering of consciousness reveals something that
> matters.[4]

Whitehead thinks that the importance that we feel in experience is objectively given, even though, of course, there is a dependence on the receptivity of us as feelers. In this respect I think that his view closely parallels that of a number of phenomenologists. Certainly Whitehead's view radically diverges from the subjectivistic analyses of value that are in common currency and that are almost always linked with a representational epistemologoy, a view strongly repudiated by Whitehead.

The experience of color vision exemplifies in a trivial way Whitehead's notion of this value dimension of experience. Unless you are color blind, you know by experience that there is an inherent value in color vision, a value experienced but not really explainable, least of all to one who has never seen color. This value, thinks Whitehead, is not just something we subjectively attach to visual experience after we have already had it, but something we find inherent within the visual experience itself as primitively given. Very specially this value dimension of experience fits essentially into Whitehead's thoroughly teleological view of creative process in general and human experience in particular. For Whitehead, building on the analogy of human experience, *all* process is teleological, goal-directed, and this means that there is given in experience the value weight not only of the determinate past but of inherent possibility felt as attractive.

I give Whitehead credit, too, for regarding the universe and experience as forming an organic whole. I mean that he recognizes that the fabric of human experience reveals itself as involving a world, things of immediate concern, and a subject. Here is one way he puts it:

> [T]he primitive stage of discrimination [of experience] is not primarily qualitative. It is the vague grasp of reality, dissecting it into a threefold scheme, namely, "The Whole," "That Other," and "This-My-Self." . . . There is the feeling of the ego, the others, the totality.[5]

Such a view is as deeply epistemological as it is metaphysical. It recognizes a basic objectivity as simply *given in* perception—that we *feel* ourselves within a wider world, a feeling that must be accepted at face value, that we focus our attention on that which is of concern to us, and that we do it from our perspective as subject, a subject to whom that other is of concern.

This then is the broader experiential context within which Whitehead's theory of prehensions, by which one entity feels the other entities of its given world, is a legitimate expression of the objectivity of ordinary sense perception. Whitehead does not have to fight his way through or past phenomena to reach the world because he finds himself already *in* a world, and the world, on the other hand, in him, through his prehensions of it.

Finally, and intimately linked with the value dimension of experience and with its organic character, one notes Whitehead's explicit emphasis on a sense of *causal derivation* as primitively given in experience. I think this is an epistemological contribution of the first importance. It recognizes causal derivations as actually *given* in experience, in a place where Hume, or even Kant, never thought of looking for it. I believe Whitehead is entirely correct in refusing to take up the epistemological question where Kant left it, but in correcting, by appeal to experience, the phenomenalistic position bequeathed to Kant by Hume and accepted uncritically (ironically enough!) by Kant. Whitehead thinks that Kant gave an ingenious solution to a badly framed problem, and I think he is right.

In all this I find a fascinating parallel to Whitehead's view in Robert Pirsig's book, *Zen and the Art of Motorcycle Maintenance*. In this book (which is really neither about Zen nor about motorcycles) Pirsig writes:

> Quality couldn't be independently related with either the subject or the object but could be found *only in the relationship of the two with each other.* It is the point at which subject and object meet. . . . Quality is not a *thing*. It is an *event*. . . . It is the event at which the subject becomes aware of the object.[6]

I suppose that, like Mark Antony, I have praised Whitehead when I had said I wouldn't, and perhaps too much at length. I now turn to wielding Brutus's dagger, and promise to do it rather more expeditiously.

After some nineteen years of working with Whitehead's thought, I confess that I have come tardily to the conclusion that his system, despite its impressive complexity, coherence, and faithfulness to many aspects of experience is, as it stands at least, metaphysically inadequate: it is inadequate as a foundational metaphysics; it is inadequate in its conception of God, especially for me as a Christian; and it is inadequate in its conception of Man.

I think it is inadequate as a foundational metaphysics mainly because, as Norris Clarke has pointed out,[7] it is ineluctably pluralistic and hence cannot found radical intelligibility. Its ultimate principle, Creativity, necessarily *presupposes* a Many to be synthesized into a new One, which then inexorably becomes part of a new Many. Furthermore, there is no ultimate reason provided, or even possible, I think, why the primordial nature of God should be its supreme instantiation. Despite Fr. John Stacer's desire to have it otherwise, I think it is just not possible in a philosophy basically like Whitehead's, to omit, as Fr. Stacer wants, "every suggestion of ultimate dualism or ultimate pluralism."[8]

Whitehead's philosophy, I say, is also inadequate with regard to God. In the first place, although it is true that a certain sense can be made within his system of a divine freedom with regard to the world, I think it cannot properly be called a divine freedom with regard to creating. For in Whitehead's system there is simply no adequate consideration given to the act of existing, Thomas's *esse,* the participation of which can alone, I think, make philosophic sense out of the Christian notion of the ontological dependence of the world on God. The Whiteheadian notion of Creativity is just not that of Thomas's *esse.* Whitehead, I think, is not concerned to ask why there *is* a world; he takes the world for granted and asks why it is the way that it is and why it behaves as it does. Fundamentally I think Whitehead's view is an essentialism rather than an existentialism. Furthermore, as Lewis Ford has pointed out, there is no room on Whitehead's principle for positing, as a variant, that God creates the *esse* of the creature, and the creature self-creates its *essentia.* For since the Whiteheadian actual occasion is not a substance but is identified with its own free act of self-constitution, there is no way God could create that particular instantiation of Creativity without ipso facto preempting the freedom of the creature to decide for itself what it is to be. Furthermore, Whiteheadian views invariably tend to introduce temporality into God (such as Stacer's allusions to God's "developing total capability"). I think that Boethius and Thomas were closer to the truth on this than Whitehead.

To bring this indictment to an end, I think Whitehead's view of *Man* is also fundamentally inadequate since it disintegrates Man into a cluster of subordinate, ontologically distinct entities, both at any moment of the person's existence and also over an interval of time. It think it is just not possible for a Whiteheadian George Washington to utter that expression of moral responsibility, "I did it!" because the "I" that did it was a different ontological entity from the "I" that says it. I find Whitehead's epochal or episodic—I almost said stroboscopic—view of personal identity through time simply unbelievable. Bergson was much closer to the truth in discerning a radical continuity of becoming in the immediacy of experience.[9] A metaphysics should account for this, not dismiss it.

Whitehead's main reason for insisting on the episodic or epochal nature of becoming, even that of a human being, was his conviction that a metaphysics of *substance* was no longer possible. I have identified for myself four distinct reasons why he held this, and I expect to show in a projected essay (number 9 of this collection) that none of them is in fact cogent. One of them, however, happens to be Zeno's paradoxes, and so I am once again haunted by a perplexity of my youth. Like the donkey turning the grindstone I have come around again in philosophy, if not full circle, at least in once again sharing with you my philosophic conscience.

SEVEN

Impossible Worlds

(1983)

The previous essay points out but does not much develop the absurdity of attributing ontological status to the now popular conception of "possible worlds." The following essay is my first detailed polemic against that very popular fiction cherished by so many contemporary philosophers but destructive of the metaphysical advance made by Aristotle when he introduced the dynamic notion of the potentiality within actual beings for as yet unrealized actuality. I argue that trading potentiality for the fiction of possible worlds is exactly the wrong way to deal with the modal ideas of possibility and necessity. Thirteen years later I focused the same central argument more narrowly and less historically in "Why Possible Worlds Aren't" (essay 14 of this volume). As far as I recall, the three principles and two corollaries that I lay out here, and which are a formalization of my Principle of Creative Synthesis referred to in the previous essay, are my own, and I use them repeatedly in subsequent writings. The reader should know that this essay is only moderately technical.

Originally published as "Impossible Worlds," *International Philosophical Quarterly* 23, no. 2 (September 1983): 251–65. Reprinted with permission.

No philosophic thicket has grown so profusely in the past twenty years as that of "possible worlds." None perhaps is so tangled. I propose not so much to untangle it as to cut much of it away. For whatever the purely logical or formal advantages of the notion (and I have nothing to say about that), I shall argue that it is entirely misguided to invoke "possible worlds" to make sense out of the actual world. For, I shall argue, "possible worlds," as usually understood, are metaphysical monstrosities: they are inconsistent with metaphysical principles that do in fact obtain, and hence are metaphysically, if not quite logically, impossible.

Let me identify a little more closely some of the shrubbery I propose to excise. Leibniz's "possible worlds" provide the classic case, and it has been argued lately (as well as long ago) that there cannot be any "best" of all possible worlds any more than there can be a greatest integer.[1] I shall argue, however, that there are no possible worlds at all, at least none of metaphysical interest.

Fascination with Leibniz's notion of possible worlds mushroomed lately because it seems to provide modal logic with a semantics, a theoretical account of the conditions under which formulae of a system are true. Thus Kripke and others have developed a paraphrase roughly to the effect that a statement of the form, "It is necessary that p," is true if and only if p is true in all possible worlds; a statement of the form, "It is possible that p" is true if and only if it is true in at least one possible world. A vigorous and complex controversy has ensued over the meaning and philosophic respectability of the very notion of possible worlds. Positions range from sheer "possibilism"—for example that of David K. Lewis, who maintains an infinity of worlds, all equally real, the possible as well as the actual—to various forms of "actualism," which holds that all references to possible worlds must reduce to references to elements of the actual world (for instance, Nicholas Rescher and Robert Merrihew Adams).

Let us take a closer look at what Lewis means by "possible worlds." He writes:

> I believe that there are possible worlds other than the one we happen to inhabit. If an argument is wanted, it is this. It is uncontroversially true that things might be otherwise than they are. I

believe, and so do you, that things could have been different in countless ways. But what does this mean? Ordinary language permits the paraphrase: there are many ways things could have been besides the way they actually are. On the face of it, this sentence is an existential quantification. It says that there exist many entities of a certain description, to wit "ways things could have been." I believe that things could have been different in countless ways; I believe permissible paraphrases of what I believe; taking the paraphrase at its face value, I therefore believe in the existence of entities that might be called "ways things could have been." I prefer to call them "possible worlds."[2]

What distinction is there, then, between possible worlds and the actual world? Lewis replies:

> If asked what sort of thing [possible worlds] are, I cannot give the kind of reply my questioner probably expects: that is, a proposal to reduce possible worlds to something else.
>
> I can only ask him to admit that he knows what sort of thing our actual world is, and then explain that other worlds are more things of *that* sort, differing not in kind but only in what goes on at them. Our actual world is only one world among others. We call it alone actual not because it differs in kind from all the rest but because it is the world we inhabit. The inhabitants of other worlds may truly call their own worlds actual, if they mean by "actual" what we do; for the meaning we give to "actual" is such that it refers at any world *i* to that world *i* itself. "Actual" is indexical, like "I" or "here," or "now"; it depends for its reference on the circumstances of utterance, to wit the world where the utterance is located.[3]

Against Lewis I shall in this essay contend that in general there are *no* "ways things could have been," even though my position is not deterministic. Thus I think that even an actualist like Rescher, who wishes to root the possible in the actual, grants too much when he supposes there are "as yet unrealized possibilities that await us in the future" as well as "the possible albeit unrealized doings of actual things such as my possible attendance at the film I failed to see last night."[4]

The shadow of Parmenides seems to lie over these discussions. For whether with Lewis one takes possible worlds to be as real as the actual, or one tries to replace them solely by the actual, the upshot seems the same: all is reduced to a planar understanding of what it means to be. In these controversies the anti-Parmenidean (Aristotelian) notion of *potentiality*, as an intrinsic character of the actual, has tended to be supplanted by *possibilities* (in the plural), Lewis's "ways things could have been," purely formal and discrete patterns. The dynamism of potentiality has been exchanged for a dust of homeless forms.

What I propose to do is the following: (1) set up some metaphysical (or cosmological) principles descriptive of the ultimate structure of the experienced world; (2) use these principles to evaluate the modem theories of Lewis and Rescher, and the classical theories of Molina and Leibniz, noting the import of these principles, especially as related to the problem of God and evil; (3) finally, come to grips with a fundamental objection against the whole contention of this essay.[5]

1. SOME METAPHYSICAL (COSMOLOGICAL) PRINCIPLES

In fashioning the few principles we shall need in order to examine the notion of possible worlds, I have in mind Alfred North Whitehead's description of speculative philosophy:

> Speculative Philosophy is the endeavour to frame a coherent, logical necessary system of general ideas in terms of which every element of our experience can be interpreted. By this notion of "interpretation" I mean that everything of which we are conscious, as enjoyed, perceived, willed, or thought, shall have the character of a particular instance of the general scheme.[6]

The sense that Whitehead here gives to the word "necessary" is delicate but crucial:

The adequacy of the scheme over every item [of experience] does not mean adequacy over such items as happen to have been considered. It means that the texture of observed experience, as illustrating the philosophic scheme, is such that all related experience must exhibit the same texture. Thus the philosophic scheme should be "necessary," in the sense of bearing in itself its own warrant of universality throughout all experience, provided that we confine ourselves to that which communicates with immediate matter of fact. . . .

This doctrine of necessity in universality means that there is an essence to the universe which forbids relationships beyond itself, as a violation of its rationality. Speculative philosophy seeks that essence. (PR 3–4)

The test of such a speculative system must be found in its power and scope, in the way it draws out fundamental insights (including non-philosophical ones) into rational connection and balance.

For a philosophic scheme ultimately reposes on principles describing our experience of the world that suggest themselves with a kind of direct immediacy confirmed by careful reflection. David Lewis almost suggests as much when he writes: "One comes to philosophy already endowed with a stock of opinions. It is not the business of philosophy either to undermine or to justify these preexisting opinions, to any great extent, but only to try to discover ways of expanding them into an orderly system."[7]

We must, with Henri Bergson, carefully distinguish between the intuitions (properly understood) that ground our metaphysics and the conceptual terms by which we attempt to articulate and communicate them. Concepts are like intellectual snapshots that, however numerous and exact, never capture *process* any more than stroboscopic photos of a bird in flight capture *flying*. No speculative scheme ever quite succeeds in articulating experience. The principles I am about to suggest, then, are imperfect, conceptual expressions of what I find, after reflection, to be fundamental features of the experienced world.[8] The (perhaps infelicitous) names I give to the principles are mainly my own, but I am indebted to the thought of Bergson, Whitehead, and Charles Hartshorne for the evidence with which these principles recommend themselves to me. And since they do not form a whole metaphysical system but only a fragment of a cosmology, I believe they are consistent also with the metaphysics of St. Thomas Aquinas. To me, at least, they gain their credibility both from their intrinsic obviousness and from the more compelling description they afford of the adventure of human experience.

Principle 1: The Principle of Determinateness: That settled actuality (past actuality, whether immediate or remote) is wholly determinate and particular.[9]

Examples: (1) *Gone with the Wind,* as completed, contains a particular set of words arranged in a determinate order. In this it differs from a novel only envisioned or in the process of being written. (2) Brahms' *Fourth Symphony* is a particular set of notes determinately arranged. (I am here referring, of course, to the symphony taken as a formal pattern, a pattern displayed in the score; I am not speaking of a performing of the symphony.) (3) The way you last passed through a doorway (whether right foot first or left, and so on).

Principle 2: The Principle of Process (or *of Determination*): That dynamic actuality (or existing actuality or concrete process) is, or at any rate involves, a process of determination whereby from the indeterminateness of potentiality there is educed the determinateness of settled actuality. This is a process of actualizing the determinate from the limited indeterminateness given in the present for the immediate future. *This is the precise location of the free act.*[10]

Examples: (1) The writing of *Gone with the Wind.* (2) The composing of Brahms' *Fourth Symphony.* (3) Your walking through a doorway. (4) Your driving a dune buggy on the beach. The surf on your right and the sheer palisades on your left set restrictions on the range of possibility for your driving; so also do the steering radius of the buggy, your speed, and other factors. Within that range of possibility, however, it is your act of driving (steering, etc.) that forms determinate tracks in the sand behind you, tracks that, prior to your driving, had no definition, were simply not there.

One may notice a strong similarity between *Principle 2* and the hylomorphic account of substantial change. That change is commonly said to be a process of "educing" from the potentiality of the matter a form not previously "there."[11] As I originally conceived *Principle 2* I assumed that this determining of the present cannot be instantaneous, but embodies, within a temporal thickness, a unique co-presence of the immediate past, the present, and the immediate future. Such a co-presence would have to be temporally thick yet not temporally divisible (following Whitehead, especially as explicated by John B. Cobb).

Principle 3: Agency alone educes the particular determinateness of settled actuality from the indeterminateness of Possibility. (By "Possibility," with an upper-case P, I here suggest the *range* for particular possibilities. Also I am using "agency" broadly, to mean originative causal activity, whether conscious and intentional or not.) Apart from such agency there do not exist possibilities but only Possibility. When one deliberately considers different possibilities for acting, one has already supplied the (intentional) agency whereby these possibilities enjoy their distinctness.

Corollary 1: Particular possibilities, particular ways of being, do not temporally precede actuality, whether settled or dynamic. This is a specification of Bergson's somewhat less guarded principle that the possible does not precede the real.

Examples: (1) *Gone with the Wind* was not even a possibility before Margaret Mitchell conceived it. This is not to say that it was *im*possible, given the existence and the health of the author. It means rather that, prior to its conception (and I am granting, for the sake of simplicity, that the novel existed in some real sense when it had been well conceived by Mitchell), there was no "it" to refer to. It was Mitchell's creative act that produced that determinateness of concepts and words that constitutes the novel. Mitchell invented it, she did not find it lying around among a preexisting collection of possibilities.

(2) The formal pattern of notes that is Brahms' *Fourth Symphony* (to be more precise: that is the directions for, or the character of, a performing of Brahms' *Fourth*) had no existence in the temporal world before Brahms conceived it. It was therefore not around even to be "possible."

This point is illuminated by asking whether "Brahms' *Fifth Symphony*" was possible before Brahms died. (I am assuming that Brahms wrote only four symphonies.) The question turns out to be illegitimate, for we have no Brahms' *Fifth Symphony* to talk about. We may inquire about *a* fifth symphony but not about *the Fifth Symphony*. There is no Brahms' *Fifth Symphony* that was or is possible for the precise reason that there never was an *actual Fifth Symphony*.

Bergson was right, then, in maintaining that the "possible" (understood determinately) arises only simultaneously with the real. The "possible" in that sense is just the *character* of the real (whether past or present)—in Lewis's phrase, "the *way* things are." But then the "possible" is by no means identical with "Possibility" or with "potentiality" (see *Corollary 2* below).

I should further clarify some of these distinctions. I take "possibilities" (or "possibles") to be Lewis's "ways things are," formal patterns of being. "Possibility" with a capital P I take to be either the total, unitary, but structured *fabric of possibilities,* or else the *range* available for real possibilities in a particular case, this range being governed by the determinate character of the settled past in its relation to Possibility as a whole. "Potentiality," however, is the power, the *potentia,* the *dynamis* residing within the real of becoming determinate, of realizing itself, in some particular new way within the given range of Possibility.

(3) In your dune buggy on the beach you have a literal width of possibility for where you can drive (that is, between the sea and the palisades), but it is the driving itself that creates the determinate tracks in the sand. They do not lie out there ahead of you, waiting to be selected. Yet the model suited to most current discussion would rather be that of a railroad engine entering a switchyard. All the tracks are already laid out there, and the activity of throwing switches merely determines which track the engine winds up on.

(4) The doorframe constitutes a certain width of possibility for how you can comport yourself in leaving the room. But precisely how you *do* walk out acquires determinateness precisely by your act of walking out.

(5) More strikingly: I have in the past pondered my own death (as you probably have your own), wondering how far it lies in the future

and what its circumstances will be. But on the above principles such speculation is meaningless. There is no such thing ahead of time as "my death," taken in the implied full determinateness. This denies neither that I shall die nor that the passage of events gradually narrows the range of indeterminacy. It asserts, however, that the precise character (and time) of my death will be determined only by, and simultaneously with, my dying.

Bergson was right, I think, in claiming that we habitually treat time as if it were a kind of space. We think of our death as lying out ahead of us in time in the same way as we would think of a boulder lying on the road around the bend. But to do this is to destroy time (as he also claimed), for it supposes that the future is already determined.

Corollary 2: The link between Actuality and Possibility lies not in possibilities but in potentiality. This potentiality is grounded in the actuality of the settled past and in the dynamic actuality of present process. Thus the new actual is always growing out of the womb of the potential, but the potential is itself rooted in and structured by past actuality.

The actualists are therefore right in denying an independence to the possible. On the other hand, to *be potentially* is a real way to be, even though it is not to be actually. And this of course is just what Aristotle said in response to Parmenides, who conceived of only one way of being, being in actuality.

Charles Hartshorne has eloquently summarized a position similar to the one I have been attempting to sketch:

> Only the past alone is fully determinate, the future is to be determined within the limits of causal possibility. These limits are just the determinateness of the past as capable of being superseded by some kinds of successors but not by other logically conceivable kinds. . . . [T]he togetherness of actuality and possibility can only be in actuality. Indeed the possibility of the future is the same as the actuality of the past and present, in their character as destined to be included in some richer total reality. The potentiality of an event is just the actuality of its predecessors.[12]

2. SOME IMPOSSIBLE "POSSIBLE WORLDS"

(1) *The "possible worlds" of David Lewis.* According to the above principles, Lewis's "possible worlds" are metaphysically *im*possible, for he
assumes them to be completely determinate cosmic histories, yet does
not furnish the agents by which to effect the determinateness.

Lewis, of course, will not be impressed by this objection. For he
maintains, as we have seen, that the agents or causes in *all* his possible
worlds are equally real, and that the term "actual," by which we think
to differentiate our world from other possible worlds, is purely indexical so that the inhabitants of other possible worlds have an equal right
to call their own worlds "actual."

There are, in effect, two assumptions operative in such a position:
(1) that it makes sense to talk about "the inhabitants of other possible
worlds," and (2) that the purely indexical use of "actual" is adequate.
Both of these assumptions have been challenged by Robert C. Stalnaker.[13] As against the first, he challenges the innocence of passing
from "ways things could have been" to "possible worlds," the "things"
that could have been otherwise. It would be comparable to confuse
"the ways people act" with "people."[14] If, then, as I would press the
argument, Lewis takes his "ways things could have been" in a sense
comparable to "the ways people act" as *distinguished* from the "people,"
then he has no agents to account for the diversity of the "ways." If on
the other hand he has shifted from talking about the "ways" to talking
about the "things" exemplifying the "ways," I should like to know
with what justification.

Stalnaker also counters the adequacy of Lewis's purely indexical
use of "actuality." It assumes that there is a kind of absolute view,
even-handed or indifferent to all worlds, and that the inhabitants of
any world are equally entitled to refer to their own world as "actual."
Thus Stalnaker remarks:

> The mistake in this [Lewis's] reasoning, I think, is in the assump-
> tion that the absolute standpoint is a neutral one, distinct from
> the view from within any possible world. The problem is avoided

when one recognizes that the standpoint of the actual world *is*
the absolute standpoint, and that it is part of the concept of actuality that this should be so.[15]

The Parmenidean flavor of a position like Lewis's is echoed in another
modern criticism, that of Phil Weiss, who writes:

> Lewis wants to understand what sort of being possibilities have.
> Things, as he says, might be otherwise than they are. Or rather,
> more accurately, things might have been otherwise than they are.
> The possibility existed that things be one of several different
> ways, but they turned out to be only this way. Lewis fastens on
> the "ways," but in doing so, he loses all the possibilities. He
> claims that these "ways" have just the same sort of being as this
> one way things turned out. But if this one way is actual, then all
> the other ways must be actual. The universe on this picture is a
> superworld of *pure actuality*. To say that a possibility exists is
> just to say that somewhere an actuality exists. This is clear from
> the definition of possibility as truth in a world. On this view of
> worlds, the only way to be true in a world is to actually obtain
> there. On this theory, then, possibility reduces to actuality—
> somewhere else.[16]

(2) *Nicholas Rescher's mind-dependent possibilities.* Moving from the
"possibilist" toward the "actualist" end of the spectrum, Nicholas
Rescher claims that unactualized possibilities are mind-dependent.
Thus he writes:

> Possibilistic claims have their principal point where the contrast
> between the actually real and the hypothetically possible pre-
> vails, and where the domain of what is or what does happen is to
> be augmented by that of what can be or what might happen.
> Now the items of this second, hypothetical sphere clearly cannot
> just "objectively be" the case. It is my central thesis that by the
> very nature of hypothetical possibilities they cannot exist as
> such, but must be thought of: They must be hypothesized, or
> imagined, or assumed, or something of this sort.[17]

This is surely a step in the right direction, and it is consistent with *Principle 3* above. But Rescher's position seems nonetheless untenable. In his preliminary remarks to the above essay he asserts: "There are as yet unrealized possibilities that await us in the future. And there are the possible albeit unrealized doings of actual things such as my possible attendance at the film I failed to see last night."[18] What, I must ask, is the agency by reason of which these plural possibilities enjoy their determinateness? According to Rescher's central thesis it would seem that each of these possibilities must meticulously be thought of, imagined, or hypothesized by a rational mind. But this is, in the context, hardly plausible. Rescher seems to be thinking of more possibilities than he has minds actually thinking *of* them. And indeed he does quickly make a substantial qualification:

> We are not saying that to be a possible (but unactualized) state of affairs requires that this state must actually be conceived (or entertained, hypothesized, and so on)—so as in fact to stand in relation to some *specific* mind. Rather, what we are saying is that possible, albeit unrealized, states of affairs or things obtain an ontological footing, that is, they can be said to "exist" in some appropriately qualified way only insofar as it lies within the generic province of minds to conceive (or to entertain, hypothesize, and so on) them.[19]

But if this absolves Rescher's theory from an unreasonable multiplicity of busily hypothesizing minds, it aggravates the problem of accounting for the assumed distinctness of the hypothetical possibilities themselves. Rescher is in fact forced to oscillate between saying that hypothetical possibilities must be *conceived*[20] and that they must be *conceivable*.[21] But by the principles worked out above, these two stances are crucially distinct, and one can't have it both ways.

At the heart of the problem lies Rescher's claim that potentiality itself is purely mind-dependent. To the objection that an acorn has in itself a potentiality to grow into an oak, Rescher replies: "Regardless of the status of the acorn as being independent of the existence of the mind, and whatever the acorn *in fact* does, the strictly *modal* aspect of what it may or may not do is not and cannot be an aspect of objective reality." Are we driven, then, he asks, to a "possibility-idealism," so that if there were no rational minds "there would be no unreal possibilities"? Yes, he answers; if rational minds were abolished, "the domain of unrealized, albeit possible, things would also have to vanish."[22]

The ease with which Rescher has shifted from speaking of *potentiality* to *possibilities* betrays the fundamental flaw of his position. By *Corollary 2,* one cannot give an account of the relation between the real and the possible without recognizing potentiality as an essential, distinct, and mind-independent ingredient of the actual,

(3) *Reflective aside.* At this point we are in a position to take a harder look at the root issues here at stake. Running like Ariadne's thread through the writings of Lewis and many others lies the unexamined assumption that there exist multitudinous, discrete "ways things could have been" even though there are no real causes responsible for the determinateness of that presumed plurality. Hand and glove with this assumption is the tendency to substitute possibilities for potentiality. Experientially we find ourselves within an actual world that in its ongoing process is constantly achieving its determinateness by the activity of real causes synthesizing settled determinateness out of a range of real Possibility (not out of possibilities). With Lewis, however, we may incautiously move from recognizing *that* things could be otherwise (recognizing potentiality) to positing *discrete ways in which* they could be otherwise (thus confusing potentiality with possibilities). With Lewis, too, we may even move to passing from these discrete ways of things to things that are assumed to exemplify the ways—to possible worlds indistinguishable, except indexically, from the actual.

According to the principles defended in this essay these discrete "possible worlds" are metaphysical monstrosities, just as square circles are logical monstrosities (Meinong notwithstanding). For the determinateness of the actual, as distinguished from the indeterminateness of the possible, is achieved precisely and only by the activity of real agents. Whereas there are actual entities that continuously found the potentiality in which the actual world weaves itself, the only actual causes we have that can account for the supposed determinateness of any one of these hypothetical states of affairs (possible worlds) is we ourselves in our thinking of them. (In this Rescher has a point.)

Even so, to what extent do we succeed in defining a possible world by thinking about it? If we take our principles seriously, its only definition will be what we explicitly give it. Inevitably we begin with imaginative material drawn from our own experience; to that extent any possible world resembles the actual world. But if we should try to construct it wholly by creative conceptualization, we find ourselves completely unequal to the infinite task of definition. Our conceptualized possible world will be almost infinitely vague and indeterminate compared to the actual world.

In this respect it is worth paying attention to the difference between the definite and indefinite articles. Before the battle one might have talked about *a* battle at Gettysburg but one could not have talked about *the* Battle of Gettysburg. The latter achieved its determinateness, about which we are now in some position to speak, precisely by the battling of the actual soldiers. Similarly, an admiral in peacetime might dreamily think of *a* sea battle tomorrow (especially if he is a Walter Mitty); an admiral in World War II might reasonably plan for *the* sea battle tomorrow (say, at Midway), if actual circumstances have made the inevitability and partial character of the battle clear. Even so, however, the battle viewed in prospect is not identical with "the Battle of Midway," and at least part of the difference lies in the complete determinateness effected by the actual battling. (Otherwise the admiral would infallibly know whether he would win on the morrow.)

Is then actuality to be *identified* with determinateness, as I may seem to have implied? Charles Hartshorne seems to think so. If one is to go along with Leibniz, he says, one "must admit that a possible world is as definite and complex as the corresponding actual one." This is quite correct. But then Hartshorne goes too far. He adds that such an admission "reduces the distinction between possible and actual to nullity. Value is in definiteness, and definiteness is 'the soul of actuality.' Were possibility equally definite it would be redundant to actualize it."[23]

Two errors lurk in this assertion. In the first place, mutual implication constitutes logical equivalence but not metaphysical identity. In the system of Thomas Aquinas, for instance, although every (finite) act of existence (*esse*) requires its actual form, and every actual form requires its *esse,* the form is nonetheless not identical with the *esse.* Similarly, for Whitehead although determinateness implies real agency, and real agency always produces determinateness, it is not the case that the agency is the determinateness. Secondly, it cannot be that "value is in definiteness, and definiteness is 'the soul of actuality.'" For Hartshorne himself grants, as we have seen, that "[o]nly the past alone is fully determinate." But then he would have to grant here that value resides only in the past rather than in the present. With Whitehead, however, I maintain that value is preeminently found in the contrast experienced by the actual entity in its present subjectivity. What has subjectively perished, the settled past, has value only insofar as it is relived in the subjectivity of its successors. If we equate determinateness with actuality we neglect the heart of reality (which is *durée* for Bergson, creative process for Whitehead, *esse* for Thomas), and we once again risk confusing potentiality with possibilities, and actuality with sterile forms.

(4) *The "middle knowledge theory" of Luis de Molina.* So far we have concentrated on "pure" possibilities, "ways things *could* have been." What about conditional possibilities, "ways things *would* have been (or would be)" in certain circumstances? And under which consideration (or both?) do we best situate our assessment of Leibniz's "possible worlds"? It is illuminating first to look at a simpler and earlier view, one with which Leibniz was perfectly familiar: the *scientia media* theory of the sixteenth-century Jesuit theologian, Luis de Molina. This theory finds a similar contemporary expression, as we shall see, in the position taken by Alvin Plantinga concerning God and evil.[24]

Molina took for granted, as did his contemporaries, that God infallibly knows both all *possibles,* everything that can or could be (this was called "knowledge of simple intelligence"), and all *reals,* everything that is, was, or will be ("knowledge of vision"). At the same time, it was held, God's knowledge cannot be passively acquired, cannot be spectator knowledge, because in that case God would be acted upon and thus in some way changed by the creature. No, God's infallible knowledge must be grounded directly in the divine creative decrees themselves. But then how can we reconcile the infallibility of this knowledge, based on a divine decree ontologically prior to the event, with the freedom of the creature's decision? It would seem that we must give up either the inerrancy of God's knowledge or the freedom of the creature.

Molina was unwilling to give up either, so he proposed the following way out of the dilemma. He posited yet a third kind of divine knowledge, a sort of intermediate knowledge (a *scientia media*) falling between knowledge of simple intelligence and knowledge of vision. Through it God knows infallibly what any free agent *would* determinately do, and do freely, in any hypothetical situation, *regardless of whether the agent is ever actually in that situation*. The particular object of this middle knowledge is that particular one of two possible contradictory acts that a free agent *would* perform if certain conditions were fulfilled. Molina referred to this object as the "contingent future"; later the term *"futurible"* was coined. The complete set of futuribles, then, is the complete set of "would be's" as distinguished from the "could be's" or the "will be's."

Armed with this simple but ingenious idea, Molina proposed the following account. In virtue of his middle knowledge God knows (eternally and infallibly) precisely what a human being, say Adam, *would* do (and even do *freely*) if placed in a certain precise situation. This situation includes very specially the exact amount of divine help ("actual grace") afforded to him. Thus, by virtue of this middle knowledge God timelessly knows that Adam and Eve, say, *would* sin if placed in the situation described in Genesis, and He knows this irrespective of (ontically "prior to") His decision to place them in just that situation. But then if, for inscrutable reasons of his own, God couples this hypothetical knowledge with an absolute decree that this situation in fact should obtain, then God's middle, hypothetical knowledge becomes knowledge of vision, of what infallibly shall occur. Thus God infallibly knows the sin of Adam and Eve antecedent to, or at any rate ontologically prior to, their historical sinning. Yet this knowledge in no way forces them to sin, for that they *would* sin in such a situation depends on them in their freedom, not on God.

Molina's theory thus stands or falls with the coherence of the notion of futuribles. But according to our principles, futuribles are metaphysical monstrosities: they posit the determinate outcome of a free agent's acting while excluding the acting itself. They are metaphysically inconsistent fictions that cannot form an object of anyone's knowledge, not even God's, since they have no possible purchase in the real.

(5) *The "possible worlds" of Leibniz.* Leibniz conceived God to have infallible knowledge, apart from (antecedent to, as it were) His creative decree, of all possible "worlds," of all possible cosmic histories in their complete detail. In accordance with Leibniz's Principles of Sufficient Reason and of Perfection, God naturally chooses to create that world in which the most perfection is realized. Any other supposition is absurd. However paradoxical it may seem from our limited viewpoint, then, this world, with all its evil, must contain on balance the greatest possible amount of perfection.

We have already seen that the very conceivability of a "best" possible world has been challenged by both classical and contemporary thinkers. But on our principles there are simply no possible worlds at *all* for God to choose from. This may best be seen by comparing Leibniz's theory with that of Molina.

Molina's principal work, *Concordia Liberi Arbitrii cum Gratiae Donis, Divina Praescientia, Providentia, Praedestinatione et Reprobatione* (1588)—Molina was not shy—was familiar to Leibniz, who summarizes it in his *Essais de Théodicée,* Première Partie, pars. 39–40.[25] Having reviewed some of the points of controversy between the Molinists and their adversaries, Leibniz proceeds to align himself exactly with Molina (as he says explicitly in par. 43) in accepting the notion of futuribles (Leibniz calls them "conditional futures" or "contingent futures"). He writes:

> [I]t will suffice if I explain how I think that there is truth on both sides. To that end I come to my principle of an infinity of possible worlds represented within the object of the divine intelligence, *where all conditional futures must be contained. . .* Thus we have a principle of certain knowledge about contingent futures,

whether they actually occur or whether they [only] ought to occur in a certain situation. For within the domain of the possibles, they are represented as they are, that is, as free contingents. . . . And although it should be true and possible that contingent futures which consist in the free actions of rational creatures should have been entirely independent of the divine decrees and of external causes, it would be possible to foresee them: for *God would see them just as they are in the domain of the possibles,* prior to his deciding to admit them to existence.[26]

Leibniz's "possible worlds," then, more clearly than those of Lewis, are worlds of "would be's" as well as of "could be's." The determinateness in these worlds is not merely a matter of "ways things could be," taken abstractly, but also of "ways agents *would freely act*" in specific situations. Yet insofar as these worlds are only "possible," the agents are only hypothetical, and hypothetical agents, in my view, are just not agents.

Leibniz's "possible worlds" are thus subject to the same fatal criticism as Molina's "futuribles." Like Molina, Leibniz tries to have it both ways: God is supposed to know the determinate outcome of an agent's free action, but without the acting of the agent. Yet it is only the acting (the act of deciding) that could produce the determinateness.

But, you might object, is God not capable of conceiving any number of possible cosmic histories, and do these not qualify to be called "possible worlds"? Indeed, is this not the traditional doctrine, defended by St. Thomas Aquinas when he asserts that God's knowledge extends not only to all that is ever actual but to that which is merely possible?[27]

God forbid that I forbid God from conceiving as possibilities any number of such hypothetical world-histories, or you from calling them "possible worlds" if you wish! But on the principles defended above, I contend that any such "possible world" is sterile in its relationship to the actual world; it is a pure fancy, metaphysically inconsequential. For instance, it cannot possibly serve in the function Leibniz assigned it, for there is no way in which it can pass from purely hypothetical to actual without robbing human agents of their freedom.

I mean that, for a purely hypothetical but completely determinate world-history, God is both the necessary and the sufficient agent effecting that determinateness. If, for example, that hypothetical world is both determinate in all details and includes a free agent P conceived as deliberately doing act q at time t, only God can provide the determinateness for that conceived scenario. If now Leibniz's God is to say, "Let that world be!" then to God must be attributed all the determinateness of the events, including P's doing q at t. No, says Leibniz: ontologically prior to His creative decree, God knew what P would freely do at t; it is just that God decrees to let that world exist. But what P is conceived to do at t cannot be attributed to P as to its author apart from P's actual *acting* at t. Hence as long as the situation is purely hypothetical, the only determinant of what P is conceived to do at t is God Himself conceiving it. Thus God, not P, is the determinant of q in that kind of "possible world."

If therefore one were to assert with Leibniz that there is some way in which such a divinely conceived and completely determinate hypothetical cosmic history could, by divine *fiat*, become actual, nothing would remain of human free agency, nor, I am afraid, could God be acquitted of responsibility for the moral evil in the world, since on that supposition God would be the only determinant of every event.

Unless therefore God is to appropriate to Himself all the determining process in the world, *there simply are no possible worlds available for Him to choose from* in creating an *actual* world. God cannot know the detailed and determinate course of world events apart from His decree that there *be* a world, for apart from that decree there are no finite agents to determine that course of events.

This conclusion shows that it is not playing metaphysical parlor games to take a stand on the ontological status of possible worlds, for that directly bears on the problem of reconciling the existence of God with that of evil in the world. If the principles adopted above are accurate, it is simply not the case that God knew, as it were ahead of time, what evils would occur in this world and then went ahead and created it any way. Yet that is the implicit attitude underlying the common question, "Why did God choose a world with so much evil in it?" If God had available for his choice an infinity of possible worlds, it is difficult indeed not to think that He chose badly.[28]

3. METAPHYSICS AND LOGIC: A CRUCIAL OBJECTION

I face, finally, a crucial objection to the procedure and the conclusions of this argument, an objection that has perhaps already occurred to the reader. Someone might protest: "Despite your intentions, you have not in fact taken seriously the notion of 'possible worlds,' and your principles, even if they were to be granted, systematically neglect an infinity of them. For your principles, besides being unprovable, apply, if they apply at all, to this actual universe. But there is nothing logically contradictory about denying any or all of them. Hence it is logically possible for other worlds (universes) to exist, exemplifying different metaphysical principles, and they precisely constitute an indefinite multiplicity of possible worlds untouched by your overzealous exorcism."

Is this objection as fatal as it sounds or is it, as Socrates might say, only a wind-egg? I frankly doubt that I shall persuade anyone who is sympathetic to this objection; nevertheless I think it mistaken.

For I deny what the objection presupposes, *that logic enjoys precedence over metaphysics.* Is it really the case that there is a paramount logical order within which various metaphysical structures must be included as so many sub-areas in a Venn diagram? Or is the logical order rather a reflection of the structure of the real (whether one calls the real "being," or "process," or "becoming")? If the latter, then insofar as one has in fact laid hold of some of the ultimate principles of the real, they are no longer negotiable. To repeat Whitehead's earlier remark: "This doctrine of necessity in universality means that there is an essence to the universe which forbids relationships beyond itself, as a violation of its rationality. Speculative philosophy seeks that essence" (PR 4).

Everything here hinges on the relation one acknowledges between metaphysics and logic. To argue this carefully, even if one could agree on the meaning of "metaphysics" and "logic," would require an essay in itself and I shall not attempt that here. I do however venture the following interconnected assertions:

(1) Whether the logical order is viewed as an abstract character of the in-some-way extramental real, or as a reflection of the structure of thought, the logically possible inheres in and depends upon the real,

not the other way around. This is already an implication of *Principles 2* and *3*, and *Corollary 1*. In that sense, the principles I have defended claim for themselves a certain autonomy. That they are unprovable is true but not a defect, for the same is true of any conceivable meta-physical principles as well as of any other genuinely basic assumptions necessarily underlying thought. The only interesting question is whether they are in fact true.

(2) That if they are true they are true for this universe and no other, is also correct but again not necessarily a fault. For it may be doubted (and I do doubt it) that it makes any sense to hypothesize other worlds in which metaphysical principles true for this world are violated. Let X stand for some world that obeys different metaphysical laws from ours. Then the assertion: "X is a possible world" is arguably an inconsistent proposition, either internally or at least in its being asserted (or both). For the "is" in that proposition is not a pure copula but has existential import. Either in the content of the proposition itself, or at least in the context of its being asserted by a thinker in this world, the character of the "is" is inevitably structured by the metaphysics of this real world. And that, I think, is why Stalnaker was correct above (in part 2), in criticizing Lewis's theory of actuality for tacitly assuming that there is an absolute standpoint, independent of the actual world, from which to view possible worlds. Rather, he says, "the standpoint of the actual world *is* the absolute standpoint, and . . . it is part of the concept of actuality that this should be so."[29]

(3) Similarly, even the objector must grant that he or she, as well as the rest of us, must perforce follow the laws of thought that obtain in *this* world, even when trying to speculate about metaphysically oddball worlds. There is simply no other way for us to think if we are to think at all. But can such thought really get us into possible worlds that dis-obey the metaphysics of our own? Or is it rather that we haven't escaped our own metaphysical structure at all, any more than (as Kant I think observed) we can imagine two universes? If we have not, then the meta-physical structure of this world provides a touchstone for evaluating the sense or nonsense of proposed possible worlds.

(4) At the beginning of this essay I disclaimed having anything to say about "the purely logical or formal advantages" of the notion of

"possible worlds." I suppose that what I have just been saying casts doubt on whether there is room at all for a purely logical, metaphysically innocuous way of speculating about "possible worlds." I am unable at present to resolve this issue. Nevertheless, since it is the metaphysical, not the logical, problem of "possible worlds" in which I am interested, I see no reason to approach it by assuming a pre-eminence of logic over metaphysics.

(5) Finally, it is worth noting that the objection draws much of its apparent strength from the seeming arbitrariness, hence replaceability, of the principles that I have set down. But is one really free to make substitutions? The picture changes considerably when these principles, which are only fragments of a cosmology, are set into the context of a complete metaphysical system. As I have said, I think those principles are compatible with the philosophies of Whitehead, Bergson, Hartshorne, and even Thomas Aquinas. Let us see what happens when we embody them in the metaphysical systems of Whitehead and of Aquinas.

For Whitehead, the metaphysical structure of reality is constituted by God in his "primordial nature." Insofar as our principles are true they must form part of that constitution. Now this constitution of a metaphysical structure, of the ways things can be related to one another, of an ultimate ground of possibility for the process of the universe, is unique. It is an *Ur*-act that is "free" in two respects: (1) it is bounded by no outside restraints; (2) it is *self*-constituting, self-creating. It is just the ultimate reason why the process of the universe is ordered as it is, and there is no reason beyond the ultimate reason. To ask for such a reason would be to make a category mistake. Further, this ultimate structure of possibility countenances, by its very nature, no alternative. It is the absolute structure for the universe, and insofar as we succeed in discerning some of its features, they have a kind of absolute status as well. This is the ground for the privileged status of the actual as over against the merely possible.

For Thomas Aquinas, God, in knowing Himself, thereby knows all the ways in which his essence (which is existence) can be shared. God is Himself the ground, the reason, why some things are ultimately possible and others not. This is "antecedent" to any divine decision to create. Also, God did not, as it were, sit down and decide what the structure of ultimate metaphysical possibility should be (as Descartes would perhaps have allowed Him to do). He is in his own essence just that structure, or the ground of it.

If that be so, once again there is an ultimate source for the metaphysical structure of the universe that gives to that structure a privileged status. The laws of being and becoming are not up for grabs, though one may want to toy with them from a purely formalistic point of view. But that is not to constitute metaphysically respectable possible worlds.[30]

EIGHT

God's Choice: Reflections on Evil in a Created World

(1984)

This short essay applies the central principles of the previous essay to the problem of evil in the world. It seemed an obvious philosophic move to make. I do not claim that it exactly solves even the narrowly defined problem laid out here, but it blunts it by showing that the most natural way in which we feel the difficulty involves wrong thinking on our part. The essay is, I believe, fairly accessible.

"Why did God create a world with so much evil in it?" In the face of the evils surrounding us, anyone who believes in the existence of a God who is infinitely powerful, knowing, and good, finds this question arising spontaneously and repeatedly.

Although I have cited this question, I have no intention of trying to answer it—not only because evil is the most formidable of problems, but because the question, as I have put it and in its natural context,

Originally published as "God's Choice: Reflections on Evil in a Created World," *Faith and Philosophy* 1, no. 4 (1984): 370–77. Reprinted with permission.

simply should not be asked. It is an unallowable question, because it takes for granted at least one of the following two illegitimate presuppositions:

(1) It may presuppose that God is a kind of Divine Playwright who has prescribed every action to take place in the world. I speak here about cosmic and human history: not only about falling sparrows and hairs on our heads but about human moral decisions for good or evil. A Divine Playwright would be the direct author of every act, including morally evil acts. Such a view is both philosophically implausible, since it makes God the sole free agent, and also religiously repugnant, since it makes God the author of moral evil. I therefore dismiss it.

(2) Alternatively, and more likely, the question may presuppose that *apart from God's free decision to create the universe*—ontologically antecedent to deciding actually to create—God knew precisely what *would* take place in human history if He *should* decide to create, and that He then (so to speak) decided to go ahead and create that universe anyway.

I do not see how this second presupposition can be defended, in view of principles that I shall briefly develop. And since the original question makes no sense except in terms of one or the other of the above presuppositions, I reject the question altogether. God's choice, I shall argue, was not among diverse competing possible cosmic histories (like Leibniz's "possible worlds"), but essentially *a choice whether or not to create a universe containing free agents.*[1]

To construct my essential argument, I need only identify a few rather obvious metaphysical (or cosmological) principles. I owe them in part to the French philosopher, Henri Bergson, but also to reflection on what seems to be the metaphysical structure of becoming as I experience it. The reader is invited to consider whether these principles do not describe his or her own experience. If they seem to, more than their opposites, that is for the present sufficient, since first principles are philosophically at the end—or rather at the beginning—of the line: you take or you leave first principles, you don't demonstrate them. Should any of these principles be rejected, however, I fail to understand what other ones could more reasonably be put in their place. The principles that I have in mind all pertain to the relation between actuality, potentiality, and possibility; between what is and what might be, including the capability of the actual to be other than it is. These principles will not found a whole metaphysical view, but only a fragment of a cosmology, a partial metaphysics of our space-time world.

The First Principle, which might be called the Principle of Determinateness, is *that settled actuality (past actuality, whether immediate or remote) is determinate, exact, unambiguous.* Thus, Dickens' novel, *David Copperfield,* consists in a well-defined set of words in a particular order. In this respect the completed novel markedly differs from the vaguer outlines of it that gradually grew in Dickens' mind. Similarly, Mozart's *Forty-First Symphony,* taken as a musical score, is (if we may assume we have a definitive edition) a precise pattern of notes to be played in an unambiguous order.

The Second Principle, which might be called the Principle of Process or Determination, states *that dynamic actuality (or existing actuality or concrete process) is, or at any rate involves, a process of determination whereby from the indeterminateness of potentiality there is educed the determinateness, the exactness, of settled actuality.* This is a process of educing an exact pattern of existence from the limited indeterminateness given in the present for the immediate future.

Putting it another way, present activity is always, one way or another, a process of creating definite patterns of existence from within a certain ambit of possibility. Dickens' activity of writing and Mozart's of composing resulted in just those precise patterns of actuality that are the completed novel and the finished symphony.

Suppose you are driving a dune buggy along a beach bounded by sheer palisades on the left and the surf on the right. This width of beach constitutes a literal width of possibility for driving: within these limits you are free to steer as you like, and your very activity of driving creates a well-defined set of tracks, tracks that simply were not there, had no existence, prior to your driving. The activity of driving *creates* the tracks within the given ambit of possibility, it does not actualize a hidden set of tracks already there. The dune buggy (and human agency) is quite unlike a locomotive entering a yard of already laid-out tracks.

The Third Principle is *that the activity of real (existing) agents alone educes the exact determinateness of settled actuality from the vague indeterminateness of Possibility.*

Several clarifications are in order here:

(a) Throughout these reflections I use the term "agent" broadly, to refer to an existential and originative cause, regardless of whether or not it is conscious.

(b) I distinguish between pure patterns of existence, "possibilities" (or "possibles"), and "Possibility," which is the range or horizon of all possibilities. In the previous example, the range of Possibility is determined by the palisades and the surf, whereas the tracks in the sand exemplify possibilities.

(c) This Third Principle is the converse of the Second. The Second holds that real existential activity entails the production of determinate patterns of existence; the Third maintains that determinate patterns of existence entail the activity of agents that produced them. By this Third Principle the exactness of determinate possibilities has to come from somewhere; it does not just "happen," for no reason at all.[2]

A *Corollary* of the above principles is *that particular patterns of existence (possibilities) do not temporally precede their actual existence as instantiated in the temporal world*. This is what Bergson meant when he said that *the possible does not precede the real*.[3]

Thus, the pattern of words that is the formal character of *David Copperfield,* or of notes that is that of Mozart's *Forty-First,* simply did not exist in time before Dickens and Mozart created them, any more than the tracks in the sand preexisted the passage of the dune buggy. They were *created* by their respective authors, not chosen out of a limbo of ghostly possibilities awaiting promotion to temporal existence. *David Copperfield* and Mozart's *Forty-First* cannot properly be said to have been even *possible* before their creation by Dickens and Mozart! True, they were not *im*possible, but antecedent to the writing or to the composing, *there existed no pattern to refer to,* no pattern that could be called either "possible" or "impossible." Only after their creation do we have anything to refer to.

To shift the example slightly: could one say that Mozart's *Forty-Second Symphony* was possible before Mozart died? (I am assuming that in fact Mozart wrote only forty-one.) If he had written yet another, presumably it would have been called *"the Forty-Second,"* but "Mozart's *Forty-Second Symphony"* was not possible before Mozart's death (nor at any other time) for the very good reason that there never was an *actual* one. Apart from its creation in time as a formal pattern (which never in fact took place), there is no existent pattern that could be referred to in any way at all; there is literally nothing to refer *to*.

What results when we apply the above principles to the second of the two possible presuppositions underlying our initial question? That presupposition, in effect, thinks of God as walking into a kind of Leibnizian metaphysical supermarket in which all possible cosmic histories are arranged neatly on the shelves and coded according to their ontological or aesthetic value. Leibniz, as we know, concluded that God would naturally choose the *best* possible world.

Now I would not boggle at God's choosing the best, if only I could believe there were any to choose from at all! I am afraid that the shelves in Leibniz's market are either quite empty or else contain only items that may not be removed from the premises.

For since these "possible worlds" are supposed to be possible cosmic histories, including the precise thoughts, words, and actions of all human beings throughout the span of history, one must ask where the determinateness of these exact actions comes from. Can it come from the individuals, the hypothetical persons? But as long as we are inquiring into what God can know *apart from,* or "antecedent to," his decision to create, the agents must be *only* hypothetical (since God has not "yet" decided to create them). But hypothetical agents are just *not agents;* they are incapable of *doing* anything at all, let alone educing the determinateness of patterned actuality from the indeterminateness of Possibility.

If, then, purely hypothetical persons cannot produce the determinateness of a human history, the only alternative, as far as I can see, is to suppose that *God* provides this determinateness. But if we make that supposition, we revert precisely to the first of the unacceptable presuppositions underlying our original question, the unacceptable presupposition of the Divine Playwright who alone has picked out all the details of human and cosmic history.

For although the principles developed above do not prevent God from envisioning as many detailed cosmic histories as He pleases, since He is certainly an agent capable of producing the required determinateness, we cannot allow that He then, so to speak, may utilize any such conjectured world as a blueprint for actual creation. For in that case God would be reserving to Himself all free agency and hence the originative responsibility for all human acts—and that I am unwilling to believe, though not by reason of the above principles. I think that God is not an author of evil, and I think that He has made us free.

To return to our analogy: God might conceivably stock the shelves of Leibniz's market, but if He does, He also prohibits Himself from taking any of these, his own hypothetical goods, out in the real world. Suppose, as a parallel, that Charles Dickens could arrange that the story he created in *David Copperfield* should take place in the actual world, right down to the last detail. Then neither young David Copperfield nor Mr. Micawber would be responsible for what they say and do, but only Dickens. He alone, after all, effected the determinateness of their words and their actions. Similarly, to suppose that the actual world is but the realization of a scenario for which God is solely responsible is to revert to the supposition that God reserves to Himself all free agency in the world, and hence has sole responsibility for every human action—and this is the other supposition that I have already rejected out of hand.

Here then are the results of applying the proposed principles to our original question:

First, the principles, if they are anywhere near correct, *rule out the availability for actual creation of any* determinate *cosmic histories* ("possible worlds") *apart from* ("antecedent to") *God's actual decision to create a universe.* Apart from that creative decree there are on the one hand no actual human agents to render human history determinate, and on the other, God Himself cannot be the source of this determinateness without robbing humans of all freedom and responsibility.

By these principles, then, it seems that "prior" to (apart from) deciding to create, God simply *did not know* what would happen if He should decide to create, for there was *literally nothing to be known,* even by God. To suppose, on the contrary, that there *was* a determinate, knowable history either posits determinateness without the necessary determining agents, or else reserves all freedom and responsibility to God—and neither option is defensible.[4]

Second, it follows that the original question, no matter how naturally it seems to arise, is in fact spurious, since neither of its necessary presuppositions can survive analysis.

Third, these conclusions go a long way toward mitigating, at least, the problem of the existence of moral evil in a world created by a good God. To speak anthropomorphically, one might say, more correctly than not, that God, knowing that the best possible universe would have to contain creatures capable of knowing and loving, and knowing furthermore that love, since it can only be given freely, may also be freely withheld, chose to take his chances, so to speak, in creating a world of free creatures.

Fourth, the above principles by no means preclude a divine transcendent knowledge of all actual events, whether (to us) past, present, or future. For such knowledge has to do with actual, not purely hypothetical, agents, and actual agents suffice to educe the determinateness of actuality from the indeterminateness of Possibility. The above principles have nothing whatever to say about the possibility of a divine knowledge that transcends time.[5]

Fifth, the application of the above principles has so far centered on moral evil, the evil of the human will and its practical consequences. What, if anything, do they have to say about natural or physical evil? What can they tell us about God's choice in creating a world in which senescence and death are the rule, a world in which a mother loses all five of her small children in a single earthquake? If God cannot be responsible for the use that humans make of their freedom, does He not seem responsible, directly or indirectly, for natural evils, for what society itself calls "acts of God"? Why did He choose to create a universe in which so much natural evil is not only possible but inevitable?

This is, in the end, Job's question, and it may be presumptuous to attempt any answer other than that given him. Still, faith seeks understanding, and it is at least worth considering whether the above principles shed any light on the question.

(a) Would it have been *possible* for God to create a material universe in which natural evils simply do not occur? The above principles do not, as far as I can see, suggest any answer to this. Independently of them, one might think such a possibility unlikely, given that extensiveness, by its very nature, grounds the possibility of division, hence of bodily dissolution. (That is, of course, unless God is to be thought of as a frantically busy divine Superman, everywhere intervening in the nick of time!) Yet—and again independently of the above principles—*some* kind of material cosmos free of natural evil can hardly be an Impossibility if we are to accept the prospect in the Letter to the Romans of a renewed creation freed from decadence.[6]

Perhaps St. Paul's notion of a transformed cosmos is a clue to God's being content with creating a universe in which natural as well as moral evil are possibilities. St. Augustine unforgettably remarked that God would never permit evil to occur in his creation if He were not so good and powerful as to be able to draw good even out of evil.[7] Can Romans 8, in effect, be an application of such a principle to the evil-laden world so keenly felt by Job?

(b) If the above principles tell us little or nothing about why God should choose to create a cosmos in which natural evil is *possible,* do they at least give grounds for thinking that God is in some sense knowingly responsible for the *actual* natural evils occurring in the world, especially those afflicting humans? For apart from human decisions and the evil that may be consequent upon them, is not God the only free agent responsible for the course of cosmic events? Would not God know, even apart from his decision to create, all the *natural* events of a hypothetical universe for which He would set all the conditions? With regard to natural events, at least, must He not have known precisely the history of this particular cosmos, including its catastrophes, apart from ("antecedent to") his decision to create? If, for instance, He set all the conditions for a Big Bang, would He not thereby know its inevitable consequences? And if so, is He not responsible for the natural evils in the world, considering that He might have chosen differently?

The answer to this question depends mainly on the sort of cosmology one adopts, and in particular, whether or not one views natural events as taking place deterministically.

Now, in the face of quantum indeterminacy anything like a pure Laplacian determinism seems out of the question. Besides, even if one *were* to adopt a rigidly deterministic view of natural events, it is difficult to see how that could satisfactorily account for a divine knowledge of cosmic events in general, given that free human agents inevitably affect what goes on in nature, whether it be by the simple burning of fossil fuels, the building of dams, or the detonation of nuclear weapons. The way a dwelling or a dam is freely built determines whether the next earthquake is catastrophic or only startling. If, as I have argued,

God apparently cannot know, apart from his actual decision to create a universe, the outcome of free human decisions made in that universe, it is hard to see how He can have any comprehensive knowledge (again, apart from that decision to create) even of the course of *natural* events, affected as they are by human decisions. By the above principles, then, it seems unlikely or even impossible that God should have a knowledge of natural evils that would befall particular human beings in a world considered purely hypothetically (apart, that is, from God's decision to *create* a world).

Furthermore, there are in general strong reasons for rejecting any rigidly deterministic cosmological view. Not only does human freedom, I would contend, become impossible in such a view, but determinism has no credentials either from direct experience or from science. This surely is not the place to argue for any particular cosmological view, but it is noteworthy that if, with anyone from William James to Whitehead, we opt for a non-deterministic cosmology, we thereby acknowledge in the course of even natural events an uncertainty of outcome that is in principle irresolvable apart from the actual occurrence of the events themselves. For if there be no freedom in natural events (and only it there is none could God infallibly know future events simply by knowing their antecedent conditions), there is no place left for human freedom (Kant notwithstanding). If, however, there is that free play in natural events that human freedom requires and that direct human experience witnesses to, then it appears once again that God could not have infallible knowledge even of specific *natural* evils apart from his decision to create a cosmos.

It seems, then, that God took his chances, so to speak, in choosing to create and to create us free. He did it, however, as Augustine pointed out, in full awareness of his own power to convert and to redeem.

God's choice in creating was thus no Leibnizian calculated selection from among diverse particular possibilities, for there were simply none to choose from. The choice was more a lover's gamble. The gamble was not without risk, as the history of Redemption shows, but it was ultimately assured of a happy ending.

NINE

Whitehead's Misconception of "Substance" in Aristotle

(1985)

My being invited to contribute to a special issue of Process
Studies *devoted to Whitehead's relation to other philosophers happened to coincide with my own eagerness to make
the following correction, as I saw it (and still do), to what
has always had the status of an unquestioned icon among
Whiteheadian philosophers, namely, the conviction that
"substance" is one of the most disastrous, though long-
cherished, philosophic concepts ever to plague philosophy.
Whitehead thought he found this calamitous concept not
only in Descartes, Locke, and Hume, but especially in Aristotle, its presumptive originator and primary disseminator.
It is past discussion that Whitehead's rejection of the notion
of "substance" played a pivotal role both in his conception
of the structure of actual entities, which were his metaphysical ultimates, and in the microatomism that he finally
adopted in his analysis of macroscopic entities such as the
human body.*

Originally published as "Whitehead's Misconception of 'Substance' in Aristotle," *Process Studies* 14, no. 4 (1985): 224–36. Reprinted with permission.

But what if Whitehead had understandably but fundamentally misunderstood what Aristotle meant by "substance"? What if Aristotle thought of substance in a dynamic and radically different sense than Whitehead supposed? This is not to assume that Whitehead would himself have been satisfied with Aristotle's conception, but it could open the possibility of some acceptable form of substance metaphysics. Such a prospect is, however, still a blatant heresy in orthodox Whiteheadian circles so that the following analysis, which I still think is sound, has had no discernible impact among them even though it was published in Process Studies. Yet I think the essay makes an important if neglected point, and may be fairly accessible even without Whiteheadian expertise.

—And indeed the question which was raised of old and is raised now and always, and is always the subject of doubt, viz., what being is, is just the question, what is substance?

—Aristotle

Aristotle's memorable sentence[1] seems as true today as when it was written. Far from settling among themselves on a metaphysical description of the world of experience, philosophers do not even agree on how Aristotle himself conceived "substance." At any rate I shall argue here that Whitehead radically misunderstood Aristotle's concept. This misconception, which has ever since flourished unquestioned among Whiteheadian philosophers, proved a powerful factor in Whitehead's ultimate adoption of an atomic or epochal theory of becoming.

Whitehead's interpretation of Aristotelian "substance" figures in a classic exchange between Leonard J. Eslick and Charles Hartshorne in the late 1950s. In his paper Eslick asserted: "I think it can be shown that Whitehead's equation of Aristotelian primary substance with Descartes' definition rests upon a gross misunderstanding. It is, furthermore, a travesty to depict Aristotle's substance as static and inert, hermetically sealed off from the causal efficacy of other entities, and devoid of any internal becoming."[2] Recognizing that Whitehead's exegesis of Aristotle is not of primary importance in evaluating Whitehead's own metaphysics, Eslick did not bother in that essay to show what he had said could be shown, and went on to other issues. Hartshorne, however, took the time to respond with some vigor that no such misinterpretation of Aristotle on Whitehead's part was evident.[3]

Hartshorne's instinct that this point is worth arguing was sound. I suspect that Whitehead's interpretation of "substance" in Aristotle had a stronger influence on the formation of his own metaphysics than is generally supposed. It was one of several factors that coalesced to convince Whitehead that no metaphysics of essentially self-identical and enduring fundamental entities is viable.[4] It encouraged him to develop a counter-theory of epochal, successive units of becoming. This alternative, for better or for worse, draws a radically different picture of the human person, for instance, than does that of Aristotle. Man himself is at stake in what one takes the fundamental constituents of being to be.

Whitehead evidently read Aristotle (or perhaps W. D. Ross's book *about* Aristotle) with the specter of modern materialistic mechanism haunting his mind, and thought he recognized in Aristotle's "substance" its remote but unmistakable ancestor. And if, as seems natural, Whitehead took Aristotle's philosophy as paradigmatic of *any* substance-type philosophy, his turn to another alternative is not surprising.

Whitehead's understanding (or, as I shall argue, misunderstanding) of Aristotle's concept of "substance" has continued to flourish, entrenched and unquestioned, among subsequent Whiteheadian philosophers. It is taken for granted, so that the word "substance" is a term of opprobrium. But whether this dogmatic antisubstance bias of modern process philosophy is well founded or, rather, stems largely from an ill-examined myth, depends on the accuracy of Whitehead's interpretation of Aristotle's concept of substance.

Here, then, is what I propose to do. I shall argue that Whitehead did in fact badly misinterpret Aristotle's concept of substance, as Eslick claimed, and I shall suggest that, far from amounting to an inconsequential error in historical exegesis, this misconception was a strong influence in turning Whitehead's metaphysics in the direction of an epochal theory of becoming. I shall maintain that Aristotle's theory conceives substances as dynamic and interrelated, contrary to what Whitehead supposed, but I shall not claim that, had Whitehead realized this, he would have been satisfied with Aristotle's conception. I shall only ask that we accept Aristotle at his own word and not transform his theory into a caricature he demonstrably never intended. I shall also suggest that a recovery of the real Aristotelian view casts doubt on the currently accepted repudiation of the very possibility of any sort of substance metaphysics.

1. WHITEHEAD'S CONCEPTION OF "SUBSTANCE" IN ARISTOTLE

We begin with Whitehead rather than with Aristotle, for Whitehead's assessment of Aristotle flows out of Whitehead's own philosophic concerns. We also take special note of what Whitehead was concerned to avoid. Bergson's observation still holds: "Is it not obvious that the first step the philosopher takes, when his thought is still faltering and there is nothing definite in his doctrine, is to reject certain things definitively? Later he will be able to make changes in what he affirms; he will vary only slightly what he denies."[5] Appropriately, Eslick writes: "It is likely the polemic against substance was originally motivated by Whitehead's reaction against mechanistic materialism, in which substances are inert, vacuous pieces of matter or stuff" ("Substance," 504).

Whitehead's polemic against materialistic mechanism is too well known to require much elaboration here. The "matter" of such a mechanism was, by its nature, static, passive, and incapable of supporting internal relationships to other bits of matter. This incapacity of relationship had its counterpart, Whitehead thought, in Descartes' definition of substance, and that in turn was a direct consequence of Aristotle's notion. In a key passage Whitehead writes:

All modern philosophy hinges round the difficulty of describing the world in terms of subject and predicate, substance and quality, particular and universal. The result always does violence to that immediate experience which we express in our actions, our hopes, our sympathies, our purposes, and which we enjoy in spite of our lack of phrases for its verbal analysis. . . .

The true point of divergence is the false notion suggested by the contrast between the natural meanings of the words "particular" and "universal." The particular is thus conceived as being just its individual self with no necessary relevance to any other particular. It answers to Descartes' definition of substance: "And when we conceive of substance, we merely conceive an existent thing which requires nothing but itself in order to exist." This definition is a true derivative from Aristotle's definition: A primary substance is "neither asserted of a subject nor present in a subject." . . .

The [Whiteheadian] principle of universal relativity directly traverses Aristotle's dictum, "A substance is not present in a subject." . . . The philosophy of organism is mainly devoted to the task of making clear the notion of "being present in another entity."[6]

Whitehead's assertion that Descartes' definition of substance is a true derivative from Aristotle's was based, claimed Eslick, on a "gross misunderstanding" of Aristotle. In the same issue Hartshorne promptly countered this claim by providing the following formal derivation of Descartes' definition from Aristotle's:

Suppose, contrary to Descartes' formula (inconsistently qualified with respect to God), a substance S' requires another substance S'', in order to exist; then S', just in being itself, is related to S'', and since related-to-S'' includes S'', S' itself must include S''. Otherwise, it must be possible for it to exist without S'', external relations being those not necessary to a thing. It follows that S'' is predicable of S' as a necessary relatum for its intrinsic relation.[7]

Thus, argues Hartshorne, denying Descartes' definition of substance logically entails denying Aristotle's, so that affirming Aristotle's entails affirming Descartes'. Aristotelian substances, therefore, are in principle mutually independent, hence intrinsically unrelated to one another. It would follow that Descartes, in defining a substance as needing nothing else in order to exist (*Principles of Philosophy*, I, 51) only spelled out what was already implicit in Aristotle's definition. This apparent incapacity of Aristotelian substances to enter into intrinsic relations with one another seems to have struck Whitehead as distinctive of matter or stuff, hence to lend itself readily to the viewpoint of materialistic mechanism.

Whitehead also saw ethical significance, says Hartshorne, in the rejection of substance. For if each person is self-sufficient to himself and intrinsically independent of all others, have we not a prescription for selfishness and self-centeredness? As Hartshorne put it:

> All genuine interests and purposes transcend the mere self. Egoism rests on a superstitious absolutizing of self-identity and consequent absolutizing of nonidentity with other persons. . . .
> Whitehead once humorously summed up the ethical objection to substance theories by remarking, "I sometimes think that all modern immorality is produced by Aristotle's theory of substance."[8]

In addition to this apparent intrinsic separateness of Aristotelian substances, Whitehead was bothered by what he took to be their static nature. He conceived Aristotle's "substances" as stolidly, changelessly, enduring through time (whatever that could mean!), while yet acquiring or losing various accidental qualities. This is the impression he got from Aristotle's *Categories*—or perhaps, instead, from W. D. Ross's *Aristotle*.[9] For Aristotle says it is distinctive of a substance that it remains numerically one and the same while nevertheless taking on varying, even contrary qualities (*Categories,* chap. 5).

This suggested to Whitehead a notion of *"undifferentiated endurance"* (a favorite phrase) almost indistinguishable from that of passive matter or "stuff." The tenacity with which the latter concept held the minds of philosophers for centuries was due, Whitehead thought, to (1) the influence of Aristotelian subject-predicate logic, and (2) a careless misconstrual of what is given in sense experience—an instance of misplaced concreteness, as we see in the following passages:

> The baseless metaphysical doctrine of "undifferentiated endurance" is a subordinate derivative from the misapprehension of the proper character of the extensive scheme.
> ... In the perception of a contemporary stone, for example, ... the immediate percept assumes the character of the quiet undifferentiated endurance of the material stone, perceived by means of its quality of colour. . . .
> Thus in framing cosmological theory, the notion of continuous stuff with permanent attributes enduring without differentiation, and retaining its self-identity through any stretch of time however small or large, has been fundamental. The stuff undergoes change in respect to accidental qualities and relations; but it is numerically self-identical in its character of one actual entity throughout its accidental adventures. The admission of this fundamental metaphysical concept has wrecked the various systems of pluralistic realism.
> This metaphysical concept has formed the basis of scientific materialism. [10]

As for Aristotle's logic, its dominance over several centuries "imposed on metaphysical thought the categories naturally derivative from its phraseology" (PR 30). Its pattern of attributing varying qualitative predicates to stable, self-contained subjects was mistakenly taken for a metaphysical description of the structure of the real. "The evil produced by the Aristotelian 'primary substance' is exactly this habit of metaphysical emphasis upon the 'subject-predicate' form of proposition" (ibid.).

Furthermore, the notion of the purely numerical identity of an unchanging subject of change seems vague or even incoherent. How can something *endure changelessly*, and in what would its supposed self-identity consist? "Numerical identity," writes Hartshorne, "has no strict meaning, once accidental qualities are admitted such that they can alter, but the thing remain that very thing" ("Reply to Eslick," 515).

In sum, Whitehead interprets Aristotle's substances (1) as self-contained, self-sufficient units of actuality, lacking the possibility of internal relationships to one another, and (2) as entities whose individual histories consist in acquiring or losing various accidental characteristics, while they, the subjects of these accidental changes, remain themselves unchanged. This interpretation arises essentially from (1) Aristotle's definition that a substance is never "present in" another substance, and (2) Aristotle's doctrine of the relation of substance to accident: that it is characteristic of substance that it itself remains numerically one and the same, while nevertheless taking on various accidental qualities.

2. WHITEHEAD'S CONCEPTION A MISCONCEPTION

Preliminary word-problem—Before taking a closer look at the evidence for Aristotle's own conception of "substance," we have to ask whether that is even the most appropriate English word. Aristotle's actual word is *ousía,* etymologically a derivative of the Greek word "to be" (*einai*). In a long and careful analysis of what *ousía* would mean to the Greek ear, Joseph Owens sets down the following characteristics of any near-equivalent in English:

> What is required is an English word which
> a) implies no prejudices in favor of any post-Aristotelian theory of Being,
> b) is more abstractive in form than "Being,"
> c) can denote the individual, both concrete and incomposite,
> d) and express to English ears an immediate relation with Being.[11]

Owens concludes that the English word "entity" comes closest to satisfying these requirements, especially if written with an upper-case E whenever it is being used to translate Aristotle's term, *ousía.*

Beyond argument, however, "substance" is exactly the *wrong* term to use, and that for several reasons:

(1) Etymologically it does all the wrong things. For it has nothing to do with the verb "to be," and derives rather from the Latin, *"substantia,"* denoting something "standing under" another, although, as we shall see, this is in a crucial sense *not* what Aristotle meant by *ousía*! *"Substantia,"* as the Latin rendition of the Greek term, was chiefly popularized by Boethius in his Latin translation of the *logical* works of Aristotle, in which the primary meaning of the term is the *subject of predication.* In his theological works, on the other hand, Boethius was careful to use *"essentia"* to translate the same term. It was, however, by his logical works that Aristotle first became widely known to the Western world, so that the Boethian logical term, *"substantia,"* stuck (Owens 68).

(2) Historically it conjures up exactly the wrong ideas—or at the very least loads the dice against an impartial examination of Aristotle's real meaning. It is especially misleading to anyone acquainted with the history of Western philosophy, as Owens points out: "Because of Locke's influence, 'substance' in English philosophical usage strongly suggests what its etymology designates. It conjures up the notion of something 'standing under' something else. The background is the view of accidents ridiculed by Malebranche. Such a perspective inevitably falsifies the Aristotelian *ousía,* and ends up by reifying the accidents as in Locke" (Owens, 69).

I shall, therefore, hereafter adopt Owens's recommendation and usually write "Entity" (with an upper-case E) to denote Aristotle's term *ousía,* rather than continue to use the unfortunate term "substance." Let us then examine Aristotle's own explanations of what he means by "Entity."

Not "present in a subject."—Here is what Aristotle actually said:

> Entity, in the truest and primary and most definite sense of the word, is that which is neither predicable of a subject nor present in a subject; for instance, the individual man or horse. But in a secondary sense those things are called Entities within which, as species, the primary Entities are included; also those which, as genera, include the species. For instance, the indi-

vidual man is included in the species "man," and the genus to which the species belongs is "animal"; these, therefore—that is to say, the species "man" and the genus "animal"—are termed secondary entities. . . .

Everything except primary Entities is either predicable of a primary Entity or present in a primary Entity, . . . and if these last did not exist, it would be impossible for anything else to exist.[12]

This is the first of the key Aristotelian definitions that bothered Whitehead, and that he and Hartshorne think leads straight to Descartes' definition of substance as "needing nothing else in order to exist." It seemed to Whitehead to insulate Aristotelian Entities from one another, so as to prevent any kind of inherence of one in another. Aristotle goes on to add: "It is a common characteristic of all Entity that it is never present in a subject" (*Categories* 3a6–7). Do not such statements vindicate Whitehead's conception of the *apartheid* of individual Entities in Aristotle?

No, they don't. To see this, we must first examine what sort of work the *Categories* is, and what Aristotle's intention was in writing it.

The *Categories* is the first of Aristotle's ordered set of treatises on the foundations of logic. In this first book he inquires into the significance of the *terms* (or, as Ross suggests, "linguistic facts") in which propositions are couched.[13] In the subsequent book, *On Interpretation,* he inquires into the relationship between multiple terms in the form of propositions. Aristotle is in effect asking, in the *Categories,* what different *sorts of entities* are named by the different terms in propositions. He refers back to this initial treatise when, in Book Delta (V) of the *Metaphysics,* he writes: "The kinds of essential being are precisely those that are indicated by the figures of predication [i.e., the categories]; for the senses of "being" are just as many as these figures" (1017a23–25).

In the *Categories,* then, Aristotle is not yet concerned to work out a metaphysics; he simply wants, as a necessary preliminary clarification, to distinguish among the many different senses in which something can be said to "be." He notices that at least the following sorts of entities or kinds of being can be distinguished: Entity, quantity, quality, relation, place, time, position, state, action, and affection (chap. 4).

And among these diverse kinds of being Aristotle notices a fundamental distinction logically dividing them into two distinct classes. One class has only a single member: Entity. It alone, of all the kinds of being, enjoys a sort of logical autonomy, whereby it can be said to "be" in its own right, whereas all the other kinds of being have an intrinsic dependence on Entity for their own being. "White" or "tall" do not exist in their own right (except as pure abstractions, and even then, as abstractions in someone's mind): they have to belong to Entities, such as a man or a tree, for instance, if they are to be at all. But "man" and "tree," as kinds of being, are not thought of as needing to inhere in some *other kind* of entity.

Aristotle works out in precise, technical terms the relationships I have just roughly sketched, and does it in terms of two careful definitions that he has already provided in chapter 2. These exact definitions are essential for understanding what Aristotle later says about Entity. (He is, after all, writing a careful, technical essay.) He says:

> Forms of speech are either simple or composite. Examples of the latter are such expressions as "the man runs," "the man wins"; of the former "man," "ox," "runs," "wins."
>
> Of things themselves some are predicable of a subject, and are never present in a subject. Thus "man" is predicable of the individual man, and is never present in a subject.
>
> By being "present in a subject" I do not mean present as parts are present in a whole, but being incapable of existence apart from the said subject.[14]

These statements define what Aristotle had in mind when he later asserted that "Entity, in the truest and primary and most definite sense of the word, is that which is neither predicable of a subject nor present in a subject" (chap. 5). When, therefore, we predicate "man" of Socrates, "man" is entity not in the primary but only in the secondary sense; it is a universal, a class. It denotes the essential nature common to Socrates and all other men. Only entity in this secondary sense is *predicated,* and then only of "Entity" in the primary sense (never vice-versa). Roughly: classes are predicated, persons aren't.

On the accidental level, however, to say that Socrates is shrewd or homely, is not to attribute to him extrinsic qualities that cling to him in about the same way as his cloak. It is to say something about *Socrates himself*. In saying, therefore, that "Entity" is never present in another as in a subject, Aristotle is not at all concerned to deny that (or even to ask whether) actual primary Entities relate efficaciously to one another. In the *Categories* he is simply not concerned to do metaphysics. He is asking, rather, how the terms of propositions denote different kinds of being, and he points out that, alone among other kinds of entities, primary Entity is conceivable, and can be discussed, without its having to be thought of as essentially inhering in some *other kind or category* of entity. Colors and shapes and relations, on the other hand, are kinds of being that of their very nature must be thought of as inhering in primary Entities if they are to be thought of as being at all. True, primary Entities do require the other kinds of entities—a man, for instance, must have some shape, yet not with that same relation of inherence. Shape is clearly in the man in a way in which it would be absurd to say that the man is in his shape.

One must conclude, therefore, that Aristotle's stipulation that one Entity is never "in another" provides no warrant for the supposition of radical, mutual exclusiveness that Whitehead read in to it. And indeed there is plenty of evidence to show that Aristotle himself never supposed that primary Entities could not be related to one another. For instance, in *Physics,* book 3, chapter 2, he says:

> The solution of the difficulty that is raised about the motion— whether it is in the *movable*—is plain. It is the fulfilment of this potentiality, and by the action of that which has the power of causing motion; and the actuality of that which has the power of causing motion is not other than the actuality of the movable, for it must be the fulfilment of *both*. A thing is capable of causing motion because it *can* do this, it is a mover because it actually *does* it. But it is on the movable that it is capable of acting. Hence there is a single actuality of both alike, just as one to two and two to one are the same interval, and the steep ascent and the steep descent are one—for these are one and the same, although

they can be described in different ways. So it is with the mover and the moved. (202a12–22)

And a few lines farther down, in reply to an objection he has posed to himself, Aristotle responds: "It is *not* absurd that the actualization of one thing should be in another. Teaching is the activity of a person who can teach, yet the operation is performed [on] some patient—it is not cut adrift from a subject, but is of *A* on *B*" (202b6–8).

This is Aristotle's way of saying that the "agent" is *in* the "patient"; that the Entity effecting change in another is, precisely in that respect, *in* the other. The resulting activity in the affected Entity is the actualization of both Entities together.

In *Metaphysics,* Book Lambda (XII) he writes:

All things are ordered together somehow, but not all alike—both fishes and fowls and plants; and the world is not such that one thing has nothing to do with another, but they are connected. For all are ordered together to one end, but it is as in a house, where the freemen are least at liberty to act at random, but all things or most things are already ordained for them, while the slaves and the animals do little for the common good, and for the most part live at random. (1075a16–23)

In the face of such passages one can suppose either that Aristotle was inconsistent in wedding his notion of primary Entity with other aspects of his system, or that interpreting Aristotle's concept of Entity in a Cartesian manner is, as Eslick suggested, a "gross misunderstanding." All the evidence points toward the latter view.

Or does it? What about Hartshorne's precise logical derivation, quoted above, of how Descartes' concept of "substance" is entailed by Aristotle's definition of Entity as "never in another"? The derivation, in fact, fails! Instead of attending to Aristotle's own careful preliminary definition of what he *means* by "*(present) in* another," Hartshorne allowed this notion of "presence in" to float ambiguously, unexamined, until it became implicitly transformed into a notion of sheer *logical inclusion.* But that is demonstrably not what Aristotle had in mind when he used the phrase.

There is a special irony in Hartshorne's providing this derivation. For not only was Aristotle highly sensitive to the perils of determining the real by means of the logical—this was, after all, his chief criticism of Plato's theory of the Forms[15]—but Whitehead himself tirelessly attacked the tendency to mistake logical relationships for the structure of the real, an ultimate case of what he called "the fallacy of misplaced concreteness." Yet in proposing this derivation Hartshorne succumbs exactly to this fallacy, since he thereby deals with the metaphysical relationship between actual Entities as if it were simply that of logical inclusion.

Entity and qualities: "undifferentiated endurance."—The other key aspect of Aristotle's definition of "Entity" that bothered Whitehead is the relation Aristotle proposes between Entity and qualities, between substance and accidents. Aristotle says:

> The most distinctive mark of Entity appears to be that, while remaining numerically one and the same, it is capable of admitting contrary qualities. From among things other than Entity, we should find ourselves unable to bring forward any which possessed this mark. Thus, one and the same colour cannot be white and black. Nor can the same one action be good and bad: this law holds good with everything that is not Entity. *But one and the self-same Entity, while retaining its identity, is yet capable of admitting contrary qualities.* The same individual person is at one time white, at another black, at one time warm, at another cold, at one time good, at another bad.[16]

We saw above in section 1 that, given the background of later Western philosophic thought, this definition provoked Whitehead to attribute the notion of "undifferentiated endurance" to Entity itself, conceived as a substrate of diverse accidental qualities that come and go. It is, he writes, "the notion of continuous stuff with permanent attributes, enduring without differentiation, and retaining its self-identity and through any stretch of time. . . . The stuff undergoes change in respect to accidental qualities and relations; but it is numerically self-identical in its character of one actual entity throughout its accidental adventures" (PR 78). This notion, Whitehead thought, has wrecked the various systems of pluralistic realism and also formed the basis of scientific materialism.

Whitehead's clearly Lockean concept of "substance" in Aristotle, besides supposing the mutual isolation of Entities one from another, seems to include at least the following characteristics:

(1) Substance is conceived as intrinsically unchanged, or unchanging, even amid its acquiring or losing accidental qualities.

(2) Substance is therefore rightly thought of as both static and passive, hence as lending itself immediately to the notion of an inert stuff or matter.

(3) Similarly, substance enjoys a kind of independence of existence from its accidental qualities; it becomes a kind of "thing" even apart from those qualities. And in a somewhat different way, qualities must enjoy a kind of ontological autonomy of their own.

I submit that attributing the above characteristics to Aristotle's notion of Entity is a mistake on every count. For Aristotle says that it is a distinctive mark of Entity that, while remaining numerically one and the same, it is nevertheless capable of admitting contrary qualities. If we read on in that same fifth chapter of the *Categories,* we find him indicating the manner in which this comes about, thereby clarifying his whole concept of "alteration" ("accidental" change, in which an Entity remains itself while undergoing change of qualities). This clarification arises in the context of an objection that Aristotle poses to himself. Propositions—which are not Entities in the primary sense—appear also to satisfy the characteristic, supposedly peculiar to Entities, of admitting contrary qualities, since the proposition that someone is sitting passes from true to false when the person stands tip. But there is a key difference, says Aristotle, between the proposed counter-example and what he has said of Entities. The difference is that the proposition changes its truth-value because of a change in something *else,* something other than itself—namely, the person who stood up. But it is different with Entities:

> It is *by themselves changing* that Entities admit contrary qualities. It is thus that that which was hot becomes cold, for *it* has entered into a different state. Similarly that which was white becomes black, and that which was bad good, *by a process of change;* and in

the same way in all other cases it is *by changing* that Entities are capable of admitting contrary qualities. . . . It is the peculiar mark of Entity that it should be capable of admitting contrary qualities; for *it is by itself changing* [κατὰ τὴν ἑαυτῆς μεταβολὴν] that it does so.[17]

There is, therefore, *no* "undifferentiated endurance" for the Aristotelian Entity. There is, on the contrary, *intrinsic development, change, becoming.* It is the Entity (the man or woman, for instance) that does the changing in passing from thin to fat or pale to tan. The reason, says Aristotle, why it is legitimate to predicate contrary predicates of the same Entity at different times is precisely because the Entity *itself* has changed: George himself, or Martha herself, has *become* tan, so that as a result "tan" is truly predicated when it would have been false before.

To identify Aristotelian Entity, then, with "undifferentiated endurance," characteristic (1) above, is, contrary to the received Whiteheadian tradition, simply anti-Aristotelian. It deserves the "pincushion" comparison used by Eslick ("Substance," 506). For on that view Entity never intrinsically *becomes* in any way; it only extrinsically acquires or loses qualities, as one might acquire or shed clothes. But in that case it is clear that characteristics (2) and (3) would also follow. For by (1), Entity has no alternative to being static and passive (2), and there must therefore be a kind of independence of existence of Entity on the one hand, and of accidental qualities on the other. For if contrary qualities do not *affect* Entity, and if they can successively be "admitted" by Entity, it seems clear that Entity and qualities all get along quite well by themselves (3).

It would be possible to construct a litany of other Aristotelian texts that indicate that, for Aristotle, Entity is dynamic and changing, rather than passive and static. Recall only that natural things, especially animals, are examples *par excellence* of Aristotelian Entities. Yet they not only change, they even move themselves to their own activities. In Aristotle's view, the self-same squirrel, by its feeding activities, moves itself to its own growth while nevertheless remaining a single, enduring Entity. Ivor Leclerc writes: "The Aristotelian doctrine is that the physical existent, by virtue of its inherent activity, is necessarily involved in internal change, while . . . the denial of internal change in matter is the one feature of the modern conception of matter which has persisted until this century."[18]

Whitehead might also have found a clue to this in Ross's *Aristotle,* with which we are certain that he was acquainted. In his chapter on Aristotle's *Metaphysics,* Ross explains:

> Aristotle does not offer in the *Metaphysics* any treatment of the categories as a whole. The categories other than substance [Entity] are, as it were, mere "offshoots and concomitants of being." Substance is prior to them in three ways:—(1) "because it can exist apart while they cannot." This does not mean that it can exist without them while they cannot exist without it. A quality-less substance is as impossible as a quality which does not presuppose a substance. The substance is the whole thing, including the qualities, relations, etc., which form its essence, and this *can* exist apart. It implies qualities but these are not something outside it which it needs in addition to itself. A quality on the other hand is an abstraction which can exist only in a substance. Obviously, if this is his meaning, Aristotle is thinking of substance as the *individual thing.*[19]

For Aristotle, then, "*The substance is the whole thing,*" and its qualities are not something outside it but rather a part of itself—that is exactly the point that Whitehead missed.

3. CONCLUSION

Insofar as Whitehead interpreted Aristotle's theory of Entity as if it were practically indistinguishable from a Lockean or even a Cartesian notion of substance, he was simply and radically mistaken. Descartes' definition of eremitical substances is *not* a "true derivative" of Aristotle's statement that an Entity is never "present in another." And the (perhaps) Lockean notion of an anonymous stuff enduring without internal change beneath a transition of superficial qualities has nothing to do with Aristotle's concept of Entity.

Whitehead's withering attack on the Lockean type of substance-philosophy proves nothing whatever against the Aristotelian concept of Entity. Furthermore, of itself it furnishes no antecedent evidence at all against the viability of at least *some* form of metaphysical system that would postulate a world of interrelated, dynamic Entities that endure in time as essentially self-identical individuals who move themselves to their own activities, and that, precisely by *themselves* changing, change their accidental qualities over time.

TEN

Intuition, Event-Atomism, and the Self

(1987)

In 1984 I had the honor of being invited to present a paper at a multidisciplinary conference held in Galveston, Texas, the aim of which was to explore the implications of Henri Bergson's philosophy for questions arising in contemporary science. Contributors to the conference came from countries as far away as Greece and from sciences as diverse as physics and neuropsychiatry. Among the philosophers was the late Charles Hartshorne, one of the great American philosophers of the twentieth century, who was a foremost proponent of Whiteheadian thinking although he developed it in his own original way. It was therefore something of a strain for me to stand only six feet in front of him and deliver this paper that favors Bergson's conception of human consciousness over that of Whitehead. Later, Hartshorne genially remarked to me that I had done as good a job as could be done with a position he absolutely disagreed with.

Originally published as "Intuition, Event-Atomism, and the Self," in *Bergson and Modern Thought: Towards a Unified Science*, ed. A. C. Papanicolaou and P. A. Y. Gunther, 38–50 (Chur: Harwood Academic Publishers, 1987). © Overseas Publishers Association N.V., reprinted with permission from Gordon and Breach Publishers.

*I'm afraid I still haven't changed my mind, but readers will
be in good company if they too disagree with my conclusions.
In any case I think the paper is fairly accessible. Readers
will recognize that it is derived from essay 4 of this collection.*

The first law to be inferred from observing the history of philosophic
experience, wrote Etienne Gilson, is that *"philosophy always buries its
undertakers."* He here uses "philosophy" in the particular sense of
"metaphysics," and goes on to say: ". . . the metaphysician is a man
who looks behind and beyond experience for an ultimate ground of all
real and possible experience. Even restricting our field of observation
to the history of Western civilization, it is an objective fact that men
have been aiming at such knowledge for more than twenty-five centuries and that, after proving that it should not be sought, and swearing
that they would not seek it any more, men have always found themselves seeking it again." [1] Those indebted to the metaphysical insights
of Henri Bergson expect that Bergson too will bury his undertakers.
Perhaps never before has so influential a philosopher so abruptly
expired within the profession at large: the Bergson who in 1913 occa-
sioned one of New York City's first traffic jams[2] does not rate today
even a bibliographical reference in most new books discussing freedom
and determinism—yet this was an area in which Bergson made original
and definitive contributions.

A chief reason, I am afraid, for Bergson's virtual demise within the
philosophic world is his uncompromising concern with real metaphysical issues. In a philosophically desiccated age, men and women jam
the halls of philosophy congresses less to discuss the metaphysics of
freedom and causality than to debate whether propositions about "the
present King of France" are referential.

Now if concern for metaphysics has proved fatal to Bergson in an
unmetaphysical age, we may with Gilson anticipate Bergson's revival—
as indeed this conference itself suggests. Misunderstanding, however,
is something else, and so is overlooking the profound implications of

Bergson's thought for an understanding both of the human person and of philosophic understanding itself.

I wish therefore to call attention to what I have belatedly come to recognize as significant but generally overlooked implications of some aspects of Bergson's philosophy, particularly of his methodic distinction between intuition and intellection. I shall do this by applying this distinction to competing analyses of becoming, especially as relevant to one's immediate experience of personal identity, and by reflecting on the metaphysical significance of such an analysis.

THE PERSON AS A SOCIETY OF OCCASIONS: WHITEHEAD

Among contemporary process philosophers, the dominant view is some form of the metaphysical system of Alfred North Whitehead. That position, as is well known, regards actual (as distinguished from merely potential) process as fundamentally atomic, corpuscular, or "epochal," as made up of "actual occasions" ("event-atoms," I shall sometimes call them) which, though intrinsically constituted by their relations to preceding occasions (and thus not atomic in the Democritian sense), nonetheless are themselves the unitary actual entities, the citizens of actuality. Thus, the apparent continuity of immediate human experience (which is, of course, an instance of process in general) is analyzed, on this view, into a rapid succession of atomic events, and ongoing consciousness is thought of as a "society" of event-atoms, which, though inheriting from their predecessors by a special affinity, nevertheless are entities ontically distinct from one another. The human person becomes at any moment a complex web of such ontically distinct event-atoms, and, over time, an historical sequence of them. Personal identity through time becomes simply the peculiarity of inheritance of countless, successive event-atoms.

Now, referring to the central vision—"image," he calls it— controlling the development of a person's philosophy, Bergson wrote:

> What first of all characterizes this image is the power of negation it possesses. . . . Faced with currently-accepted ideas, theses which seemed evident, affirmations which had up to that time

passed as scientific, it whispers into the philosopher's ear the word: *Impossible!* Impossible, even though the facts and the reasons appeared to invite you to think it possible and real and certain. Impossible, because a certain experience, confused perhaps but decisive, speaks to you . . . because it is incompatible with the facts cited and the reasons given, and because hence these facts must have been badly observed, these reasonings false.[3]

Something like this reaction has lately been taking place, I believe, among several philosophers, otherwise deeply indebted to Whitehead, with regard to Whitehead's epochal (atomic) view of becoming in general and of the human person in particular. "*Impossible!*" whispers the voice of Bergson's "image," a voice he compared to the one that warned Socrates against missteps. For on this epochal (I might almost say stroboscopic) view of the self it is no longer possible to say, "I did it!" with that sense of "I" that experience seems to warrant. The entity that *says* "I did it!" can never be ontically the entity that in fact did it. Indeed, it would presumably require *hundreds* of successive entities to constitute a linear society of entities long enough even to span the *Augenblick* it takes to say, "I did it."

The ranks of philosophers sympathetic to Whitehead's thought but who find this event-atomic analysis of the human self unbelievable are, as I suggested, growing,[4] and I take this to be an instance of Bergson's negating image. Bergson's own view of the self, however, seems quite the opposite.

THE PERSON AS A CONTINUITY: BERGSON

For Bergson, the person—the self—luminously constitutes a continuity over time. "There is one reality, at least," he writes, "which we all seize from within, by intuition and not by simple analysis. It is our own personality in its flowing through time—our self which endures."[5] In fact, the duration that is immediate experience is the primary object of Bergsonian intuition: "The intuition we refer to . . . bears above all upon internal duration. It grasps a succession which is not juxtaposition, a growth from within, the uninterrupted prolongation of the past into a present which is already blending into the future. It is the direct vision of the mind by the mind. . . . Instead of states contiguous to states, . . . we have here the indivisible and therefore substantial continuity of the flow of the inner life" (CM 32).

The flow, then, of immediate experience (*durée,* as Bergson calls it) is not a continuity in which successive states are set beside one another, contiguous to one another, as are quantitative parts. It is rather the continuity of a melody, in which, precisely *as* a melody, the previous notes still linger in the present and the future notes are at least vaguely anticipated. The same holds true, of course, for speech: a spoken sentence could not convey meaning unless the earlier words are held together in experience with the later.

It is a favorite claim of Bergson's that the mind tends to view reality through the "prism" of space. Thus, in introspection, the mind tends to treat its own experiencing (*durée*) as if it were continuous in the same way that space is—that is, as if it were a *continuity of quantitative homogeneity,* indefinitely divisible into less of the same. In fact, however, by more careful and direct inspection (by "intuition," as Bergson uses the term), we discover a *qualitative heterogeneity,* a fluid unity in which the past so blends with the present in an anticipation of the future that it is impossible, except artificially, to mark off boundaries. As in a melody, the experienced past, and to some extent the anticipated future, give themselves as part of the present.

On the face of it, then, Whitehead's analysis of the person as a society of ontically discrete entities, and Bergson's contention that the self is an unbroken continuity, seem antithetical to one another.[6]

GROUNDS FOR THE EPOCHAL VIEW

If, as Bergson claims, direct intuitive inspection of immediate experience discloses continuity rather than discreteness, what are the essential reasons that persuaded Whitehead to embrace an atomic or epochal interpretation of personal identity?

The chief argument for the epochal theory derives from a Zenonian analysis of experience. For if the process that is immediate experience is through and through continuous in the ordinary sense, we cannot in principle find a locus for any responsible act. On the supposition of pure continuity we are driven, as was St. Augustine (*Confessions* XI, 15), to squeeze any "present" into a temporally inextensive instant in which there is literally no time nor any action. The only rational alternative seems to lie in positing, as did Whitehead, that there is "a becoming of continuity but no continuity of becoming."[7] And in a later passage he states: "The conclusion is that in every act of becoming there is the becoming of something with temporal extension; but that the act itself is not extensive, in the sense that it is divisible into earlier and later acts of becoming which correspond to the extensive divisibility of what has become."[8]

These "acts of becoming" that occupy temporal extension but that internally are not temporally divisible are Whitehead's "actual entities," the ontic quanta of becoming.

At this point we seem faced with a choice: either we give a rational analysis of human experience, an analysis that forces us to interpret it as fundamentally atomic or corpuscular in nature and to give a correlative account of personal identity in terms of an historical succession of ontically discrete actual occasions inheriting from one another, or else we content ourselves with providing a purely phenomenological description of an only apparent continuity that cannot withstand critical analysis. The multiplicity of the analyzed self seems incompatible with the unity of the apparent self.

I for one am not prepared to admit that we find ourselves, in fact, in this either-or position. I propose, rather, that Bergson's own distinction between intuition and intelligence rescues us from this dilemma. I propose further that if this be so, his distinction calls attention to a peculiarity of the very function of metaphysical explanation.

BERGSON'S DISTINCTION BETWEEN INTUITION AND INTELLIGENCE

Bergson, as is well known, distinguished between two different ways of using the mind: *intuition* and *intelligence*. In the former, we place ourselves, through our attention, within the immediate duration in which we act. It is a deliberate mental effort reflectively to understand the act from within rather than from without. By intelligence, on the other hand, the mind orders itself to practicality. We view the rush of experience in terms of stable patterns mirrored in concepts that are, as it were, snapshots of reality.

These two modes of mental activity are naturally correlative to two different aspects of reality. Just as for Plato the different modes of knowing—opinion, reasoning, and understanding—correspond to different levels or depths of reality—the sensible world, the mathematicals, and the Forms—so for Bergson the two main ways of using the mind—intuition and intelligence—correspond to two different aspects of the real, two kinds of process or duration. He writes:

> We should . . . distinguish two forms of multiplicity, two very different ways of regarding duration, two aspects of conscious life. Below homogeneous duration, which is the extensive symbol of true duration, psychological analysis distinguishes a duration whose heterogeneous moments permeate one another; below the numerical multiplicity of conscious states, a qualitative multiplicity; below the self with well-defined states, a self in which *succeeding each other* means *melting into one another* and forming an organic whole.[9]

Bergson reaffirms this distinction in *Matter and Memory:* "The duration *wherein we see ourselves acting,* and in which it is useful that we should see ourselves, is a duration whose elements are dissociated and juxtaposed. The duration *wherein we act* is a duration wherein our states melt into each other."[10]

Bergson thinks that by intelligence we grasp homogeneous, extensive duration; by intuition we grasp heterogeneous, continuous duration. This explains the sense of the outside-inside symbol that Bergson announced at the beginning of his *Introduction to Metaphysics:* "[Philosophers] agree in distinguishing two profoundly different ways of knowing a thing. The first implies that we move round the object; the second, that we enter into it. . . . The first kind of knowledge may be said to stop at the *relative;* the second, in those cases where it is possible, to attain the *absolute*" (IM 21).

In categorizing immediate experience, intelligence makes conceptual blueprints, intellectual snapshots of experience seen as if from the outside, in its wrapping. Though this conceptual description provides precision and intellectual satisfaction, it correspondingly loses that direct reflection of ongoing process that is attainable only by intuition.

This difference of mental approach to reality is perhaps most vividly evident when applied to the human act in the immediacy of its freedom. Freedom is intuitively felt in the ongoing immediacy of decisive acts; it is only the specious difficulties arising from a nonintuitive, extensive analysis that later persuade us to doubt the veracity of this feeling. If, that is, we proceed to try to provide a conceptual (intellectual) definition of this felt freedom, we find that, like water through a sieve, freedom has escaped our conceptual net, so that its very existence seems questionable.[11]

Again, Bergson writes: "Freedom is the relation of the concrete self to the act which it performs. This relation is undefinable, just because we are free. For we can analyse a thing, but not a process; we can break up extensity, but not duration. Or, if we persist in analysing it, we unconsciously transform the process into a thing and duration into extensity. By the very fact of breaking up concrete time we set out its moments in homogeneous space; in place of the doing we put the already done; and, as we have begun by, so to speak, stereotyping the activity of the self, we see spontaneity settle down into inertia and freedom into necessity" (TFW 219–20).

A PROPOSED RECONCILIATION

It is essential for our present purpose to ask how intuition and intelligence relate to each other. Bergson, I am afraid, made plainer how they differ than how they interrelate. It is clear enough, however, from what has been said, that they are complementary functions of the mind, two different avenues to reality, which correspond to two different aspects of reality. It should be no surprise, then, that the respective descriptions they provide should, like the blind men's diverse descriptions of the elephant, appear at first sight antithetical, whereas in fact they are complementary to each other.

I propose that this is exactly the situation we are faced with in the apparently antithetical descriptions of personal identity through time that are provided, respectively, by Bergson's affirmation of the continuity of duration and by Whitehead's theory of the self as a society of successive actual entities. The descriptions do not oppose but rather complement each other, drawn as they are from complementary mental functions operating on different aspects of experience.[12]

Look at the main argument that induced Whitehead to adopt an epochal theory of reality: the application of Zeno's analysis of continuity to the experience of personal identity over time. Now, Zeno's analysis applies precisely and only to a continuity of quantitative homogeneity, the continuity of space. But, as Bergson decisively established, that is not the continuity of immediate experience, of *durée*. It is rather the continuity that experience takes on after we have with our intelligence refracted it through the prism of space. In other words, the very decisiveness of Zeno's argument for an epochal theory of becoming constitutes proof that the analysis therein undertaken is a function of intelligence, not of intuition, and that the experience analyzed is not immediate but derivative, abstract.

A suasive illustration confirming this conclusion is provided by asking this question: If Whitehead's analysis of personal identity through time is accurate, why does one not notice the successiveness of the multiplicity of the actual entities required by the theory for even the shortest of ordinary human experiences? Immediate experience, after all, seems continuous by and large, as Bergson has eloquently shown, rather than successive. The apparently ready reply—namely that, as in a well-made motion picture, the frequency of the successiveness is too rapid to be noticed—must be disqualified, since it implicitly swallows a contradiction hidden within the question itself.

For the question asks why one does not *notice* this successiveness. But on the Whiteheadian analysis, noticing must pertain to the internal subjectivity of actual entities, whereas successiveness belongs to actual entities as they relate to one another in their externality, as they are "objectified" in one another, or, in other words, as they relate to one another not in their subjectivity but in their objectivity, what Bergson might perhaps call their "outer shells." To put it another way, succession as such is, in principle, a characteristic that could be "noticed" only from outside the series, as when one stands beside the embankment and counts the cars on a passing train (impossible to do from within the train). But the noticing in question must of necessity lie within one or more entities of the series. The question, therefore, is internally inconsistent in demanding that one simultaneously stand both within and without the series.

The atomic successiveness, then, of personal identity, on the Whiteheadian analysis, belongs not to the immediacy of the experience of the subject or subjects, but rather to an abstraction derived artificially by the intelligence from this lived immediacy. The living reality of personal identity through time, a reality that is disclosed from within by direct intuition, shows itself as an unbroken but growing and varied unity, a continuity of qualitative heterogeneity. The "I" of personal identity is constituted by this very continuity. When one takes account of the diversity of methods of analysis, the Bergsonian insistence of the unity and continuity of the self through time is not only compatible with the Whiteheadian societal model, it is also more fundamental.

Whitehead himself implicitly grants a similar diversity of modes of analysis, and perhaps even grants the fundamentality of the intuitive. It will be remembered that he compares philosophic discovery to the flight of an airplane. "It starts," he says, "from the ground of particular observation; it makes a flight in the thin air of imaginative generalization; and it again lands for renewed observation rendered acute by rational interpretation" (PR 5).

Now the Whiteheadian analysis of personal identity as an historical society of corpuscular entities is the clear product of abstract, conceptual generalization; it is not a mirror or exact counterpart of actuality. Its very genesis as a Zenonian analysis of becoming proves its remoteness from direct experience, for in order for Zeno's argument to apply, becoming must be understood to enjoy that continuity of quantitative homogeneity peculiar to space, rather than the continuity of qualitative heterogeneity peculiar to ongoing immediate experience.

Yet some of Whitehead's best metaphysical insights spring from an acute intuitive observation of experience. Striking examples abound. His theory of perception in the mode of causal efficacy recognizes the genuineness of our immediate experience of causal derivation and of the value dimension of experience. Similarly, he appeals to a direct, and I would say Bergsonian, intuition when he says that our immediate experience "dissects itself" into "the Whole, That Other, and This-My-Self."[13]

Professor P. A. Y. Gunter has in several places pointed out how, in Bergson's view, intuition and intelligence reinforce each other. "Intuition," he writes, "and intelligence can function only *in terms* of each other. Their functioning involves . . . a continuing interaction."[14]

One way in which intuition assists intelligence is by suggesting which intellectual models more effectively approach actuality. For although no intellectual model can fully capture the actual, some models prove richer and more suggestive than others.

Whitehead's own model of the nontemporal successiveness of the phases of concrescence of an actual occasion is an instance of such a model. He stipulates that there is a succession of phases, such that some are prior to others, but that this succession is nevertheless not temporal, so that one phase cannot be said to come temporally before another (PR 283). This apparently anomalous relationship among the phases has constituted a notorious source of difficulty for Whiteheadian scholars.[15] But in the light of what I have said about the diverse kinds of continuity appropriate on the one hand to subjective immediacy and on the other to time as usually understood, the difficulty should vanish. The time in terms of which the phases are not "before" or "after" one another is the intellectually derivative version of time, which has the quantitative homogeneity of space, whereas the time in which the phases stand in genetic succession to one another is clearly the primordial time of subjectivity, Bergsonian *durée,* a time of radically different continuity from that of space. Nevertheless it is not unenlightening to consider subjective becoming by means of the intellectual model of a successiveness of different phases of development.

Whitehead, then, like Bergson, begins his metaphysical analysis by intuitive appeal to direct experience. He promises to return to it, and indeed he did so to some extent in his later works, as in his extraordinary meditations on truth, beauty, adventure, and peace in *Adventures of Ideas.* Nonetheless, discussions among Whiteheadians about personal identity continue to take as apodictic the event-atomic conceptualization of the self, and that bespeaks a reluctance to return to the immediacy of experience.

CONCLUSIONS

(1) Bergson's distinction between intelligence and intuition enables us to resolve the apparent conflict between his view of the self and that of Whitehead. These two images of the self—the one, of an unbroken continuity that nonetheless enjoys ceaseless qualitative diversity, and the other, of a complex historical route of ontically distinct actual entities—are recognized as the products of two different modes of analysis that implicitly attribute to the self different kinds of continuity. As such, these images can be taken as complementary to one another rather than antithetical, though the Bergsonian image is the more fundamental.

(2) But does not the Bergsonian image of the self as a unity within ongoing qualitative diversity amount to something like a new substance-type philosophy, even though we are not here speaking of a substratum underlying the experience itself?

It seems to me that much of the aforementioned dissatisfaction with the Whiteheadian epochal analysis of becoming stems from a growing awareness of a need to reinstate something closer to a substance-type philosophy than the metaphysics of Whitehead allows.

Furthermore, the way to such a development lies open, contrary to what is usually thought. I am prepared, on some other occasion, to argue that of the several considerations that persuaded Whitehead that no substance-type philosophy is metaphysically feasible, none is cogent.[16] If that be so, the almost a priori assurance with which many philosophers dismiss the notion of any substance-type philosophy as definitively discredited, so as even to use the word "substance" as a term of opprobrium, is without real foundation.

(3) Bergson's distinction between intuition and intelligence also sheds new light on the range and function of metaphysical descriptions in general. It cautions us against confusing the result of conceptual, intellectual analyses with reality itself. It warns us, if you will, against an extreme case of what Whitehead dubbed "the fallacy of misplaced

concreteness." Philosophers following a philosophical tradition are in constant danger of being deceived by this sort of metaphysical mistaken identity. The abstractions enshrined in the philosophical categories of the founding thinker tend to get treated by his followers, if not by himself, as the unquestionable furniture of reality rather than as intellectual models.

I wonder, in fact, whether there is not a parallel here to the situation physicists found themselves in in the third decade of the twentieth century. In some circumstances light seemed certainly to be a wave; in others, just as certainly to be particles; and it seemed impossible to reconcile these descriptions. Light seemed almost like a square circle. Eventually physicists came to realize that the concepts of waves and particles, drawn as they are from the macroscopic world of ordinary human experience, are inadequate models of the micro-world of light and the atom. Such models, however helpful for practical understanding and for prediction, must not be mistaken for exact images of reality.

In a somewhat similar way, Bergson's analysis of the function of intelligence cautions us against confusing the result of intellectual analysis with reality itself. Whitehead, too, tells us to land the plane— to return from the realm of intellectual abstraction to that of direct observation—and Bergson explains at length just how we do this: by returning, through painstaking intuition, to the ongoing immediacy of our concrete experience.

When we do this, we recover the unbroken unity of our selves, a unity that seems hopelessly atomized by intellectual analysis. We also put the conceptualizations of intelligence into their proper metaphysical place.

ELEVEN

Faces of Time

(1987)

The following essay appeared in Thought, *a Fordham University journal that unfortunately is no longer being published. Though fairly easy to read, the essay clarifies and develops a Bergsonian idea, already alluded to, of the two radically different conceptions of time that arise from two different ways of using the mind. In particular I suggest, perhaps originally, how the future can be thought to inhere in the present as well as how the two different kinds of time are interrelated.*

—Time is our own more than commonly supposed.

Most of us have shared St. Augustine's frustration in his candid, even desperate, admission that although he knows what time is if no one asks him, he cannot explain it to anyone who does (*Confessions* XI, 14).

Originally published as "Faces of Time," *Thought* 62, no. 247 (December 1987): 414–22. Reprinted with permission.

In that remark there is as much philosophic wisdom as candor. Further-more, in those same reflections Augustine implicitly distinguished two different kinds of time, or two different aspects of time, both of which seem undeniable yet mutually incompatible. Though the following reflections are not a study on Augustine, they will suggest that Augustine was right in noticing these diverse aspects of time and that they are not so incompatible as at first appears.

Time is part of the fabric of our lives yet tends to evanesce when we try to look it in the face. Like an actor of ancient Greece, time seems to prefer appearing to us only behind masks. In Augustine's meditation on time we seem to discern two of these masks. Perhaps there are others. But since I think that the two manifestations of time noticed by Augustine are among the most fundamental—and seemingly the most irreconcilable with each other—I shall concentrate only on them. I propose to reflect on their interrelationships with a view to discerning the face of time behind its masks.

CLOCK TIME

The first mask is the time of lectures, air schedules, and the morning alarm clock: the time we carry around on our wrists. In our techno-logical culture—though notably not for peoples sometimes called "primitive"—it is what first answers in our minds to the name "time." This is the kind of time Augustine was thinking of when he asked how long is the present and found it shrink before his intellectual gaze into a timeless instant, since every supposed present, like any other tempo-ral width, is itself divided into past and future by the razor-edge of an instantaneous present (*Confessions* XI, 15). But since the past exists no longer and the future not yet, Augustine was left with the paradox that only the present is real yet cannot itself embody time, since it can be no more than a timeless instant. Let us call this mask "clock time" and take a still closer look at it.

Clocks, by imitating the rotation of the earth on its axis, enable us accurately to coordinate our activities with that common motion and with each other. We thus use the motion of a body in space as a mea-sure for other motions, and this is, of course, what Newton called "relative" time. Clock time, then, exactly fits Aristotle's definition of time as "the number [measure] of motion [in space] in respect of 'before' and 'after' [in the motion]."[1] It is object time, the time by which we measure the intensity, so to speak, of the motion of bodies in space. It is not precisely the motion itself but rather a measure, a gauge of that motion. The asymptote, as it were, of clock time—its ultimate distillate—is Newton's "absolute time":

> Absolute, true, and mathematical time, of itself, and from its own nature, flows equably without relation to anything external . . . : relative, apparent, and common time, is some sensible and external . . . measure of duration by the means of motion, which is commonly used instead of true time; such as an hour, a day, a month, a year.[2]

Newton's immediately subsequent definition of space exactly parallels this definition of time: "Absolute space, in its own nature, without relation to anything external, remains always similar and immovable." Time, as Newton has defined it, shares most of the essential characteristics of space.

Thus, like absolute space, which is "always similar," absolute time is homogeneous, "flows equably." Because of this steady thrust of absolute time, the clock time that is relative to it can itself be regarded as homogeneous, each hour being as long as every other. Furthermore, by reason of this very homogeneity, one part of clock time—one minute, say—is distinguished from any other minute solely by its relative position in the total manifold of clock time, not by any qualitative difference. To us, time may sometimes seem to drag, but we do not believe that it drags in clocks—or in clock time.

Clock time, again like absolute space, is indefinitely divisible into shorter and shorter segments (as Augustine assumed in his analysis of the present). It is, consequently, fatally vulnerable to Zeno's relentless dissection that reduces any supposed present interval to a timeless instant.

Furthermore, the parts of clock time exclude one another, as do the sections of a chalkboard or the panels on a wall. Quantitative parts are set apart from one another by their very nature as parts: each extended part is distinct from every other precisely by its position. But the same is true of the different parts of clock time: they exclude one another precisely by being successive. Augustine mused that his boyhood no longer existed now that he had passed to manhood (*Confessions* XI, 18). And as Alice in the looking-glass house learned from the White Queen, the rule of jam yesterday and jam tomorrow means never jam today.

In sum, clock time seems fairly described as object time that is uniform (homogeneous, its parts differing not qualitatively but only quantitatively), exclusive (each part set apart from all others), and objective. It thus shares most of the characteristics of space, since the continuity that it enjoys is, like that of space, an exclusive continuity of quantitative homogeneity.

LIVED TIME

I call the second mask "lived time." It is the time of the boy Wordsworth's "splendor in the grass," a time of qualitative diversity from that of his manhood, a time, he wrote:

> when meadow, grove, and stream,
> The earth, and every common sight.
> To me did seem
> Apparelled in celestial light.
> The glory and the freshness of a dream.
> It is not now as it hath been of yore . . .[3]

The man and the boy are one, yet the time of his manhood puts a different quality as well as a different measure on his mature experience. He simply does not experientially encounter the same wondrous world as before. What sort of time is this that thus transforms the world of the boy to that of the man?

In general, this lived time, this *time of our lives,* has the opposite characteristics from those of clock time. Whereas clock time is the time of objects, of bodies in motion, and so can be called "object time," lived time is the time of a subject's experience as a subject: it is "subject time." This is not to say that it is illusory, manifesting pure appearance. Nevertheless, subject time is apt in our culture to be regarded as purely phenomenal.

Lived time is anything but homogeneous, as Wordsworth movingly pointed out. It is heterogeneous, each part differing from every other. Furthermore, this heterogeneity is qualitative rather than quantitative. We experience it as "longer" or "shorter" precisely because we feel it as burdensome or exhilarating; the parts of its flow, while coherent, are colored by different brushes. Lived time does not count our experiencing of the world nor weigh it nor hold a stopwatch to it. It feels its qualitative diversity from all our other experiences. It is the time by reason of which, as Thomas Wolfe wrote, you can't go home again. It is why Augustine and Wordsworth as men can no longer experience the world of their boyhoods.

By reason of this qualitative heterogeneity, lived time resists indefinite analysis into shorter and shorter parts, and hence is not vulnerable to Zeno's relentless subdividing. For we are aware on reflection that a deliberate, responsible, human action constitutes a unity such that the act itself is lost if it is dissected.[4] Besides, Zeno's argument depends for its efficacy on the exclusive apartheid of each part from every other, from their mutually exclusive side-by-sideness. But lived time will be seen as a continuity in which the present includes rather than excludes the past. The parts of such an inclusive continuity cannot thus be set alongside one another so as to found that possibility of endless, exclusive division that Zeno's argument requires.

The parts of lived time, we find, may be inclusive of one another. We are so accustomed to thinking of time as if it were space, with its mutual exclusivity of parts, that it initially strikes us as absurd to assert that past and future are somehow simultaneous with the present. Yet this togetherness of past, present, and (in a special sense) future is an integral part of our constant experience.

Two obvious examples clarify the point. Consider any melody. A melody is a pattern of several successive notes. These notes cannot be simply isolated from one another; otherwise, once again there is no melody. A melody requires that several different notes not only succeed one another but that they be held together in a unity. The earlier notes must be held present, though as past rather than as present. Furthermore, the experiencing of a melody entails also a certain anticipation of the immediately future notes. Now the unity of the melody, the togetherness of its earlier and later notes, exists only within consciousness itself, certainly not in the instruments or the concert hall. Furthermore, it is an inclusive unity of the parts, unlike the exclusive unity, the distinct side-by-sideness, of the parts of a spatial manifold or the different segments of clock time.

The same fact of inclusion occurs in speech. For the words are spoken successively, and the first word is physically gone long before the sentence ends. Yet all the words must be held in a unity if there is to be comprehension of meaning, and that unity is precisely the conscious experience of the hearer.

The immanence of the past in the present is so ingrained an aspect of experience that it is difficult to notice. Yet without it there simply would not be any intelligible experience. It is an inclusive unity within consciousness of the past with the present, together with a certain felt anticipation of the immediate future.

This inclusive, conscious unity of past, present, and future is the other kind of time that Augustine recognized, at least implicitly. Having puzzled over the paradox that time in the ordinary sense (clock time) is divided into three mutually exclusive parts, Augustine tentatively suggested an alternative way of thinking about time:

> It is now, however, perfectly clear that neither the future nor the past are in existence, and that it is incorrect to say that there are three times—past, present, and future. Though one might perhaps say: "There are three times—a present of things past, a present of things present, and a present of things future." For these three do exist in the mind, and I do not see them anywhere else: the present time of things past is memory; the present time of things present is sight; the present time of things future is expectation.[5]

It may even be that Augustine thought of memory not so much as a phenomenon in the present as a way in which the past inheres in the present. For Augustine thought of the soul as a kind of time-traveler. It does not move in space, since it is immaterial and thus not in place at all, but it does move in time, traveling backwards in memory and forwards in anticipation.[6]

In thus recognizing a present of the past, Augustine implicitly recognized, because he inwardly felt, the lived time that I have described. This time is very different from time in the ordinary sense, the time in which, he thought, every present, on shedding its nonexistent pasts and futures, must shrink into an indivisible instant.

Lived time, then, in contrast to clock time, manifests itself as qualitatively heterogeneous, inclusive of its parts, and pertaining to the subject as such. Therefore, it is subject time, an inclusive continuity of qualitative heterogeneity, whereas clock time, we have seen, is object time, an exclusive continuity of quantitative homogeneity.

FURTHER REFLECTIONS ON LIVED TIME

The qualitative heterogeneity of lived time brings us back again to "long" and "short" times and to the splendor in the grass. It explains why you can't go home again, since it is always a different "you," summing within yourself (by inclusion) your previous experiences. I wonder if this is part of what T. S. Eliot meant when he wrote:

> Fare forward, travellers! not escaping from the past
> Into different lives, or into any future;
> You are not the same people who left that station
> Or who will arrive at any terminus.[7]

The cumulative inclusiveness of ongoing experience is altogether natural as we live it—indeed, it is indispensable to its intelligibility. For if we lived solely in an exclusive, knife-edge present, that present would be entirely without meaning or intelligibility; in it we could only blindly respond to stimuli.[8] Inclusive or subject time only seems paradoxical when instead of simply living it amid our ordinary concerns, we try to make it a direct object of reflection. Better, subject time, which we live (or even, perhaps, which we are in our living) only becomes paradoxical when we endeavor to turn it into an object, something we can analyze and measure and generally treat as if it were not part of our selves even in the very act of analyzing, measuring, or doing anything else.

At this point we can notice some significant implications of the previous considerations. First, correlated with the distinction we have already drawn between subject time and object time, we have begun to notice two different ways of being aware of something in experience: one way that is immediate and more or less ineffable; another that is mediate, conceptual, definitional. Concepts are like intellectual snapshots that we take of the real when we are treating the real like an object, like something to be analyzed at arm's length. Concepts frame for us patterns within the flow of experience. But such patterns, themselves timeless, cannot capture the dynamism of the flow itself or of the subject. Small wonder, then, that time, which has the character of such a flow, always escapes from conceptual cages. Every formal definition states an interrelation among concepts, so that whatever cannot be conceptualized cannot strictly be defined either.

On the other hand, we can pay direct attention to immediate experience in such a way as to enter into it without making it into an object and without conceptualizing it. I think that despite the poor press that the notion of "intuition" has received, Bergson was fundamentally right about its existence and its importance. He wrote, for instance: "There is at least one reality which we all seize from within, by intuition and not by simple analysis. It is our own person in its flowing through time, the self which endures."9

A second point is that in the foregoing discussion I have long since drifted from talking about time as if it were a measure outside of or independent of the flow of experience and have rather been describing the character of experience itself. But I think this is not a methodic error so much as a philosophic advance. I am not alone in rejecting the ontic reality of any absolute time such as Newton described, a time thought to exist in its own right. Time (and space, too) seems rather to be an aspect of the concretely real, of events or instances of becoming in their interrelationships, an aspect that, by a process of abstraction,

we are able to isolate for consideration even though ontically it is insep-
arable from that becoming.

When therefore we ask about the continuity of the masks of time,
we are really asking about the continuity either of the becoming itself
that is fundamental time (subject time) or of the mental model of time
that we have implicitly or explicitly constructed for ourselves (object
time). To understand lived time is to grasp in our awareness the flow of
ongoing, immediate experience, an experience that is nothing at all like
the motion of bodies in space and that cannot therefore be described in
terms of clock time.

This conclusion reverses the order of priority usually assigned
to the objective and subjective aspects of time—what I have called
object time and subject time. It indicates that subject time rather than
object time is the more fundamental. This fundamental time is lived
time, the time of your life; it is Bergson's *durée*.

A third implication of this suggested view has the form of a question that has implicitly arisen as to the precise manner in which the
future exists in the present. To this I venture the following suggestions:

(a) In speaking of the "future in the present" we cannot mean that
there already exists, but simply has not yet come on stage, a queue of
specific, successive events waiting in the wings. There are simply no
such particular, future events.

(b) If we take Augustine's "expectation" of the future simply in
Hume's sense as that of a function of our own habit of mind, it proves
nothing at all about a "present" of the future. There are, however, other
possibilities.

(c) There is an expectation, I hold, that legitimately arises out of a
feeling for the character of the immediate future. This feeling, I have
elsewhere argued,[10] is grounded in our immediate perception of the
continuity of experience, the perception that the immediate future
stands in continuity with the present and its immediate past.

(d) The present, by its very nature as the present of lived time, is an
openness to a future. From this present a future issues. (Leibniz said
that the present is pregnant with the future.) The lived present is not
like a point on a geometric line nor like a geometric plane, bounding

past and future but in itself sterile. The lived present, rather, is precisely what generates a future, as a mother generates a child. The living present, just in being itself, inclusively embodies its past and is continuously giving birth to a future.

(e) A final aspect of the presence of the future, is the future-oriented dimension of final causes. If one grants that the dynamism of the universe is essentially teleological, then there is a sense in which an ideal future lures forward the struggling, present world.

INTERRELATION OF THE TWO TIMES

We can now, in conclusion, notice how these two masks of time relate to one another. In the first place, clock time is constructed by subjects and does not exist apart from human experience. This is not to deny that prior to the human race there were bodies in motion. It is rather to deny that apart from human beings there ever exists a quasi-quantitative and exclusive togetherness of past, present, and future, as on a time line. Clock time is of our own making and everywhere bears our own fingerprints: those of the human race, in clock time's being a unity at all; those of our Western culture, in its affinity to space. Secondly, lived time is our very experiencing itself. It is the natural, internal time of subjects. It turns out, therefore, not to be a mask at all. Thirdly, that time manifests itself to us in diverse ways appears to result from the following three ontological or epistemological polarities:

(a) The different aspects of time result from the soul-body nature of the human person. For we are aware in our own intelligent reflecting that we thereby transcend the space and the clock time that describe our bodies. The ability to be an Augustinian time-traveler belongs not to the body but to the intelligent soul.

(b) The two manifestations of time also result from the subject-object poles of analysis, wherein the subject pole is the pole of free agency, the object pole that of stubborn facts. Thus, subject time is the time of freedom, object time the time of machines.

(c) The diverse manifestations of time are a function of the difference between intuitive and conceptual self-awareness. Awareness of subject time arises from an immediate intuition of our experience as we subjectively live it; awareness of object time arises from a conceptual analysis of the experienced world taken as an object.

In the end we have had to correct our figure of two masks of time. For a mask is primarily an object for an audience, and hence is suitable only for describing object time, clock time. Clock time is generated when the subject tries to see itself as an object. Lived time, on the other hand, is the subject subjectively aware of itself in its own act of experiencing the world.

Yet I suppose that for the Greek actor a mask was something to be lived as well as looked at, almost a part of himself. And indeed, the conclusion seems to be that in whatever way we succeed in unmasking time, the face we disclose is our own.

TWELVE

Fatalism and Truth about the Future

(1992)

This essay first appeared in The Thomist, *and subsequently as a chapter in my book* Making Sense of Your Freedom. *It does not pretend to cover this whole issue of the relation of truth to time, controverted since Aristotle, but it may provide an accessible introduction to some aspects of the problem. It stakes out what I still think is a defensible position. Professional philosophers familiar with contemporary literature on the issues will rightly recognize these reflections as the work of a beginner in the field, for they are my first serious and independent reflections on the topic. Perhaps what they lack in erudition may partially be balanced by the freshness of one person's new start. Right or wrong, some parts of this essay may be difficult sledding by reason of the topic.*

Originally published as "Fatalism and Truth about the Future," *The Thomist* 56, no. 2 (1992): 209–27. Reprinted with permission.

When we speak of future events, does today's truth mean tomorrow's necessity? The question is as old as Aristotle's "sea battle tomorrow," so the last ships should long ago have been sunk, but after two thousand years the textual analysis of Aristotle's position is still controverted. Yet I think something new can be said about it if we consider afresh the philosophic issues themselves.

What philosophic consequences must we accept if we suppose that *predictions,* that is, propositions referring to future events, are either true or false antecedently to the events to which they refer? In particular, if a prediction be true now, does its present truth imply a fixity inherent in the future such that fatalism is unavoidable?[1]

It has been argued that it does. Aristotle sketched such an argument (not necessarily his own) in the sea battle passage already alluded to:

> [If anything] is white now it was true to say earlier that it would be white; so that it was always true to say of anything that has happened that it would be so. But if it was always true to say that it was so, or would be so, it could not not be so, or not be going to be so. But if something cannot not happen it is impossible for it not to happen; and if it is impossible for something not to happen it is necessary for it to happen. Everything that will be, therefore, happens necessarily. So nothing will come about as chance has it or by chance; for if by chance, not of necessity.[2]

If, then, a prediction is true in the present or false in the present, its very truth value today seems to create an ineluctable fixity upon tomorrow's event such that fatalism would be unavoidable. And as is implied in Aristotle's example, it seems natural to suppose that a prediction must, after all, be either true or, if not true, then false. Does not the law of excluded middle demand this?

Thus the logic of truth relations seems to impose a fatalistic view of events. Indeed, fatalism is sometimes defined precisely in terms of logic, so that a contemporary author writes: "Fatalism is the thesis that the laws of logic alone suffice to prove that no man has free will, suffice to prove that the only actions which a man can perform are the actions which he does, in fact, perform, and suffice to prove that a man can bring about only those events which do, in fact, occur and can prevent only those events which do not, in fact, occur."[3]

I shall, however, argue that (1) neither the law of excluded middle nor any other logical consideration requires that predictions be true or else false when they are asserted; (2) the antecedent truth (or falsity) of predictions would not necessitate fatalism by reason of any logical considerations, (3) though it could necessitate fatalism for causal reasons; and (4) predictions are never, absolutely speaking, true nor false before the occurrence of the events to which they refer, though they may be true or false in an attenuated, relative sense.

— *Thesis 1: Neither the law of excluded middle nor any other logical consideration requires that a prediction be, prior to the event, true or, if not true, then false.*

I understand the law of excluded middle (LEM) to mean that, for any meaningful proposition p, it is (logically) necessary that p be true or, if not true, then false.

By ordinary usage a proposition referring to a state of affairs in the world, as distinguished from one referring to logical relationships, is called "true" if and only if that state of affairs obtains. The proposition "I am sitting" is true just in that case when I am sitting.

This usage normally presupposes that the object or event described in the statement is available as a referent. Thus if Mary should say "I am taller than my sister," when she has no sister at all, there is a clear sense in which her statement could not be regarded either as true or as false.[4] The existence of the referent for comparison can thus be a necessary condition for applying LEM.

Now it may reasonably be doubted, and I do doubt it, that a future event, as future, is available as a referent in the present. A prediction is dubiously true now (or false now) when the event it refers to has not yet taken place. As Mary's phrase "my sister" provided only a nominal definition of an object of predication (since there was no actual object), so a prediction provides only a nominal definition of a state of affairs until that state of affairs exists. But can a non-existent "state of affairs" function to fix the present truth or falsity of the prediction that refers to it? Only if that state of affairs is somehow available in the present, I should think, can LEM be applied to the statement.

I hold that LEM itself cannot meaningfully be applied to a prediction prior to the occurrence of the event to which the prediction refers because it is a necessary condition for the truth relation embodied in LEM that the referent of the prediction be available for comparison.

One may object that the present obviously does cast its shadow on the past, as in the argument indicated by Aristotle. For common sense supposes that if X is the case today, an assertion made yesterday that X would be the case today must yesterday have been true.

Yet this supposition of common sense is purely gratuitous. While the proposition that I am sneezing is true now if I am sneezing, it does not thereby follow that it was true yesterday that I would be sneezing today. For though *I* existed yesterday, *today's sneezing me* did not. To claim in general that the true description of any present fact must always have been true (not, of course, that the *fact* always obtained) is to utter what William James would call a *Machtspruch*, a decree that closes the case before it is heard. It implicitly appeals to what one may call the Logic of the Future, and it supposes that truth is *omnitemporal:* that what is true at any time is true at all times.

An objector might instead propose that the truth of propositions is not omnitemporal but atemporal, literally timeless. Thus, though my sneeze is a temporal event, the truth of the proposition that I sneeze at such and such a time is not itself temporal. The truth of the proposition, on this view, does not come into existence with my sneeze nor with the proposition's entertainment by anyone. If, then, propositions are atemporally rather than omnitemporally true, it does not seem sensible to speak of a proposition as true "now" or "then" or at any other time. Furthermore, the atemporal truth of propositions referring to the future would be sufficient for the fatalistic argument indicated by Aristotle. For there is obviously nothing one can do to change an atemporal truth nor, consequently, to avoid the matter of fact that it atemporally describes.

This latter form of the objection, however, involves the same presupposition as the former: that the future is as much a fact as the past. For whether one regards the truth of propositions as omnitemporal or as atemporal, as reaching across all time or as having nothing whatever to do with time, one implies that future events as well as past belong to a unitary whole that is itself not temporal. A common conception of this whole is that of a four dimensional space-time manifold in which all temporal events are naturally situated according to the time and place of their occurrence. This is the sense in which time can be said to "flow" only in the way that a fence "runs" across the property.

I submit that to adopt this unitary view of temporal events, hence to adopt an omnitemporal or an atemporal view of the truth of propositions referring to those events, is to make an arbitrary and dubious presupposition that locks one into an untenable metaphysical position. It gives to space and time, or to space-time, an ontological priority over actual events instead of making space-time derivative from events. It tacitly presupposes the metaphysical priority of a space-time manifold that embraces within itself all space-time events and thus unites the future with the present. Such a unity would be requisite if logic would require one to hold that predictions must be true or be false antecedently to the events.

I do not grant, however, that space-time is ontologically prior to actual events in their interrelations; consequently I accept neither the omnitemporality nor the atemporality of the truth of propositions referring to temporal events. I must on the other hand provide a sense in which propositions can be said to be true at some times while not at others, and indeed a sense in which predictions *become* true or else false within the passage of events. This sense will, I believe, become apparent in (and stand or fall with) the argumentation for Thesis 4 below.

At present I tentatively suppose that it makes sense to speak of propositions as true *at* some time, and I return to the question whether any logical considerations require that predictions be true or else false when they are asserted, prior to the occurrence of the events to which they refer.

So far there have been found no compelling reasons, either from LEM or from other logical considerations, for holding that they are. In Thesis 4 I shall provide strong positive reasons for thinking that, in an absolute sense, predictions can in fact never be true nor false prior to their events. If that be the case, then no logical consideration could possibly require that predictions be true before the fact, and thus Thesis 1 will be proved indirectly. At this point, however, I have only claimed that LEM cannot even be applied to predictions unless the future events referred to are available for comparison, and also that there are no evident reasons requiring one to think that future events are thus available.

— *Thesis 2: The truth or the falsity of predictions prior to the occurrence of the events to which they refer would not logically entail fatalism.*

By *fatalism* I mean the view that whatever happens, happens inevitably and could not have happened otherwise. It is reductively the view that the actual and the possible coincide, for if nothing could happen otherwise than as it does, then the actual exhausts the possible.[5]

The most common argument for fatalism, as in that already quoted from Aristotle, goes roughly like this: "Let q stand for any proposition referring to a future 'contingent' event—say the proposition 'I shall tell a lie tomorrow.' Since logic assures me that either I shall tell a lie tomorrow or I shall not, it seems that q must either be true today or be false. But if it is true today, then, as in a Greek tragedy, I cannot avoid telling a lie tomorrow. And if q is false today, I shall be quite incapable of telling a lie tomorrow. And since this trivial example can be generalized, it follows that no events are in fact contingent, but everything happens of necessity."

But this argument is unsound. In the first place it assumes that LEM requires that q be true today or else false today, and that, as we have seen, is at best dubious. Secondly, the argument illegitimately transfers the hypothetical necessity of the proposition (that q is true) to the human act.

For if q be true now, what can be said to follow logically? That I shall tell a lie tomorrow; that I shall not fail to tell a lie tomorrow; that I shall not not tell a lie tomorrow. But it does not follow that I *cannot* fail to tell a lie tomorrow; that I shall not be able not to lie tomorrow. In the fatalistic argument sketched above, however, this logical misstep has been taken. The element of necessity has been wrongly transferred from the logical situation to the act of telling the lie. That is, as long as we assume that q is true, it necessarily follows, on that assumption, that I shall in fact tell a lie tomorrow. But it does not follow that in telling the lie I shall do it necessarily.

This becomes clearer when we turn the time around. If today it is true that I whistled "Dixie" yesterday, then, on that supposition, it is necessarily the case that I did whistle it. But the necessity is only the necessity of the supposition that it is true that I whistled it yesterday; it does not follow that yesterday I couldn't help whistling it.

To return to the argument for fatalism described by Aristotle (not necessarily as his own), we find two distinct steps, which I shall call (i) and (ii), both of which have now been called into question:

(i) "[If anything] is white now it was true to say earlier that it would be white; so that it was always true to say of anything that has happened that it would be so." This assertion is rejected by Thesis 1 above.

(ii) "But if it was always true to say that it was so, or would be so, it could not not be so, or not be going to be so. But if something cannot not happen it is impossible for it not to happen; and if it is impossible for something not to happen it is necessary for it to happen. Everything that will be, therefore, happens necessarily. So nothing will come about as chance has it or by chance; for if by chance, not of necessity."

Thesis 2, however, claims that there are no grounds in logic for the assertion (ii) that today's truth entails tomorrow's necessity. The first "could" in (ii) is logically unjustified; "would" is all that one is logically entitled to. Similarly unjustified are the words "cannot" and "impossible" that follow the "could." If it was always (or at any past time) true to say that something (say, X) would be so, then indeed X *would* not not be so, but it does not logically follow that X *could* not not be so. The necessity of the hypothesis that it was true to say that X would be so cannot legitimately be transferred to the event itself.

On the other hand I think it must be granted that the present truth or falsity of predictions could indeed entail fatalism, though not by reason of logic.

— *Thesis 3: If predictions be absolutely true or else false prior to the events referred to, fatalism would be inescapable, but for causal, not logical, reasons.*

Thesis 2 has already argued that the truth of predictions does not entail fatalism by reason of logic. It should also be noticed that the point at issue is independent of anyone's *knowledge* of the events. It is irrelevant to the argument whether anyone, including God, somehow knows that a prediction is true. The question is, rather, whether a proposition referring to future events can itself be said to be true, independently of anyone's knowledge of its truth.

To explain and support Thesis 3, I must (a) explain the meaning of the term "absolutely," then (b) identify the necessary condition for the truth of such predictions before their events.

(a) "Absolutely" refers to the following case. (Though extreme, it is not really all that rare and will serve as a useful reference point for more ordinary cases.) Let us suppose a kind of Laplacian Intelligence, or perhaps a supercomputer, and further suppose it able to formulate a definite, though perhaps infinitely complex, proposition that describes with absolute precision the entire detailed state of the cosmos for all future time. This megaproposition would constitute the complete World Book of the Future. It would be a detailed expression of the sort of future that is conceived as part of the unitary whole discussed under Thesis 1. It would, in other words, be a complete script of that definite future that is envisaged as occupying the space-time manifold of actual events in the direction of the future. Such an assumed future would correspond to the future that is assumed when one supposes that logic alone entails fatalism: "Que será, será."

I call "absolute" the hypothetical future thus conceived as a complete and definite (exact) totality, and accordingly I call "absolute" the truth or the falsity of propositions referring to this concept of a future.

(b) What would be the necessary condition for the present truth or falsity of a proposition referring to such an absolute future?

Any proposition about temporal events is called "true" only when the events it describes occur as stated. In considering Thesis 1, I suggested that future events, as future, do not seem available as referents for such a comparison. I now wish to give more precision to this notion of *availability* and to do it in terms of *definiteness*.

The predicate of the typical proposition, including a prediction, assigns a certain definiteness to its grammatical subject. For instance, the prediction may assign a sneeze to "tomorrow's me." But "tomorrow's me" is only a linguistic dummy, a kind of nominal definition, until "tomorrow's me" becomes definite in every particular. Will "tomorrow's me" actually include an act of sneezing? Tune in again tomorrow to find out, for only then will "tomorrow's me" become a real, and hence a definite and determinate me.

Today's real me is an openness to a whole spectrum of "me's" for tomorrow. Or more exactly: today's actual me opens onto a possibility-spectrum for "tomorrow's me." The future as future is always characterized by a certain vagueness, a lack of definiteness. So too, tomorrow's me, like a slide projected unfocused onto a screen, awaits the definiteness, the focusing, that only the actual events between today and tomorrow can give it.

But we are presently in search of the necessary condition under which a proposition referring to tomorrow's event could be called true, hence be said to match that event exactly, even today. Indeed, in the present extreme example we seek the necessary condition for the truth of the megaproposition describing the total future.

Now only to the extent that all indefiniteness is even today excluded from tomorrow's events can today's prediction about them be called true. Otherwise there is no precision to tomorrow itself that can serve as a basis for the truth relation today. Only if today's set of events already fixes the definiteness of tomorrow's events can today's prediction be now true of tomorrow.

But to suppose that the definiteness of tomorrow is already settled today is to embrace the doctrine of determinism. By "determinism" I mean the hypothesis that for every event Q, there is an antecedent event (or set of events) P, such that P constitutes a sufficient condition for Q. Thus every actual event or state of affairs (this is a universal hypothesis) would be the inevitable outcome of the previous state of affairs, since, by hypothesis, the previous state of affairs is a sufficient condition for the present state. And since the sequence of matters of fact is not the result of purely logical relationships, I do not hesitate to call such determinism "causal."

If universal causal determinism accurately describes the world, then every state of affairs today was already in the cards yesterday, so that yesterday's prediction referring to today's event must yesterday have been true or else false, inasmuch as even yesterday there would have been no indefiniteness about the exact character of today's events. The correctness of the hypothesis of determinism would, then, be a sufficient condition for the truth or the falsity of predictions prior to their events.

Conversely, only if determinism be correct could there yesterday have been complete definiteness about today's events. For what was to remove the vagueness, the indefiniteness of today's events, so as to guarantee their exact fit to yesterday's predictions, if not an impossibility, intrinsic in yesterday's events, that today's events could turn out otherwise than precisely as they do? Only such an impossibility could furnish yesterday the definiteness for today that is requisite for yesterday's truth or falsity of predictions about today.

But to say that yesterday's events render today's events absolutely definite is just to say that yesterday's events constitute a sufficient condition for the definiteness of today's, and that is precisely the claim of causal determinism.

Determinism, therefore, is both a necessary and a sufficient condition for the present absolute truth of the hypothetical megaproposition referring to a total future. If that proposition can even now be true, then the hypothesis of determinism must be correct.

But if determinism is correct, then every state of affairs, every present, is the inevitable outcome of its own past, and this is exactly the doctrine of fatalism. Therefore if predictions are absolutely true or absolutely false prior to their events, fatalism is entailed because causal determinism is entailed. And this is the central assertion of Thesis 3.

Is this "absolute" sense of truth, however, a straw man? Have I defined absolute truth in such extreme terms that the thesis has no real practical application?

No, I don't think I have. I had two reasons for saying earlier that the hypothetical megaproposition describing the total future is not really all that rare. The first is that it is natural, almost instinctive, to regard the future as a totality of definite events that lie ahead of us, much as the highway lies ahead of us around the bend, even though we may now be unable to see it. Insofar, then, as we suppose that our expectations about any particular detail of the future are basically correct, we tend to suppose that they shine a spotlight, as it were, onto parts of that tacitly assumed, given totality. The Logic of the Future seems to bind all events together so that particular predictions imply that supposed totality that I have called "absolute."

The second reason is that it is again natural, from a purely logical point of view, to suppose that even the outcome of a free decision also lies unambiguously ahead. But to suppose this is once again to suppose that there exists that totality of the future just considered, since the hypothetically free decision, as free, could enjoy definiteness in the present only insofar as it forms part of that very totality.

The extent to which an analogue of Thesis 3 would apply to more ordinary propositions, propositions not referring to such an absolute future, will become apparent from the considerations supporting Thesis 4, to which I now turn.

— *Thesis 4: Absolutely speaking, predictions are never true nor false antecedently to the occurrence of the events to which they refer. In a relative sense, however, some predictions can be so regarded.*

Before giving reasons directly in support of this thesis, I must offer some preliminary suggestions concerning (a) some relations between logic and metaphysics, and (b) the relation of determinism to the thesis.

(a) At the heart of this issue lies the fundamental question, mentioned earlier, of the relation of space and time, and perhaps even of logic generally, to metaphysics. On the one hand it seems natural to construct out of the abstract ideas of space and of time a kind of logical, four-dimensional space-time manifold onto which all temporal events can be mapped. The truth or the falsity of propositions referring to events in this manifold would then lie outside the manifold itself, hence be atemporal.

But such a construction implicitly presupposes that the space-time structure enjoys logical, even perhaps ontological, priority over actual events. For the "before" and "after," the "here" and "there" of temporal events is then thought of as at least logically prior to the events themselves rather than derivative from them.

Paradigmatic of such a view is Newton's conception of an absolute space and time that serve as infinite, unaffected repositories for all spatiotemporal events. Analogous to this is the contemporary fascination with interpreting the actual world (actual cosmic history) in terms of an infinity of hypothetical "possible worlds," possible cosmic histories. More than that, the metaphysics of the actual world is thought of, implicitly at least, as exemplifying one particular set of principles out of an infinity of possible ones. In such a conception, metaphysical principles are mapped onto a broader logical structure tacitly accorded a priority, in principle if not in time, to actual events and to the metaphysical structure they exemplify.

I, however, proceed on the assumption—though this is not the place to argue it—that, whether the logical order is viewed as an abstract character of the extramental world or as a reflection of the structure of thought, logical structure and the structure of space-time inhere in and depend upon the structure of actual events, not the other way around.[6]

(b) By Thesis 3, if predictions be absolutely true or absolutely false prior to the occurrence of the events to which they refer, fatalism is entailed because causal determinism is entailed. Conversely, if determinism in fact holds, all predictions could be considered true or else false prior to their events because all indefiniteness of the predicted events would already have been excluded at the time the prediction is entertained.

If therefore the hypothesis of determinism be correct, Thesis 4 cannot stand. But is determinism correct? It would clearly be unfeasible here to re-examine that complex and hoary question. It is, however, appropriate to note that the hypothesis of determinism is just that—a hypothesis and, indeed, a hypothesis that, in the nature of things, cannot be proved. You can never *observe* that a particular event—let alone all events—could not have turned out otherwise. Neither can you *demonstrate* this on purely logical grounds. You cannot in fact argue to determinism at all. You take a stand on it and you take the consequences. Since I hold that we are, at least sometimes, free agents responsible for our decisions, and since I also hold that determinism is incompatible with freedom, I make no apology for assuming in what follows that determinism, as a universal thesis, is false. Furthermore, the principles that I am about to propose in support of Thesis 4 themselves serve as plausible reasons why determinism cannot be a correct doctrine.

I now return to the consideration of Thesis 4 itself. The thesis was adumbrated in a preliminary way in the considerations supporting Thesis 1, by which the availability of future events for a truth relation in the present was called into question. Furthermore, the antecedent truth of predictions was seen not to be required by what I have called the Logic of the Future. One can not claim, without simply begging the question, that the truth value of propositions is omnitemporal, as if once true, always true, in the past as well as in the future. It is just not evident that a description of today's fact must have been true yesterday—at least not unless one is prepared to accept the claim of causal determinism. For if the description was already true yesterday, of what use is today? Unless indeed, as determinism would assert, today adds no determinations to yesterday but only an ineluctable production of what is already causally necessitated. Similarly, it is gratuitous to claim that tomorrow's fact must be describable by true propositions today, for that presupposes that tomorrow's fact is settled even today. If so, of what use is tomorrow?

These questions are of course tendentious, and deliberately so. They appeal to a metaphysical insight into the processive nature of reality as we experience it. Let me describe this insight more exactly in the form of the following proposed metaphysical principles. I say "proposed" because, like all metaphysical principles, they cannot be demonstrated but only pointed out as more plausible, closer to experience, than their opposites. The reader must judge whether they ring true. The principles, however, in concert with a rejection of determinism, constitute the metaphysical reason why predictions can never be absolutely true prior to their described events.

— *Principle A: Past actuality, whether immediate or remote, is definite, exact, unambiguous.*

For instance, an essay or a novel, when the author is finished with it, is just that particular assemblage of words. So too with the definite-

ness of events. The Battle of Gettysburg was, in the event, just those
definite soldiers firing just those definite shots. Closer to home: each of
us has lived a very definite personal history. Our present memories
about where we were or what we did at any particular time may be
uncertain, but we suppose nevertheless that at every moment, past and
present, we were just "there" doing just "that."

— *Principle B: Present actuality involves a process of determination,
whereby from the indefiniteness of potentiality there is created the
definiteness of settled actuality.*

The writing of a novel or an essay, for instance, is a process by
which the indefiniteness of the author's initial vague ideas takes on the
definiteness of the finished product. Principle B claims that something
like this is happening all the time—that this is exactly what "happening" amounts to.

The present therefore is always creating itself out of what is given
from the past for the present; it is not simply instantiating the necessities inherited from the past (as determinism would have it). If that be
correct and determinism mistaken, then the present has to be taken
seriously as a kind of creation, a creation in which genuinely new, and
consequently unforeseeable, events and details may take place. The
exact history of our individual lives is the indelible trace of what we
have chosen to make out of the situations we found ourselves in.

— *Principle C: Only actual events create this definiteness of settled actuality within the given width of possibility.*

Principle C is roughly the converse of Principle B, and if any aspect
of my position is the most controversial, this is probably it. Principle B
asserts that actual events always exemplify, because they produce, definiteness, an exact pattern of actuality. Principle C, conversely, asserts
that such definiteness, such exactness of pattern, requires actual events
as the origin of that definiteness. Possibility as such is always vague,

poorly defined, whereas actuality is definite and precise by reason of its own activity. Actual events, therefore, imply definiteness (Principle B), and definiteness implies actual events (Principle C).

The possible ways, for instance, in which you can next walk out the door of your room are limited by the doorframe, but within that limitation there is no end to the different ways you can walk out. But the actual way you do walk out—say, left leg first, etc.—gets its definition precisely and only from your act of walking out.

Similarly, the actual writing by a real author is required not only for the resulting novel as a whole but for the creation of the pattern of words that constitutes its form. Dickens literally created the literary pattern that is *David Copperfield;* he did not select it from an array of pre-defined (or even of atemporal) patterns within some limbo-library of possible novels available for actualization.

An immediate consequence of C is that *the definiteness of the actual (its formal pattern) never precedes the actual in time.* Prior to the Battle of Gettysburg the generals involved doubtless speculated on the possibility of a battle at Gettysburg. But one can only refer to *the* Battle of Gettysburg after a battle has been fought and has, by the fighting, transformed "*a* battle" into "*the* battle." The phrase, "the Battle of Gettysburg," supposes that exactness of detail that was supplied only by the fighting. The same would be the case for a musical creation. Only after Mozart had conceived it, at least, did there exist the definite and marvelous pattern of notes that we call his *Fortieth Symphony.* Mozart created that pattern in his thinking and his writing, and prior to his act of creating the pattern simply did not exist, not even to be talked about as a possibility.

This Bergsonian point is illuminated by noting that it would be odd if someone were to entitle a book *On Preventing the Next Air Disaster* but not odd to call it *On Preventing Another Air Disaster.* For unlike "another air disaster," which is vague and indefinite, "the next air disaster" sounds as definite and precise as "the last air disaster." Yet "the next air disaster" cannot be definite if it is in fact prevented and so never happens at all.

Now if the precise pattern of an actual event never precedes the event in time, neither does the possibility of an absolute truth relationship between that event and a prediction making an assertion about it, for there is as yet no complete definiteness to the event that the prediction can be compared with. The event is not available for comparison precisely because it is indefinite. Since this is the case, however, predictions can never be absolutely true nor false prior to the occurrence of the events to which they refer. And this is the primary assertion of Thesis 4.

Predictions, therefore, that directly or indirectly refer to a total future, as do predictions about free decisions (as we have seen), are never true nor false antecedently to their described events.

Yet aside from these absolute cases there does seem to be a large class of predictions that can be considered as antecedently true or false in a relative sense. These are predictions about events that, quite apart from the thesis of determinism, seem physically necessitated, given our present understanding of nature and given the factual situation at the time the prediction is made.

Consider, for instance, the proposition, "Tomorrow the moon will be at a distance of one light-year from the earth." It seems obvious from our understanding of nature that this proposition cannot possibly be true; that it is even now false. One need not hold determinism to recognize the absurdity of this proposition; one need only know a little physics.

In considering Thesis 3, I granted that present predictions could even now be true in a deterministic universe precisely because in such a universe the present would already fix the definiteness of the future. In an analogous way, to the extent that physical laws at work in the present fix the margins of the future, just to that extent can predictions about the future be said to be even now true or false. This, however, is truth or falsity in a relative sense—relative, namely, to that width of possibility fixed for the future by physical laws operative in the present. And this is the meaning of the latter part of Thesis 4.

Consider a more ordinary example of predictions. What about tide tables? Are the predictions about the height of future tides true now? I think we should say yes, but in the relative sense. After all, it is neither logically nor even physically impossible that some cataclysm should occur (such as the sun exploding) prior to some predicted tide, so that the prediction might prove false after all. Hence the tide tables cannot be true in an absolute sense, as if they were giving us a sneak preview of the future. Granted that, however, and granted our solid knowledge of the gravitational and kinetic forces at work, we seem justified in regarding these predictions as true relative to those factors. Ask any sailor.

Tide tables, however, may be less a description of the future than a formalization of our own expectations about it. In any case, most predictions fall in a gray area between predictions of an absolute future, none of which can be true before their events, and blind guesses. But the truth or falsity of most predictions is exactly relative to the constraints of nature and is, therefore, a relative kind of truth or falsity. But this relative truth of propositions referring to the future affords no argument for a doctrine of fatalism.

I conclude, then, that arguments for fatalism based on considerations of logic are mistaken; that predictions about an absolute future are never true nor false; and that predictions about particular events can be true or false at most in an attenuated, relative sense.

The philosophic scent of many philosophers has therefore been accurate in sniffing fatalism whenever predictions were taken to be unqualifiedly true or false in the present, yet almost all of the barking has been directed up the wrong trees: the Tree of the Law of Excluded Middle, wrongly thought to entail the truth or the falsity of predictions antecedently to the occurrence of their described events; and the Tree of the Logic of the Future, wrongly thought to entail that what will be, cannot not be. The barking would better have been directed up the Tree of Causal Determinism where the serpent of fatalism actually lurks, tempting us to take the fatal bite of supposing that what we say about an absolute future can even now be true.

THIRTEEN

Relational Realism and the Great Deception of Sense

(1994)

The Modern Schoolman *was the birthplace of this short piece, an essay that I consider significant, not because I am saying something quite original (I really am not), but because of the importance of the issue for a sound philosophical understanding of sense perception. The basic thesis reaffirms in modern terms the essential view of St. Thomas Aquinas, and does it in stark contrast to a view of perception that, although not new in itself, found strong adherence in the thought of Descartes, Locke, and Hume, and thus largely dominated, with disastrous effect, Western philosophical thinking ever since. The position I here develop, which I dare to think is Thomistic in modern expression, was already inchoately in my mind when I criticized Whitehead's epistemology in essay 5 on Whitehead's elephant. This essay should be easy to read; I develop the position more fully in my book,* Human Knowing: A Prelude to Metaphysics.

Originally published as "Relational Realism and the Great Deception of Sense," *The Modern Schoolman* 71 (May 1994): 305–16. Reprinted with permission.

ANATOMY OF THE DECEPTION

This is an attempted exorcism. I shall be trying to get rid of a ghost that has haunted Western philosophy with baleful effect for at least 350 years. More exactly, the ghost is a myth that, in the way of many myths, has mainly lived on forged credit. Though one finds its influence even in the atomists of ancient Greece, it fairly dominated the thinkers of the seventeenth and eighteenth centuries, and it remains a common view today. Thomas Hobbes, who believed in the myth but was troubled by it, called it *"the great deception of sense."*[1] Roughly it is the doctrine that we do not find ourselves directly confronted with colored, noisy, and smelly objects, but merely with our own sensations of color, sound, and smell. Our own sensations are what we find; the world that provoked them can only be inferred.

For a twentieth-century instance of this myth, notice how it pervades the first chapter of Bertrand Russell's early book, *The Problems of Philosophy*.[2] There he considers a table and notes that its visual appearance changes as he walks around it or sees it in a different light, yet he does not believe that the table itself (the "real table") thereby changes. But if the appearances change while the table does not, it seems to follow both that the appearances are not the table, and that appearances alone are what is immediately given us. As Russell puts it: "Thus it becomes evident that the real table, if there is one, is not the same as what we immediately experience by sight or touch or hearing. The real table, if there is one, is not *immediately* known to us at all, but must be an inference from what is immediately known" (11). And again: "What we directly see and feel is merely 'appearance' which we believe to be a sign of some 'reality' behind" (16). What we do feel and see he calls "sense data," and he defines "sensation" as "the experience of being immediately aware of these things [sense data]" (12).

But at the dawn of the modern era, the same ghost already haunts the views of Galileo[3] and Newton[4] among scientists, and of Hobbes, Locke, Descartes, Hume, and indeed of most later philosophers.

Locke, for instance, takes the myth for granted but also confesses to the immediate problem that it poses:

3. 'Tis evident the Mind knows not Things immediately, but only by the intervention of the *Ideas* it has of them. Our *Knowledge* therefore is real only so far as there is a conformity between our *Ideas* and the reality of Things. But what shall be here the Criterion? How shall the Mind, when it perceives nothing but its own *Ideas,* know that they agree with things themselves?[5]

THE ABSURDITY OF THE MYTH

How indeed? But then it may fairly be asked whether we have to live with this doctrine at all. To begin with, it flies in the face of the interpretation that we tend naturally to give to sense perception. Ordinary people not yet perplexed by philosophy think that they see, feel, smell, and taste apples, not the appearances of apples. They will report that they applied the brakes because they saw a red light, not because they had noticed an impression of a red light.[6]

But the myth would have us lock ourselves within a dream world of appearance while assuring us that the "real" (that is, non-mental, material) world is forever beyond our immediate grasp. Yet if this be a "dream," we normally take it for reality, and that is just why Hobbes calls it "the great deception of sense." The myth in effect canonizes Plato's allegory of the cave: it sentences us forever to the fate of the prisoners who can view only images of reality, not reality itself, without the possibility of comparing the images to the real.[7]

Furthermore, this world of appearance is very little like the world of reality that is supposed to lie behind it. According to the myth, all the smells and colors and sounds are entirely within us, not in the world itself, which is a world of bodies in motion that merely provoke such sensations in us.

Another problem with the myth's world of appearance is that the succession of different sensations is, so far as we can ever know, entirely arbitrary, as Hume emphasized later in his *Enquiry.* Though our minds are quick to form habits of expecting similar sensations to follow those of the past, as also did Plato's prisoners, there is no intrinsic connection of any one sensation to the preceding one. Sense perception, in this view, is simply a display of unconnected impressions succeeding one another with no more necessity of connection than that by which one image follows another in a PowerPoint lecture. Each sense datum is self-contained and contains no intrinsic pointers to any other.

More than that, the myth takes for granted that no sense datum can contain an intrinsic pointer to an external event that could be supposed to have provoked it. Although Locke simply took for granted that his sensations were evoked by objects in a world around him, Hume claimed that even for those events that we call "cause" and "effect," each is just simply itself and cannot disclose to us anything beyond itself. Consequently we are, and must be, altogether ignorant of the supposed causes, if any, of our sensations. For what warrant do we have for assuming the existence of an extramental object that provokes the sensation? Aside from pure habit of mind, it seems that the only such warrant would lie in a clear causal relationship between the sensation and the object. But that, according to Hume, is exactly what we can never have, for the reasons just mentioned. It is easy therefore to see how the myth, in this form at least, puts us immediately on the road either to subjective idealism, like that of Berkeley, in which all reality is taken to be mental, or to skepticism.[8]

SYSTEMATIC GROUNDS FOR THE MYTH

If neuroses can sometimes be overcome by discovering their roots within past experience, it may be possible to exorcise this myth of the deception of sense by uncovering and severing, not necessarily its historic but its systematic roots. By "systematic" roots I mean the underlying pressure of philosophic presuppositions and principles that naturally entail the myth. To this end I venture the following assertions.

(1) The myth radically misconceives the possibilities for the direct object of perception. It assumes that if the external object were the object of perception, it would be a purely independent object, a thing in itself. Since this assumption will not survive analysis, the myth supposes that the

only alternative to an external object, so conceived, is the *appearance* of the object within the perceiver.

To see how this works, let us return to Russell's table. He notices that the mental appearances (sense data) of the table change as he walks around it, while the table itself presumably does not change. The appearances therefore cannot be identical with the table, and he seems certainly to be experiencing the appearances. Russell cannot therefore admit that he is experiencing the table rather than its appearances.

In this bit of reasoning, seemingly so conclusive, Russell has distinguished between the appearances of the table on the one hand, and the "real" table on the other, and then tacitly presupposed that the object of perception must be either the one or the other. Since the "real" table, so conceived, is presumed to be the table in itself—stable, unchanging, independent of the constant variations in the ongoing act of perceiving—it cannot be the direct object of this shifting perception. We are left then with the *appearances* of the table.

But this overlooks a third possibility, that the object of perception is *the appearing table*. The appearing table, as I use the term, is indeed the real table but not an independent table, a table somehow taken in itself, a non-relational table. The true object of perception is, rather, *the table in relation to the perceiver within the act of perceiving*. It is a relational table, the table that is the immediate object of the perceiver's act of perceiving, and so a table that, as such, necessarily involves the perceiver.

The perceived table, as such, cannot be divorced from the act of perception. The world actually encountered in the act of perception is bipolar. It bears witness, as we shall see, to its own potential transcendence of the act of being perceived, and it carries an ineradicable relation to its actual perceiver, for the perceived object is also the actuality of the perceiver.[9]

Thus we have to distinguish the contents not of two but of three concepts: (a) the "real" table, as Russell puts it, an independent table conceived as insulated from the act of perceiving; (b) the pure appearances of the table, admittedly proper to the perceiver; and (c) the perceived, appearing, relational table. It was thus a false dichotomy between the table itself, considered as independent, and the appearances of the table that implicitly forced Russell to conclude that, since the "real" table, so conceived, cannot be immediately perceived, what is perceived must be only the appearances of the table. But this conclusion systematically overlooks the third possibility, that what is perceived by means of those appearances is precisely *the appearing, the relational table*.[10]

(2) *The myth presupposes an inadequate conception of causality.* Hume thought it obvious that the events we call "cause" and "effect" are entirely separate from one another. "The effect," he says, "is totally different from the cause, and consequently can never be discovered in it."[11] This view has been part of the myth ever since. Thus it is taken for granted that there can be nothing of the cause in the effect, except in our own anticipations that a similar event will follow upon familiar and similar antecedents. This aspect of the myth is usually thought too obvious to merit discussing. Yet it is not evident that it must be so, and the price we pay for supposing it to be so is to lock ourselves within the dream-world of appearance postulated by the myth.

For it is usually presupposed by those under the sway of the myth that the external world itself acts upon us through our senses in such a way as to produce particular sense data within us that we then take to be representative, more or less, of the external world. The sense data that we do experience *represent* to us a "real" (material) world that we do not experience, and so the myth involves a "representational" theory of perception.

Yet if Hume is right about causality, there is no known intrinsic relation between the sense datum that we call "effect" and anything in an external world (if there is one) that may be its "cause." Thus even the *representative* relation of appearance to reality cannot be maintained with any assurance. For on that view of causal connection—or of the lack of it—there is nothing to take us beyond bare appearances except a naive hope, a mere inclination to think that on the other side of appearance must lie a reality that provokes the appearance within us. Hume himself was not happy about having so little assurance of the existence of anything beyond appearance, and he contented himself with practice rather than theory. "Nature will always maintain her rights," he observed, "and prevail in the end over any abstract reasoning whatsoever."[12]

But Hume's separatist notion of cause and effect is not an obvious truth. Aristotle maintained long ago that *the activity of the cause is in the effect* and not distinct from it. The mover and the moved, he says, form a single actuality: "[T]here is a single actuality of both alike, just as one to two and two to one are the same interval, and the steep ascent and the steep descent are one—for these are one and the same, although they can be described in different ways. So it is with the mover and the moved."[13]

This Aristotelian notion of efficient causality assumes the intrinsic togetherness of the cause and the effect within the causal act. Break this intrinsic connection between the causal, external world and its effect on the human senses, however, and you immediately transform the person from a perceiver to a beholder; from someone who perceives a world related to him- or herself in and through the perceptive act, to someone who beholds only a display of appearances little different from the images on a movie screen or the shadows on the wall of Plato's cave.

Hume's arbitrary and systematic exclusion of the cause from the very effect it produces also prevented him from recognizing how this causal connectedness gives itself to us immediately within perception. Thus we have a third factor contributing to the myth.

(3) The myth also involves an inadequate recognition of the causal dimension included within sense experience. In examining the origin of the idea of causal influence, Hume invites us to consider one billiard ball colliding with another, and then asks whether we discover within our experience any sensation of the *influence* exerted by the first ball on the second.[14] He makes a convincing case that we do not, and hence consigns the origin of the idea of causal influence solely to the tendency of our mind to expect one usual thing after another.

But Hume chose the wrong kind of example with which to rule out the experience of causal influence. There is no reason to think that what goes on causally between two billiard balls forms any part of our own sense experience, but there is plenty of reason to think that if one were struck in the head by one of those balls, one would directly and immediately *feel influenced* by it. Indeed, even in the perception of the two balls colliding with one another one feels some causal influence of both balls on oneself simply as presenting themselves within the perception.

This immediate feeling of the influential presence of the world around us—the feeling of a world that makes a difference to us—is a constant (hence also little noticed) part of our experience.

To illustrate this feeling of causal influence Whitehead suggests the situation of a man in a darkened room. Suddenly the lights are turned on and the man blinks. If you ask him why he blinked, Whitehead proposes, the man will say, "The light made me blink," and if you ask him how he knows that, he will say, "I know it because I felt it."[15] Whitehead thinks that an adequate philosophy of perception should take the man at his word and accept the authenticity of such feelings of causal influence.

But the myth of the great deception of sense systematically overlooks or disregards the immediate feeling of the influence of the surrounding world upon us within our perception. After all, just because this feeling is all-pervasive it is hard to notice. Besides, our attention is normally focused on particular things of practical concern to us. We can even, in fact, focus our attention—like an impressionist painter—on our sense impressions themselves rather than on the world giving itself to us in those impressions.

Yet if we are sensitive to this feeling of causal influence within our experience, we find ourselves facing not an impenetrable screen of appearances within our own psyche, but an efficacious world making an impact on us in and through our sense experience.

RELATIONAL REALISM

Where then does this leave us? I think that when we have corrected the above errors underlying the myth, we find ourselves in a position of *relational realism.*[16] By "realism" I mean a theory of perception that holds not only that there is an external world but that the things in the external world form the direct and normal objects of our perceiving. I beg leave to illustrate this by returning once again to Russell's table.

Russell thought he could not actually be perceiving the "real" table since he supposed that the real table leads an independent, impassive existence insulated from the vicissitudes of the conditions of perception. So conceived, such a table would be self-enclosed and self-contained, an unrelated table. The only alternative object of perception, in Russell's mind, was pure appearance in the mind of the perceiver.

In fact, however, Russell was perceiving a *related table,* an *appearing table,* the table precisely as related to him in his own act of perceiving it. The experiential table is necessarily a related table, not a purely independent table. And of course the experiential table, which is the appearing table, varies under changing circumstances such as lighting or the perspective of the viewer.

The appearing table is thus a relational table such that the relationship necessarily includes the perceiver. Now there could be no appearing table without appearances of the table in the perceiver. Nevertheless the pure appearances of the table are not themselves the appearing table but only the *medium by or through which* the extramental table appears to the perceiver.

Here is an analogy. Only with the aid of corrective lenses do many people see the world clearly. But in thus seeing things clearly they are not looking at their lenses, they are looking at the world *through* the lenses. The lenses serve as a medium *by which* they see, not in the manner of a motion picture screen *on* which one sees the projected appearances of a world. The lenses are thus not a medium *in* which, but rather a medium *by* which, one sees.

But according to the myth, the sensations or sense-data provoked in us by the external world do not function as a medium by which the world appears to us, but rather as a medium *in* which it does, for sense perception is supposed to terminate in the appearances, even as it does at the images on the motion picture screen. Sense perception itself, on this theory, is barred from proceeding farther; only by shaky intellectual inference do we form any opinions as to what may lie beyond that screen.

To further articulate this view of relational realism, I propose the following alternatives to the erroneous presuppositions underlying the myth:

(1) *Through sense perception we immediately encounter not sense data but an external world.* Common sense is right about this, as against the extreme views of the myth on the one hand and Berkeley's idealism on the other. It is objects in that extramental, material world that we normally confront in our acts of sense perception.

(2) The world encountered in perception, however, and as *encountered in perception, is not an independent world, a world in itself.* Galileo and the others were right about this. A world in itself would be a non-relational world, hence a world that could not enter into that relationship with our own sense powers that makes perception possible.

Objects intrude themselves upon us in sense perception as making a difference to us, as part of the environment that affects us and that we must deal with. They act causally on our sense organs and thereby make themselves ontologically present to us since, as Aristotle said, the actualization of one entity (the cause) is *in* the other (the effect).

This point is strikingly developed by W. Norris Clarke in the essay referred to in note 16 above. He writes:

> Not only does every being tend, by the inner dynamism of its act of existence, to overflow into action, but this action is both a self-manifestation and a self-communication, a self-sharing, of the being's own inner ontological perfection, with others. (67)

> For Aquinas, as for Aristotle and Neoplatonism, every being, by the very fact that it communicates itself through action, also produces in the recipients of this communication an ontological *self-expression,* a likeness or image of itself. The reason for this flows from the nature of the cause-effect relationship: every effect must in some way resemble its cause, and vice versa. (69)

More than that, in virtue of the natural function of the sense organs, extramental objects are at the same time *intentionally* present to us in virtue of that activity. By nature we aim ourselves at them exactly as at the proper objects of our senses.

Also, in acting on us causally in perception, sense objects thereby *reveal themselves as autonomously capable of activity,* and thus as in themselves transcendent of their activity on us and of our perception of them. Yet we perceive them not in their transcendence but rather in their relatedness to us. Though they make themselves present to us precisely through their activity on us, that same activity reveals their own ontological independence of their being perceived by us. In causally giving itself to us in perception, the perceived table (which is a relational table) at the same time manifests its ontological independence from our act of perceiving, so that we can reasonably *speak* of the table's own existence apart from its being perceived, even though we can never possibly catch it in the act of existing, never *experience* it, independently of our perceiving it.

Such independence, however, need not imply a denial of any intrinsic relatedness of the object to other things apart from its involvement in our act of perception. One need not take this independence to mean that Bertrand Russell was right in his early surmise that "the universe is exactly like a heap of shot,"[17] rather than like the parts of an organism.

The legitimate notion of a table existing in its own right, independently of our perception of it though never *perceived* that way, invites a comparison with Kant's doctrine of the "thing in itself." In what ways is the independent, unperceived table like, and in what ways unlike, Kant's noumenal "thing in itself"?

The real and independent table has affinities to Kant's "thing in itself" insofar as neither is encountered *as such* in sense perception. The only table we can possibly perceive is a relational table, a table acting causally on our sense organs in such a way as to stimulate their appropriate responses, with the result that it is the causally active (hence related) table that we directly apprehend in sensation. It is not only physically, it is even logically impossible that we perceive a table just as it is in itself—that is, as an utterly unrelated, wholly self-contained table.

Yet the independent table of which I have spoken is nonetheless a spatial object, and that of course cannot be said of Kant's *Ding an sich*. For according to Kant, space itself, as a form of sensibility, is contributed to the experienced object by the mind. Kant's "thing in itself," which is never experienced, cannot itself be spatial. But a non-spatial table is a contradiction in terms. Kant's thing in itself, because it is not spatial, cannot possibly be a table or any other object of perception. As Kant put it:

> The transcendental concept of appearances in space . . . is a
> critical reminder that nothing intuited in space is a thing in

itself, that space is not a form inhering in things in themselves as their intrinsic property, that objects in themselves are quite unknown to us, and that what we call outer objects are nothing but mere representations of our sensibility, the form of which is space. The true correlate of sensibility, the thing in itself, is not known, and cannot be known, through these representations; and in experience no question is ever asked in regard to it.[18]

(3) The world we encounter in perception is the appearing world, a relational world. The appearing world, as has been said, is a relational world involving both the external world and ourselves in the act of perceiving. Berkeley was right about this insofar as he claimed that the sensed world is identical with the real world. He was wrong in further claiming that the sensed world is only mental.

But what about hallucinations? Don't they prove that sense data rather than external bodies are the immediate objects of perception? And do they not thereby refute perceptual realism and verify the validity of a representational theory of perception?

No they don't. In the first place, the very fact that they are abnormal, deceptive, perhaps even pathological, means that they should not be made the paradigm for a theory of perception. Secondly, hallucinations exemplify rather than form an exception to the causal relationships described above. During an hallucinatory experience I may indeed find myself influenced by extramental causes—drugs, for instance—and it is not very surprising that diverse causes might sometimes produce similar physiological effects on the perceptual organs, so that I may misinterpret the nature of the cause that is acting on me. (The epistemological analysis here may not be very different from that of the oar that appears bent in the water.)

We may accept, then, that ordinarily the appearing world is just that colored, noisy, fragrant world we have always supposed it to be. The so-called secondary qualities, such as color and sound, do really belong to the encountered world, though they do not belong to a world in itself, because a world in itself is never what we grasp in our perceiving. Neither are they only appearances in our own minds (at least not usually). I perceive a *red apple,* not a sensation of red that I inferentially attribute to an extended something or other presumably causative of my sensation. The appearing apple, rather, is a physical, external apple, yet an apple with which I am intimately involved within the relational act of perceiving. Consequently:

(4) *The appearing world is a relational world, and is not mere appearances, sense data,* and

(5) *The appearing world is a unity of the external world and me, the perceiver,* for it is the actualization of both it and me in the perceptual order.

FOUNDATIONS FOR RELATIONAL REALISM

What are the philosophic foundations required to support a theory of relational realism such as I have sketched? This is no place to work them out but only to point toward them. And indeed they scarcely need working out, since that has already been done more than once, as I shall mention.

(1) For one thing, one must clearly recognize within the immediate experience of sense perception the *feeling of causal influence,* contrary to the conclusion of Hume. But Hume was looking in the wrong place, as we have noted. The influence we feel in perception is not that of one external object upon another (Hume's billiard balls), but of the *external world acting upon us* within the mutual activity that constitutes sense perception.

Whitehead has convincingly described this dimension of experience, which he calls "perception in the mode of causal efficacy," and has shown how it fits indispensably within a realistic epistemology.[19]

More recently, John R. Searle has affirmed this causal dimension of sense perception. Thus he writes: "On my account the visual experience does not represent the causal relation as something existing independently of the experience, but rather part of the experience is the experience of being caused."[20] And again: "I get a direct experience of causation from the fact that part of the Intentional content of my experience of perceiving is cased by the object perceived, i.e., it is satisfied only if it is caused by the presence and features of the object" (130).

Now Searle, in emphasizing as he does the *logical* requirements for the intentional act of perception, is less interested in the phenomenological aspect of the feeling of causal influence than was Whitehead, and one might at first wonder whether he succeeds in escaping Hume's position after all. For it is not enough to assert that causal influence forms a logical ingredient of sense perception as we understand it, or would like to understand it. One must also point out within sense experience that impression of the causal influence of the object upon us that Hume sought in vain. But Searle does this, in passages such as the following:

> Hume's question was how can the content of our experiences tell us that there is a cause and effect relation out there, and his answer was, it can't. But if part of an experience is that it itself causes something or is caused by something then there can't be any question as to how an experience can give us an awareness *of* causation since such an awareness is already part of the experience. The causal nexus is internal to the experience and not its object." (125)

(2) On the level of metaphysical principles, we need a theory of cause and effect, unlike that of Hume, in which it makes sense to say that the cause in its causing is literally in the effect rather than insulated from it. But such a theory of causality is already at hand, for instance in the metaphysics of Aristotle and of Thomas Aquinas, as well as in Whitehead's theory of "prehensions."[21]

(3) Correlative to this theory of how the perceived object is present to the perceiver through its own causal activity, one needs a theory outlining how the perceiver, in virtue of the object's causality upon the perceiver, exercises its own causality in the intentional order, an activity by which, in a unique but quite literal sense, it *becomes* the object sensed.

Once again, such theories of intentional activity are at hand explicitly in the philosophies of Aquinas and of Whitehead, and implicitly in that of Searle (this enumeration is not meant to be exclusive).

Thus we are on rationally respectable grounds in affirming that the sunset really is red and roses fragrant without at the same time being in

peril of the kind of mentalism that Berkeley thought the only alternative to the myth. For the world that we sensibly perceive is indeed the
real, material world, but it is perceived *as relational,* related to us in our
very act of perceiving. And though the world gives itself to us precisely
as our own world, we do not thereby deprive it of its own pole of transcendence. We can legitimately *think* of it as existing on its own, apart
from our perceptions of it.

There is therefore no good reason to remain haunted by the myth
that tells us sense perception is a deception and that we can never
escape from Plato's cave.

FOURTEEN

Why Possible Worlds Aren't

(1996)

*This essay is parallel to "Impossible Worlds" (essay 7 in
this volume), but more sharply focused on the issue itself
with less attention to its historical background. Once again
I could not resist attacking the contemporary philosophic
penchant for thinking that the concept of "possible worlds"
illuminates rather than obfuscates the basic metaphysical
relation between possibility and actuality, a relation that
was brilliantly elucidated by Aristotle when he introduced
the concept of potentiality. That concept has largely been
lost today and needs to be reinstated, since possible worlds
are a most unsatisfactory substitute for a fundamental
philosophical wheel that already worked just fine. The essay
is, as I think, accessible, and readers can judge the issue for
themselves.*

Originally published as "Why Possible Worlds Aren't," *The Review of Metaphysics*
50 (September 1996): 63–77. Reprinted with permission.

Here is an uncommon argument for doubting the existence of possible worlds. It calls into question the whole spectrum of supposed possible worlds, from the late David Lewis's radical plurality of worlds to the world-stories of Robert Merrihew Adams and Alvin Plantinga. More than that, the argument challenges the tacit presuppositions of most of those who have attacked those views. Yet despite its strangeness I cannot but think this unorthodox position is correct. I shall furnish metaphysical reasons for thinking that it is, and then proceed to show why the possible worlds taken for granted in contemporary discussions are based on a misconception, a metaphysical mistake that we would be better off without.

We are faced here with the deliberate choice of philosophic first principles, not with demonstrations proceeding from commonly acknowledged or even tacitly presupposed principles. So there can be no knockdown argument for such a choice, only reasons for thinking it better than its alternatives. Lewis himself has noted that "one man's reason is another man's *reductio,*"[1] and, after arguing against "ersatz" substitutes for his thoroughgoing modal realism, he advises: "Join the genuine modal realists; or forsake genuine and ersatz worlds alike."[2] On the view that I shall propose, Lewis's modal realism turns out to be itself a *reductio* rather than a reason, and so I must set it aside with all its variants, ersatz or otherwise.

Though philosophic beginnings are chosen, their consequences are not. As Etienne Gilson put it: "Philosophers are free to lay down their own sets of principles, but once this is done, they no longer think as they wish—they think as they can."[3] These first principles are chosen not only for their initial plausibility, but most importantly because they appear to make more intelligible sense of experience than do their opposites. Consonance with experience is the final criterion for accepting or rejecting any philosophic standpoint. As Whitehead mentioned, it has been said that systems of philosophy are never refuted, they are only abandoned, either by reason of the mutual incoherence of their principles or because they are inadequate to account for experience as we find it.[4]

I begin this consideration, then, by recommending the plausibility of three metaphysical principles that suggest themselves, both initially and in their consequences, as characterizing our immediate, ongoing, changing experience.

THREE PRINCIPLES OF BECOMING AND BEING

These principles[5] are meant to express, at least partially, the character of human experience viewed in terms of its changing patterns over time. They link the dynamism of activity with its own formal patterns; they link temporal actuality with possibility.

— *Principle (A): Past actuality, whether immediate or remote, is definite, exact, unambiguous.*

Lady Macbeth observed that what's done cannot be undone. But also, what's done, being done, has its own definite character. Though knowledge of the past fades, including knowledge of one's own past self, this past is not in itself ambiguous. We have to cope in the present with what has in fact been decided, by us and others, in the past. The pattern of that past is settled, now and always. And how does this settled pattern come about?

— *Principle (B): Present actuality involves a process of determination whereby from the indefiniteness of what might be (within the width of possibility) there is created the definiteness of what actually is (actuality).*[6]

Take the writing of a philosophic essay. It is a process by which more general initial thoughts take on the definition of exact formulation, a process by which the vagueness of what might be written takes on the definiteness of what is written. A more vivid analogy is that of a dune buggy on a beach. The margin in which you can drive is perhaps already determined by the surf on one side and sheer palisades on the other, so that these two factors literally determine a *width of possibility* for your driving. But within that width you can drive (steer) as you please, and it is just your activity of driving that determines the track that you make in the sand. The definiteness, the pattern of that track is created precisely by your act of driving.

— *Principle (C): Only actual events create this definiteness of settled actu-*
ality within the given width of possibility.

Principle (C) is roughly the converse of Principle (B). (B) asserts
that actual events always exemplify—because they produce—definiteness, an exact pattern of actuality. (C), conversely, asserts that such
definiteness requires actual events for its own creation. Of itself the
width of possibility leaves undetermined the particular patterns that
may be defined within it.

This principle embodies the central point of controversy around
which this essay pivots. It is derived from reflection on our experience
of the creation of the patterns of ongoing temporal events. Thus the
pattern of tracks in the sand is created precisely, and only, by the driving, just as the exact way in which you will walk through the next doorway will be created precisely, and only, by your act of walking through
it. The act, by its very nature, creates its own pattern. Better, you by
your act of walking create the pattern.[7]

As a natural but further specification of Principle (C) there
follows:

— *Corollary (1): In temporal events at least, the definiteness or pattern of*
the event does not temporally precede the event itself.

This is what Henri Bergson meant by saying that the possible does
not precede the real:

> As reality is created as something unforeseeable and new [because
> previously undefined], its image [its pattern of definiteness] is
> reflected [mentally] behind it into the indefinite past; thus it
> finds that it has from all time been possible, but it is at this pre-
> cise moment [of temporal creation] that it begins to have been
> always possible, and that is why . . . its possibility, which does
> not precede its reality, will have preceded it [for the mind] once
> the reality has appeared. The possible is therefore the mirage of
> the present in the past.[8]

This viewpoint is so unusual and so critical to the argument of this essay that it bears more illustration. Thus, the pattern of the actual track in the sand had no existence in the world prior to the driving that made the track. But when we look at the track already made, we naturally suppose that that pattern must have been possible even before it was made—that it must have constituted a particular possibility preceding the making of the track. We suppose that this particular possibility was only one of an infinity of such exact possibilities awaiting realization by the driving. Yet we make this supposition only by means of mental rearview mirrors. Only after the track is made do we have a pattern to refer to and then to project mentally into the past as having been antecedently possible.

It is almost impossible to exaggerate the seductiveness of this natural tendency to relocate the present back into the past. Yet we deceive ourselves when we suppose that the pattern in fact preexisted the driving.

This becomes more evident if we consider the production of a piece of literature or of music. Mozart created the pattern of notes that is his *Fortieth Symphony*. Once created, this definite pattern can be thought of as having always been possible—otherwise how could it have been created at all? But only with the actual creative activity that went into the composition of the symphony does there exist a pattern, a single "possibility," to talk about at all. Prior to its creation by Mozart it was not, of course, *im*possible—that is, there were no intrinsic impediments to its creation—yet there was no definite pattern of notes at all, to be called possible or even impossible. There was literally nothing specific to talk about or think about.[9]

To think otherwise is to suppose that the exact pattern of notes that is the *Fortieth* existed as such, perfectly defined, in some ghostly limbo of possibilities (one is reminded here of Quine's "slum of possibles"),[10] awaiting the infusion of actuality by Mozart. On such a view there would never be artistic creation or novelty, only selection from among pre-given definite possibilities.

To return finally to the dune buggy: according to the common way of thinking of the possible and the real, there is an infinity of possible tracks lying ahead on the beach, and, by your driving, you select one for realization. This way of thinking implicitly likens the beach to a railroad yard, where the locomotive enters upon one of several tracks already laid down in advance. But in fact there are no preexistent possible tracks in the sand just because there was nothing to define them ahead of time. Yet a single track does get created by the actual driving. Only after the driving, however, is there a particular track that one can talk about or suppose, by hindsight, to have been possible prior to its creation.

In the wording of Corollary (1) I added the qualification, "in temporal events at least." By this I meant that the form or pattern of an actual event (its *way* of being or becoming) has no existence in *time* prior to the event itself. Prior to the event its own form simply *is not,* and (as Parmenides or even Wittgenstein would say) cannot even be spoken of. This I consider to be an ineluctable conclusion if one seriously supposes that novelty does arise in the world. More than that, I now propose to remove the above qualification, and to state, more broadly:

— *Corollary (2): No definiteness of form obtains at all, temporally or atemporally, except in virtue of the activity of a real agent.*[11]

This doubtless is my most controversial claim. Yet given what I have contended in justification of Corollary (1), it seems intuitively plausible to make an analogous assertion concerning patterns of definiteness ("possibles") conceived just in themselves, apart from any emergence in the temporal world. So conceived they are atemporal, not of themselves involved in time.[12]

Some examples of such pure, self-standing patterns of possibility would be Plato's Forms, the "futuribles" of Molina, and Whitehead's "eternal objects."[13] But if one accepts that a particular pattern of definiteness is realized (in the literal sense: becomes part of a *res*) in temporal events only as the result of the defining activity of an agent, it seems to me reasonable to think that definite patterns of pure possibility, apart from any temporal realization, also require the activity of a defining agent. This seems more plausible than supposing that such distinct, definite patterns simply exist on their own, in their very distinctness, within the general range of possibility.

I have noted that with regard to first principles, such as the above, there can be no knockdown argument one way or another. Rather, we are at a level at which we must in effect play philosophic cops and robbers. "Bang, I got you!" "No, you missed me!" As the saying goes, You pays your money and you takes your choice.

WHY POSSIBLE WORLDS AREN'T

Let us now apply the above principles to current notions of possible worlds, and—because of its fundamentality and lucidity—first of all and chiefly to the possible worlds of David Lewis. How does he conceive possible worlds, and why does he think they exist? Here is his well-known reply:

> I believe that there are possible worlds other than the one we happen to inhabit. If an argument is wanted, it is this. It is uncontroversially true that things might be otherwise than they are. I believe, and so do you, that things could have been different in countless ways. But what does this mean? Ordinary language permits the paraphrase: there are many ways things could have been besides the way they actually are. On the face of it, this sentence is an existential quantification. It says that there exist many entities of a certain description, to wit "ways things could have been." I believe permissible paraphrases of what I believe; taking the paraphrase at its face value, I therefore believe in the existence of entities that might be called "ways things could have been." I prefer to call them "possible worlds."[14]

Twelve years later, looking back at the controversies his view had stirred up, Lewis took pains to insist on the existential import of what he is claiming:

> I must insist that my modal realism is simply the thesis that there are other worlds, and individuals inhabiting those worlds; and that these are of a certain nature, and suited to play certain theoretical roles. It is an existential claim, not unlike the claim I

would be making if I said that there were Loch Ness monsters, or Red moles in the CIA, or counterexamples to Fermat's conjecture, or seraphim. It is not a thesis about our semantic competence, or about the nature of truth, or about bivalence, or about the limits of our knowledge. For me, the question is of the existence of objects—not the objectivity of a subject matter.[15]

That is what Lewis claims; he does not pretend to be able to prove it, but rather to offer plausible reasons why it is so. In *On the Plurality of Worlds* he only argues that modal realism is useful, whereas in the above argument from *Counterfactuals* he had made a stronger claim. But if the above principles are right, Lewis's argument runs right off the rails at its second step. That is where he supposes that saying that "things might be otherwise than they are" is equivalent to saying that "there are other ways things could have been." The first statement, however, reflects how the present state of affairs arose within a general *range of possibility* set by its antecedents, while the second statement posits the existence of a *multiplicity of distinct, particular possibilities,* none of which has been actualized by the course of events.

These are not two different ways of saying the same thing; they are two different statements altogether. To say that the track in the sand could have had a different shape does not entitle one to say that there exist other definite shapes that it could have had. What agency has produced the definiteness of these supposed "other shapes" whereby we may talk of them? And what agency has produced the definiteness of the multiplicity of "other ways things could have been," Lewis's possible worlds? Agents in this world determine the events in this world, together with their definite ways of being, just as you, in your act of walking, will determine the way in which you next walk through a doorway. But where are the agents that define all the other ways things *could* have been, all the hypothesized possible worlds? Lewis tells us that he is making an existential claim about these possible worlds. In his view there is the same existential definition to these worlds as there is to the one we happen to inhabit, in which exactly these events obtain and others do not. What can possibly be the agent or agents that give their respective definitions to Lewis's plurality of possible worlds?

Modal realists such as Lewis, however, would doubtless challenge the presuppositions inherent in that question. They would say that I am presupposing a distinction between the agents of this world and their hypothetical ("counterpart") agents in other possible worlds; that I am attributing an ontological priority to the former; that I am making an indemonstrable distinction between this real world and the other worlds posited as possible, such that only agents of this (real) world are really agents, in contrast to so-called but unreal agents of possible worlds.[16]

I willingly grant the accuracy of this charge, but I deny that it is a fault. Cops and robbers! I think, though I cannot prove it, that a possible or hypothetical or counterpart agent just isn't an agent. It can't *do* anything.[17] I think, though I cannot prove it, that there is an ontological difference *as ways of being* between possibility (I would rather say *potentiality*) and actuality. Lewis, on the other hand, writes: "Nor does this [actual] world differ from the others [other possible worlds] in its manner of existing. I do not have the slightest idea what a difference in manner of existing is supposed to be."[18]

On the view here proposed, to *be potentially* is a real way of being that differs essentially from being actually.[19] But potentiality necessarily inheres in what is actual. Thus the range of what is possible is determined by what is in fact actual, just as the range for driving the dune buggy is set by the actuality of the cliffs and the surf. Relations of possibility and necessity presuppose and depend on what is actual.

Potentiality as such cannot consist in a set, even an infinite set, of distinct, definite possibilities. It is rather the inherent *capacity* within given actuality for any such definite possibilities to be realized by the activity of appropriate agents. Potentiality as capacity differs ontologically from any set of forms of definiteness that it makes possible. Hence to confuse possibility, in the sense of potentiality, with a set of hypothesized possible patterns is to make a category mistake. And it leaves unanswered and unanswerable how one is to account for the definite distinctness of the hypothesized possibilities.

There is a remarkably apposite passage in Aquinas in which he not only makes roughly the same point, but practically puts modern theories of possible worlds into that perspective. In a digression in his commentary on Aristotle's treatise *On Interpretation* he writes:

There are various opinions about possibility and necessity, about *can be* and *must be*. Some people, like Diodorus, distinguish these by reference to what happens, saying that *can't be* never happens, *must be* always happens, and *can be* sometimes happens and sometimes doesn't. The Stoics, however, distinguished them by reference to external obstruction, saying that the truth of *must be* can't be obstructed, of *can't be* is always obstructed, and of *can be* can sometimes be obstructed and sometimes not. Neither way of distinguishing them seems adequate. The first way gets things back to front: it is not that things must be because they always happen, but that they always happen because they must be, and similarly for the other definitions. And the second way appeals to something extrinsic and so to speak inessential: it is not that things must be because nothing obstructs them, but that nothing can obstruct them because they must be.[20]

By extrapolation, Thomas would say that it is getting things backwards to say that something is necessary because it is found in all possible worlds (if there are any), rather than to say that something is found in all possible worlds because that thing is necessary. Thomas evidently takes possibility and necessity to reside primitively within the relations of what is actual. Class inclusion is derivative from those relations, not definitive of them.

Since I am persuaded by the above principles, I must conclude that there can be no possible worlds in the sense required by Lewis's modal realism, for there are no agents to produce the definiteness of their patterns. Possible worlds, in his sense, cannot be existential objects as he supposes; they can at most be his own *conceptions* of possible worlds.[21]

But what about other current conceptions of possible worlds— what Lewis calls "ersatz" possible worlds? It will suffice here to examine one such conception, for all of them suffer from the same defect. Lewis is right in maintaining that genuine and ersatz possible worlds fall together if they fall at all.

Let us now consider in a general way the *world-story* or *world-book* interpretation of possible worlds suggested respectively by Robert Merrihew Adams[22] and by Alvin Plantinga.[23] Instead of thinking of a possible world as another object like the real world, as Lewis does, one can think of it as a set of propositions forming a story or book describing a world. If a proposition can denote a state of affairs, then suppose there exists a maximal, consistent set of propositions describing a totality of states of affairs. It is maximal in the sense that no further proposition can be added to it without either duplicating or contradicting some proposition already contained in it. One such world-story will, further-more, be distinctive, in that all its propositions will in fact be true. That is, it alone will describe the real world.

It would be pointless here to review the alleged advantages of world-story possible worlds over those of Lewis, for if the above prin-ciples are sound it is evident that world-stories are as metaphysically specious as are his. For world-stories are presumed to enjoy definite-ness of and on their own. The multiple—even infinite—possible world-stories are simply taken as *given* in all their detail. Only on that suppo-sition does it make sense to distinguish one of them from another and to allege that one has the distinction of being wholly true. Yet no agent can be assigned that is capable of having made up the stories—at least no agent short of God.[24] Certainly no human mind could invent the complete story of a universe.

Once again, then, I must conclude that there are in fact no existing possible worlds for us to deal with, either genuine or ersatz, inasmuch as no agent is available to have created their alleged definiteness.

What, however, shall we say about Lewis's contention that a good reason for thinking there are possible worlds is that it is useful to do so? Here is how he puts it:

> Why believe in a plurality of worlds?—Because the hypothesis is serviceable, and that is a reason to think that it is true. The famil-iar analysis of necessity as truth at all possible worlds was only the beginning. In the last two decades, philosophers have offered a great many more analyses that make reference to possible worlds, or to possible individuals that inhabit possible worlds. I find that record most impressive. I think it is clear that talk of *possibilia* has clarified questions in many parts of the philosophy of logic, of mind, of language, and of science—not to mention metaphysics itself.[25]

Lewis spells out a number of such instances, and it is not possible here to examine them individually. I submit, however, that in each case Lewis fails to show that it is useful to think of possible worlds as *ontologically existing,* as modal realism asserts, rather than that certain possibilities, or even very vaguely defined possible worlds, are simply *conceived* by us. Conceptions suffice in every case; there is no need for, or an agent determinative of, a plurality of existing possible worlds.

POSSIBLE WORLDS AND PLATONISM

Anton Pegis has described the Platonic method of philosophizing as "the method of modeling the properties of existing beings on the abstractions of the human intellect. In other words, it is the method of thinking that being takes its characteristics *as being* from what it reveals of itself *in the state of being thought.*"[26] Pegis intended, and so do I, to distinguish Platonism from the contrasting viewpoint of Aristotle or the adaptation made of it by Aquinas, and I doubt that one could find a more striking instance of philosophy in the Platonic manner than the contemporary possible-worlds ontologies, especially the modal realism of David Lewis. Plato and Aristotle embodied two fundamentally different ways of regarding the world and of doing philosophy that characterize thinkers in the whole course of Western philosophy. It is therefore illuminating to set theories of possible worlds into this thematic and historical context. I close this essay, then, by pointing to the Platonic strain that is paramount in the ontologies of possible worlds.

First of all, there is in Lewis's thought an identification of definiteness with actuality, and to make this identification is precisely to adopt the Platonic viewpoint. The identification underlies his indexical theory of what it means to be actual, so that the inhabitants of other worlds, who are assumed to be just as definite (and apparently just as active) as we, are supposed to have as much right to call their worlds actual as we do ours. For Lewis, all possible worlds are as real as our own, differing only in their spatio-temporal locus; they do not differ in their manner of existing.

Thus Lewis has in effect accepted the conclusion that Charles Hartshorne reached, that belief in possible worlds erases the distinction between the possible and the actual. As Hartshorne put it: "One must admit that a possible world is as definite and complex as the corresponding actual one. This, I hold, reduces the distinction between possible and actual to nullity. Value is in definiteness, and definiteness is 'the soul of actuality.' Were possibility equally definite it would be redundant to actualize it."[27]

Again, in Lewis's argument for the existence of possible worlds, the conviction that things could be otherwise becomes the conviction that there are other ways things could have been. "Otherwise" has become "other ways," and that is exactly a Platonic move. Because we can conceive of other ways, those other ways are assumed to be constitutive of extramental reality.

In this regard, we may note the affinity between modal realism and the quintessentially Platonic "ontological" argument for the existence of God. When I conceive "that than which no greater can be conceived," I must *ipso facto* conceive "a necessarily existing being." Therefore such a being exists. This, however, slips in the tacit assumption that what I have conceived in my mind has an extramental counterpart, and that is 24-carat Platonism. Similarly Lewis, because he conceives other ways of being, including other possible worlds, habitually supposes that these other ways of being extramentally exist.

Again, *potentiality* for determining a particular pattern within a width of possibility becomes, for Lewis, an already existent set of *possibilities,* discrete, definite, conceivable patterns of being. Aristotle's *dynamis* for originating a determinative action has been replaced by an assemblage of conceivable patterns. Lewis has passed from *potentiality* to *patterns.* But this is to regress past Aristotle to Parmenides. It nullifies Aristotle's solution to Parmenides' dilemma of becoming, for it denies any intrinsic distinction as ways of existing between *being actually* and *being potentially.*

The same pattern of thinking is apparent in the way Lewis relates causality to counterfactuals. He conceives that the way the letters appearing in his book causally depend upon the keystrokes of his word processor is just that if he had touched different keys, different characters *would* have appeared. "That," he says, "is how the letters depend causally upon the keystrokes."[28] Thus the causal *power* of actuality has passed into counterfactual *patterns* of possibility. Attempting to describe causal relationships in this way has left him lost in the "woulds" of counterfactuals.

And they are dark woulds as well, since they do not in fact succeed in describing *causal power*. They substitute instead a pattern of conceived hypothetical possibilities. These possibilities are not only purely conjectural, they even tacitly presuppose the causal power that they are meant to define.

Confiding to Dorothy why everything in Emerald City was green, Oz explained: "When you wear green spectacles, why of course everything you see looks green to you."[29] Everyone, I suppose, wears philosophic lenses of one prescription or another, and Lewis has chosen to see everything through the lenses of possible worlds. He admits that this entails a vast expenditure of entitative suppositions, but nevertheless insists that the price is right.

The argument of this essay implies that the price, far from being right, is simply exorbitant. Possible worlds, in the currently accepted senses, are the monstrous issue of a metaphysical mistake; they are unnecessary for realizing the advantages Lewis seeks; and investing in them promotes rampant metaphysical inflation at a time when the credibility of philosophers' currency is already badly undermined.

FIFTEEN

Proposal for a Thomistic-Whiteheadian Metaphysics of Becoming

(2000)

This essay is my first tardy response, after some twenty-nine years, to my own invitation (essay 2) to attempt to fuse the better elements of the respective metaphysics of St. Thomas Aquinas of the thirteenth century and Alfred North Whitehead of the twentieth. It was about time—and also about being and becoming. A notion of how such an unlikely merger might be effected had gradually taken shape in my mind and is expressed in the following essay. I followed the ideas fairly closely in the fuller expression of the book Coming To Be *(2001) and more perfectly in its sequel,* Aims: A Brief Metaphysics for Today *(2007). It is my perhaps narcissistic impression that I have at least partially achieved that goal by devising a new way in which Whitehead's metaphysics can be adapted so as to enrich*

Originally published as "Proposal for a Thomistic-Whiteheadian Metaphysics of Becoming," *International Philosophical Quarterly* 40, no. 2 (2000): 253–63. Reprinted with permission.

that of Thomas. The following essay attempts to draw the
broad outlines of such a revised metaphysics and is perforce
moderately technical.

"It has been remarked," wrote Whitehead, "that a system of philosophy is never refuted; it is only abandoned."[1] There can be no demonstration of its falsity, but after being seriously tried it may eventually be found wanting in its ability to interpret the multifarious aspects of human experience. It has become unbelievable, often under the impact of criticisms from competing systems, and in any case after deeper introspective reflection on the part of the philosopher. The search is on for another view, one that is intellectually more satisfying because it rings truer both to immediate experience and to what science progressively tells us about experience.

In adopting this view of the eclipse rather than the refutation of one philosophic system by another, Whitehead anticipated in philosophy what the late Thomas S. Kuhn later said about scientific revolutions. Kuhn pointed out that difficulties or apparent anomalies are never enough to disprove a theory and, consequently, that scientists never abandon a theory until they have a better one to put in its place.[2]

This essay, of course, is addressed more to philosophers than to scientists, and indeed to philosophers who, whether of one school or another, are unfashionable enough to take metaphysics seriously. The breed has never been entirely extinct. As Etienne Gilson put it: "It is an objective fact that men have been aiming at such knowledge for more than twenty-five centuries and that, after proving that it should not be sought, and swearing that they would not seek it any more, men have always found themselves seeking it again."[3] More specifically, I invite process philosophers indebted to the thought of Alfred North Whitehead, and Thomists inspired by that of Saint Thomas Aquinas (hereafter "Thomas"), to ask themselves whether their respective systems do not suffer from anomalies sufficiently grave to call for abandoning those systems as they presently stand and devising a better alternative rooted in, but transforming, those two systems.

Whiteheadian process philosophy and contemporary Thomism have been jostling each other for some sixty years, and their mutual criticisms have not only proved salutary to each view but seem to point toward the possibility of a new paradigm derived by adapting both systems in such a way as to form a new synthesis embodying the chief advantages and avoiding the disadvantages of each system as it now stands. At least that is the possibility that I should like to point to in this essay, although in only a very preliminary way. I make the proposal with fear and trembling, haunted by the poet Horace's warning in his *Ars Poetica* of how silly it would look if an artist were to paint a human head onto a horse's neck, together with assorted feathers. But before applying brush to canvas, I review in more detail the revolutionary state of affairs.

TWO COMPETING METAPHYSICS

1) *Process philosophy's criticisms of Thomism* were often inaccurate or misplaced, attacking only a caricature of Thomas's doctrine and lumping his thought indiscriminately with that of other medievals. Yet they did point to real weaknesses and provoked a salutary rethinking on the part of Thomistically oriented philosophers.[4] These criticisms are familiar and I mention them only in passing.

Among them looms the charge that Thomas's God is admittedly not really related to this world, and hence seems neither an appropriate object of religious worship nor plausibly to be identified with the caring and involved God described in the Scriptures. This criticism, which was Whitehead's, was elaborated with great effect by Charles Hartshorne.[5]

More generally—and this is a related criticism—Thomas's substances, like Aristotle's, have not appeared to process thinkers to stand in active relationship with one another. Thomas seems to stress the autonomy of his substances to the detriment of their inter-relatedness. He also has appeared to favor the static over the active. Certainly he interprets becoming in terms of being, rather than the other way around.

This criticism focuses especially on Thomas's Aristotelian conception of substance, supposedly that of an "enduring substrate" that changelessly underlies the acquisition or loss of accidental features, much as a person might put on or shed clothes. One may fairly call this the "pincushion model" of substance that Whitehead found in Descartes and Locke and read back into Aristotle.

To these more usual criticisms of the Thomistic system, I venture to add a special criticism against Thomas's interpretation of temporal becoming in terms of Aristotle's theory of matter and form, the theory of hylomorphism. Now I grant the indispensability of something equivalent to the Aristotelian-Thomistic principle called "substantial form" if one is to make metaphysical sense of the identity and the transformations of material things, as Terence Nichols has recently pointed out.[6] Yet I cannot think that hylomorphism as Thomas understood it can account either for the individual unity of material things or for their evolutionary transformations as we now understand them. For in the first place, hylomorphism traces the individuation of the material substance to its located spatial continuity as to its ultimately determining principle. The form or nature is individuated by its "matter" (its "proto-matter," as Nichols well puts it), but since the proto-matter is of itself amorphous and unindividuated, it derives its individuation from its quantitative determinations, which allow it to be exactly here and not there. The substance is one and individuated ultimately because it forms a located spatial continuum.

This theory was, I think, uncomfortable enough even in Thomas's day when the human body was less well understood in its complexity. It now seems to me quite incredible inasmuch as we must today take into account such ingredients of the human person as the water and elements that are undoubtedly contained in and function peculiarly in the blood. As Nichols argues, it is no longer enough to say with Thomas that such elements are contained in the human body only *virtually* and not actually.[7] Is it not time to rethink the Thomistic conception of substantial unity? Should not that unity be conceived rather as a matter of dynamic, telic function than of three-dimensional spatial location?

The other aspect of temporal becoming that Aristotelian hylomorphism seems incapable of interpreting is the evolutionary advance now recognized in nature. Despite the overall increase of entropy, there is an urge toward life, sensitivity, and intelligence, toward new and more sophisticated forms of existence. Hylomorphism may give a plausible account of how cats generate cats, but I am afraid that it cannot explain how a primate got ready to be a human. Indeed, hylomorphism seems ill suited to account for any irruption of novelty into nature at all, let alone novelty of a higher order. For such an account, Whiteheadian metaphysics seems much better adapted.

2) *Thomistic criticisms of process philosophy* are less widely known and I merely cite some of them. Once again we begin with God. Many Thomistically inspired philosophers find Whitehead's "God" too limited to fit either Christian belief or the ultimate necessities of ontological explanation. One recalls Huston Smith's charge that Whitehead arbitrarily limited the range of his Categoreal Scheme to specifically human experience, thus allowing no room for a God who transcends the very existence of the world.[8]

Furthermore, Whitehead's ontology is basically a pluralism: it supposes a "many" endlessly in search of unity. This is for Whitehead the whole sense of process. As he puts it, "The ultimate metaphysical principle is the advance from disjunction to conjunction, creating a novel entity other than the entities given in disjunction" (PR 21). Thus in Whitehead's analysis the many enjoy an ontological priority over the one toward which they are ordered. One sees this in the starkest way in the presumed relation between creativity's ur-instantiation, the "primordial nature of God," and everything else, the "world." For Whitehead, God and the world are both simply given disjunctively, though neither is conceivable apart from the other. God is not responsible for the very existence of the world but, like Plato's demiurge, only for its ordering. This contrasts strongly with Thomas's conception of all reality flowing from and returning to God as to the ultimate source of both being and intelligibility.

Whitehead's arguably unsatisfactory conception of God appears to me related to his lack of interest in the *ontological dimension* of existence, which plays such a central role in Thomas's thought. I call this the "vertical" dimension. It is the dimension of the question, "Why does anything exist at all?" This question differs radically from asking why anything is the way that it is. It is the latter question that exercised Whitehead. He wanted to make sense of the swirling processive advance of which he found himself a part; he wanted to understand how things get to be the way they are. He was, I think, wholly concerned with what I call the "horizontal" dimension of existence, the dimension of temporal becoming. He was both accurate and candid when he sub-titled his central philosophic work "an essay in cosmology" rather than in ontology. But Thomists see this as a radical lacuna in Whitehead's philosophy.

Regarding the analysis of the things we find in experience, White-head's rejection of the notion of substance—that is, of the (numerical) self-identity over time of a unitary being that is nevertheless itself in transition—leads him to reduce ordinary things, and the human being in particular, to a vast concatenation of individual microevents that perish and succeed one another with great rapidity. These microevents are taken to be the ontological ultimates, yet no one of them can have the characteristics of a person despite Whitehead's avowed intention of modeling his metaphysical ultimates on the structure of human experi-ence.[9] Thomists tend to regard this stroboscopic picture of the person as an unfortunate distortion of experiential fact.

There have been other criticisms from the Thomist vantage point, but I add just one more that has perhaps not been given enough recog-nition. It is that Whitehead, at least in the opinion of William Chris-tian, Ivor Leclerc, and Lewis S. Ford, in the end identified the being of his ultimates, his "actual entities," with their own act of becoming. From the point of view of Thomas's metaphysics, however, such a move would amount to a category mistake because it confuses three distin-guishable existential acts: coming-into-being (*fieri*), the act of existing (*esse,* so-called first act), and activity (*agere,* second act). Such a position would destroy the possibility of a theory of interactive agency.

3) *A Thomistic reaction to Whiteheadian criticisms:* Impressed by pro-cess criticisms of the apparent unrelatedness of Thomas's God to the world, W. Norris Clarke, who calls himself a Thomist-inspired phi-losopher rather than a Thomist, has developed a new view that is arguably an extrapolation of Thomas's own position when one takes into account what Thomas says as a theologian when speaking about

the concept of person, particularly as that is found in the doctrine of the Trinity.[10] Consequently Clarke is able to affirm, as at least compatible with Thomism, that God is related to the world in a personal relationship, a relationship in which God can, in a carefully defined sense, receive from creatures as well as give to them. If Clarke has this right, as I think he does, then a main process criticism of Thomas's doctrine of God has been answered, to the enrichment of Thomism itself, and I therefore set it aside in what follows.

As for the apparent lack of interrelation of Thomistic substances to one another, this objection is in part answered by rectifying for process thinkers the true meaning of "substance" for Thomas. I have argued elsewhere[11] that Whitehead misunderstood Aristotle's concept of "substance," attributing to it the notion of "undifferentiated endurance" that he found in Locke and the exclusiveness that he found in Descartes, and missing the dynamic and changing nature of substance as Aristotle conceived it. Another part of the answer to this objection is found in the Aristotelian-Thomistic theory of efficient causality whereby the activity of the cause lies precisely in the affected being. The effect is related to the cause intrinsically, not just extrinsically.

Yet difficulties remain in the Thomistic account of temporal becoming inasmuch as hylomorphism, if my previous analysis is correct, is unable to account either for the individual unity of the substance or for evolutionary, creative change. This leads me to ask why it would not be possible, within a modified Thomism, to replace hylomorphism with a modified Whiteheadian account.

I now wish to examine, at least in a preliminary way, the feasibility of thus retaining the essentials of the Thomistic ontology (the "vertical" dimension) and coupling it with a theory of "horizontal" temporal process analogous to Whitehead's system and taking the place of the hylomorphic analysis of temporal becoming. To this end I require that the new system be compatible with Thomistic ontology. Thus it must be compatible with Thomas's theory of the participation of creatures in the act of existing and with the analysis of being in terms of potency and act. I name the ontological ultimates of the system *primary beings* (replacing Whitehead's "actual entities" and Thomas's "substances") and require that, like Aristotle's and Thomas's substances, they be units of being that retain their own ontic self-identity, each over a span of time appropriate for it, while at the same time undergoing internal development or change. I retain the Thomistic distinction between the very act of existing (the *esse*) of primary beings and their proper activity (their *agere*).

PROPOSED ANATOMY OF A PRIMARY BEING

1) The activity of the primary being is essentially experiential (as it was also for Leibniz and Whitehead), but with Thomas I require that the primary being includes, as an essential internal principle, something equivalent to Thomistic substantial form. That is, it must contain a principle grounding its particular nature and moving the primary being to its activities, somewhat as Thomistic substantial form functions as final, efficient, and formal cause of the substance and its activities.

2) As experiential, the primary being requires an appropriate span of time within which it retains its ontic self-identity while simultaneously engaging in self-development.[12] This requisite span of time depends upon the natural exigencies of what it takes to fulfill the primary being's subjective aim, and may range from microseconds for the most primitive primary beings to a human life span.

3) We thus reintroduce into the structure of a primary being the stipulation that it is ontologically, hence numerically, *self-identical over time*. This is not, however, the notion of "undifferentiated endurance" (Whitehead's *bête noire*). For experience can be neither instantaneous nor a succession of instantaneities, but (as Whitehead himself held) *takes time*. This is manifest not only phenomenally but as a logical requirement for the very possibility of an experiencing subject.[13] The primary being, then, is a genuine substance in the Aristotelian sense, neither static nor unrelated nor separable from its qualities.

4) Whitehead employs the concept of subjective form when considering the particular feelings or experiential acts that make up the actual entity, and this subjective form is governed by the actual entity's subjective aim, which amounts to a self-ideal. In the new system I propose to widen the scope of subjective form so as to apply it to the primary being as a whole. Let us then call it the *essential form* of the primary

being, and retain its subordination to the self-ideal of the primary being. For that self-ideal I retain Whitehead's term *subjective aim.*

We thus have in the new system the notion of essential form as a function of the subjective aim of the primary being. Also, subjective aim, taken together with essential form, is our correlate of Thomas's substantial form. Like the latter it may be said to ground the nature of the primary being in that it is the determinant of what it is and how it acts. Also, the essential form is itself a particular capacity or potency for *esse,* the act of existing, as well as an active potency for *agere,* activity.

5) Every primary being, then, essentially includes a subjective aim and an essential form. But such a simple analysis cannot succeed in accounting for the varied activities of the things we find around us. The primary being must be more complex than that. With Whitehead—or at least with Whitehead's original intention—the primary being should model the natural unities that we experience, including very especially our own personal but complex unity. Therefore we have to allow for primary beings that are ontologically one yet internally complex. Aristotle and Thomas provide for this in terms of diverse *principles* of substances that are not themselves little substances. We have to suppose something similar but seem to be faced with a more difficult problem than was Thomas. For, as I indicated above, it is no longer adequate to say with Thomas that the substance is exactly one being, and so informed by just one substantial form, so that its intrinsic components have at most only a "virtual" self-identity within the whole (and thus are not actually informed by their own particular substantial forms).

6) Let us instead assume that the primary being, although itself a functional unity, may contain within itself "subordinate entities" (such as the water or various chemical elements in the blood). These subordinate entities resemble primary beings in that each is an experiential entity governed by a distinctive subjective aim, but the subjective aim of each subordinate entity is subordinate to the subjective aim of the primary being that constitutes the whole. One might appropriately say that the subjective aim of the subordinate entity *participates* in the subjective aim of the primary being to which it is subordinate.

7) The experiential activity of the primary being is informed by the unique subjective aim of the being. There is then a kind of hierarchy among the subordinate entities included within the primary being, a

hierarchy dependent on the degree of participation in the subjective aim that obtains for each subordinate entity. Some are more intimately subordinated than others in their contribution to the activity of the primary being as a whole.

8) A consequence is that the unity and individuation of a primary being are determined by its subjective aim, as is its essential form. Located spatial continuity is not the primary ground of individuation as it is for Thomas, but the uniqueness of the subjective aim, which in turn uniquely specifies the essential form.[14] For the spatiality of the primary being and its subordinate entities is a function of their activity, in its limitations and its potentialities. Thus neither the primary being nor its subordinate entities can be thought of as constituted by extension (the Cartesian idea). Rather, their extension is derivative from the functionality of the entities (as both Whitehead and Leibniz supposed).

9) It is necessary to distinguish between the subjective aim of the primary being taken as a whole—what one might call the general self-ideal of the primary being—and its *particular aims* in its successive, repeated activities. These latter, ranging from changing the channel to adopting a state of life, always are meant to contribute toward the global subjective aim as described above, and can be said once again to participate in that subjective aim.

A complete account would also take into consideration Whitehead's distinction (not always emphasized) between "initial aim," which is the very first realization of the subjective aim, and the "subjective aim" as it is progressively modified by the entity through its own particular decisions. The internal history of a primary being involves above all its own self-induced modifications, sometimes for the worse, of its own initial self-ideal.

10) The above model for *the internal constitution of the primary being,* for instance the human being, avoids conceiving the human being as a multiplicity of microscopic ultimates standing in historical relationship to one another. At the same time it tries to allow for the undeniable complexity of material beings. My proposal is parallel to suggestions made by several Whiteheadian thinkers who have been bothered by Whitehead's event-atomic reductionism, and who have suggested alternative models of compound or inclusive entities.[15]

11) Although the above model suggests how the primary being affects its subordinate entities through their subjective aims, nothing has been said about how subordinate entities affect the primary being, but an answer to that problem readily presents itself. The number and character of the subordinate entities set natural limits to the possibilities—or better, to the width of possibility—that can be aimed at by the subjective aim. Thus, without the requisite, particular activities of the brain it is not possible to aim at bodily motion or perception or understanding. In this way subordinate entities limit the possible scope of the subjective aim and hence the subjective form of the whole. Conversely, those activities of the brain, whatever they may be, constitute it as *my* motion and *my* thought through their participation in my subjective aim. I reject the common presumption (which is neither Thomas's nor Whitehead's) that my brain thinks for me. Rather, *I* think with my brain, and that is exactly consonant with Thomistic thought.

12) This rough account of the internal constitution of a primary being has included a sort of mutual causality between the primary being as a whole and its subordinate entities. The latter are affected by the former inasmuch as their respective subjective aims participate in the subjective aim of the whole, whereas the primary being is affected by the subordinate entities inasmuch as they set a limit to the possible scope of that subjective aim. But since the subordinate entities change over time, this mutual influence between the primary being and its subordinate entities is an ongoing process. And because the subordinate entities are constantly affected by the aim of the primary entity, the theory is open to giving a reasonable account of the recently discovered evidence within physics for a simultaneous influence of a whole upon its parts, in what seems at first blush a violation of the principle that information cannot be transmitted at a speed greater than that of light.

THE GENESIS OF A PRIMARY BEING

But how shall we account for the genesis of a new primary being? How can we suppose that it comes into being? As a rough sketch I propose the following account.

1) The primary being can be thought to come into being in close accord with Whitehead's analysis, namely with the fusion of experiential feelings that include as their objects the primary beings that make up its "actual world," though unlike Whitehead we are leaving open the possibility that some of those primary beings may be contemporaneous with the primary being in question. Normally the primary being will be complex, and the components that will become what I have called its subordinate entities are already in existence. It is precisely those experiential feelings that get fused into the complex, unitary feeling of the nascent primary being under discussion.

2) But what can we mean, in our new, quasi-Thomistic system, by such a fusion of feelings into the feeling of a single experient? The key to the individual identity of the primary being is its subjective aim. That aim governs the essential form—the "how" or particular character—of the subject's experiential feeling, and consequently orders it to actual existence (*esse,* its first act) as a potentiality ordered to its actuality, and also orders it to its peculiar activity in existence, its *agere,* or second act. The identity and unity of the primary being thus resides in the unity of its *esse* and its experiential activity, its *agere,* but the defining principle of that unity is its subjective aim.

This means that I as a human person, a "primary being" in the new system, exercise one act of existing. *I* act in my every particular activity, even though my subsidiary entities, such as those that constitute my organ of seeing, make these particular activities possible and also share in the personal identity of these, my acts, by reason of participating, in their own particular ways, in my own subjective aim.

3) Thus, when the multiple experiential feelings of the components are suitable for coalescing into a higher-order feeling, there arises a feeling of—or rather, a feeling for or toward—a possible realization of a novel value that incorporates them all into a new unity that is nevertheless coherent with the given order of things. This feeling for a new possibility for value is precisely the *initial subjective aim* of the nascent primary being. It gives to the new primary being its unity and its individuality so that the particular experiential feelings of the subordinate entities now share, by a kind of participation, in that subjective aim.

Lest all this sound like only an exercise in fantasy, let us consider a particular example. How about a human sperm and egg? Singly neither is a human being nor ready to be a human being, but together they have that potentiality. (It is irrelevant to this consideration whether the new human being comes into existence at the moment of penetration of the egg by the sperm or at a later stage of development.) Let us now suppose that that potentiality has in fact been actualized. Why would this development not fit the above description of the provision of a higher subjective aim, thus bringing into existence a complex primary being of a higher form, namely, a human being?

4) Now it is a fact of experience that the feeling for as yet unrealized but relevant possibilities for value does constantly arise in the world. Yet those values, precisely because they are not yet realized, are nowhere to be found or perceived in the world. Furthermore although they are felt as adapted to the particularities of the given situation, by and large they fit harmoniously into the overall structure of the whole universe. How is it possible that these novel but apt possibilities thus present themselves as lures for activity? I do not at present see why one may not accept Whitehead's own account of how they arise, namely, by the involvement of God with the world. Thus Whitehead writes:

> Apart from the intervention of God, there could be nothing new in the world, and no order in the world. The course of creation would be a dead level of ineffectiveness, with all balance and intensity progressively excluded by the cross currents of incompatibility. (PR 247)

5) This "intervention" by God is not conceived as extrinsic to the nascent primary being, but rather amounts to the primary being's feelings of God's propositional feelings for *it* precisely in its situation in the world. This constitutes the primary being's own fundamental ontological feeling in virtue of which alone relevant novelty arises in nature.[16]

Such an account of the origin of subjective aim appears perfectly compatible with the Thomistic theory of the creature's participation in the structured act of existing provided by God. For in Thomas's view the order of the universe reflects God's own conception (ST I, 15, 2). God's particular conceptions stand as the existential patterns of all creatures (ST I, 15, 1), and every creature aims at its own perfection, which is itself a finite image of the divine goodness (ST I, 44, 4). From the perspectives, then, of both Whitehead and Thomas, God is the most plausible source of both the novelty and the stability of the universe.

SUMMARY AND CONCLUSION

The above suggestions sketch the general outlines of a metaphysics intended to incorporate into the fundamental ontology of Thomas Aquinas a quasi-Whiteheadian analysis of temporal becoming in place of Thomas's hylomorphic account. The obvious and pressing question arises: does such a hybrid account work? To answer this we must first ask whether this hybrid view is internally consistent or rather the kind of monstrosity that Horace envisioned. One way to test its consistency would be to try working out the scheme in some detail, and such an elaboration would in any case be the next step in the experiment.

In carrying out such a development, or in just examining its consistency, it is useful to notice in an explicit way how the proposed system agrees or disagrees with the proto-metaphysics of Thomas and of Whitehead.

I believe I have been able to retain the ontological or vertical dimension peculiar to Thomas's view. The primary being (which, according to Aristotle, is where the action is), is constantly dependent on God for its act of existing, whatever its intrinsic constitution may be. The distinction between the activity of the primary being and its fundamental act of existing is perfectly Thomistic, but according to several interpreters is a distinction that Whitehead finally forbade himself to make. Also, I have argued that the subjective aim and the essential form of the primary being effectively play the role in the proposed system of substantial form in Thomistic hylomorphism.

Though I have proposed to substitute a quasi-Whiteheadian analysis for Thomistic hylomorphism, the divergences from Whitehead, explicit or implicit, loom very large. Here are a few (doubtless not all) of them:

1) In accepting the Thomistic ontology of participation I have rejected Whitehead's disjunction between God and creativity, though this has not been a subject of very explicit discussion.

2) I have on a most fundamental level rejected what was, in the view of several notable scholars, Whitehead's ultimate identification of the being of an entity with its act of becoming and with its activities. According to that interpretation, Whitehead ultimately reversed the roles of cause and effect in his analysis of efficient causality, so that causal efficiency lies only in the internal activity of the actual entity experiencing its past rather than in the efficacy of the past laying its hand on the present entity. Such a restriction of the being and activity of an actual entity to its own self-creation would present an insurmountable obstacle to any effective theory of efficient causality between actual entities.

3) I have, at least implicitly, rejected what I take to be Whitehead's supposition that only entities that are completely determinate and "satisfied," and thus are no longer subjectively active, are available to be experienced by other entities. I assume on the contrary that only subjectively active entities can causally affect others (in the sense of efficient causality). Such active entities act only in virtue of their subjective aims and essential forms and thus of their already having a sufficiently determinate nature to be causal agents, even though their subjective aims are not yet completely fulfilled.

4) Concomitantly I do not follow Whitehead in promoting the Einsteinian epistemological definition of simultaneity into a metaphysical principle whereby only past actual entities can possibly be experienced. Rather, the first phase of sense experience consists in the simultaneous presence of the object *as* experienced to the experiencer by means of the sense organs. This is another instance of the Aristotelian-Thomistic doctrine that the causality of the efficient cause is *in* the affected entity.

5) I reject, as do a number of others, Whitehead's microatomism whereby, contrary to his original intention of making human experience a paradigm of the structure of reality, he was forced to regard the human being not as an entity that retains its numerical self-identity over time but as a serial ordering of successive entities. Presumably a main motive for his choosing this view was his wish to avoid a philosophy of "substance" conceived the way Locke or Descartes or Hume did—which, it appears, was the only doctrine of substance that concerned Whitehead.

When we review this sampling of divergences, we may very well ask whether anything much is left of Whitehead other than some borrowed terminology and a general interest in evolutionary becoming. True, I have utilized Whitehead's concepts of subjective aim, subjective form, and even his account of the God-given origin of novel subjective (or initial) aims, but the former concepts turn out to correlate almost exactly with hylomorphic substantial form.

What Whitehead chiefly brings to Thomas in his analysis of temporal becoming is his explicit interest in the origin of *ordered novelty* as it arises in the world, an interest he shared with Bergson. That eye toward novelty and evolutionary progress together with Whitehead's explicit attribution of its origin to the telic activity of God in the world are, I believe, consonant with Thomistic metaphysics but naturally go beyond it as a reflection of a later age.

Inasmuch as one is convinced of the lasting value of Thomas's central ontological analysis of being in terms of participation in *esse,* yet also of the impotence of hylomorphism any longer to account for evolutionary becoming, one naturally turns to an evolutionary philosophy, such as Whitehead's, for an already available model to serve as a coherent substitute for hylomorphism as Thomas conceived it. Whether a revision such as that suggested above can be carried through successfully, remains to be seen.[17]

SIXTEEN

Epochal Time and the Continuity of Experience

(2003)

This is the presidential address delivered to the Metaphysical Society of America at its meeting at Santa Clara University in March 2002. It is as much an essay on metaphysical method as on time, and it draws on ideas developed in earlier essays, especially essay 4 of this volume. I hope the reader will forgive the repetition of some of the principles already invoked, since I still stand by them. But I do confess now to one misgiving. In the following essay I apparently accepted John B. Cobb's assumption that no action can occur in a timeless instant. I am now inclined to question that assumption. (See note 10 to essay 4 in this volume.) For the action most in question is that of deciding, of choosing to pursue one particular possibility. This is the essential act of internal freedom, and we already saw that it belongs not to clock time but to lived time. It does not involve any movement of bodies in space; neither is it itself part of the antecedent consideration of possibilities and motives. It is

Originally published as "Epochal Time and the Continuity of Experience," *The Review of Metaphysics* 56 (September 2002): 19–36. Reprinted with permission.

*the decisive, self-originative act of internal freedom that
opts for one possibility out of indefinitely many others. It is
not clear to me that such an act need take any time at all. It
is not an "event" in the ordinary sense of the word. It is a
transition-point, if you will, within lived time, and as we
have seen, lived time is simply not measured by clock time.
So perhaps Cobb's elegant analysis (alluded to in essay 4
and summarized below) explicative of Whitehead's difficult notion, that the free act is temporally thick yet not temporally divisible, is unnecessary.*

*As the reader may have gathered, aspects of the fol-
lowing paper may be somewhat dense though I hope not
obscure.*

I should like to examine the plausibility and consequences of a particular view of the nature of metaphysics, especially in its relation to immediate human experience, which it is designed to illuminate. In order to
make the consideration concrete I shall apply this interpretation to a
familiar controversy about the nature of time. One view, accepted by
Whiteheadian process philosophers, is that time is actually episodic,
atomic, epochal. The contrasting view, that of Henri Bergson among
others, is that time is continuous, even though it embodies temporal
qualitative variations.

These contrasting opinions bring out, in their clarity and relative
simplicity, important consequences of the interpretation of metaphysics that I shall propose. My primary aim, therefore, is not so much to
resolve that particular controversy as to show its dependence on divergent views of metaphysics, although I shall indeed draw some conclusions that tend to favor one of those views over the other.

I

To start with I lay some metaphysical cards right on the table. For one
thing I assume that metaphysics is a philosophic enterprise that is neither futile nor meaningless. This of course runs counter to a powerful

philosophic tradition since Hume, as well as to popular conceptions.[1] I agree with Etienne Gilson who held that failed metaphysics are instances of bad metaphysics, not exercises in a priori futility.

Secondly, I take for granted a certain form of epistemic realism. It is not, I think, a naive realism, and certainly it is neither an idealism like that of Kant nor a representationalism like that of Locke and Hume. It is a *relational realism,* and is a fundamentally Thomistic view put into a modern context.

Thirdly, I assume that the more fundamental issue is not whether time itself is epochal or continuous, but whether *becoming,* especially the becoming that is immediate experience, is such. For time, whether the time of bodies moving in space or the time of consciousness, is not itself a fundamental entity but a derivative one. Bergson prefers to talk about *duration*—the duration of experiential becoming—and the Whiteheadian view of time as epochal is really the view that *becoming* is basically atomic or epochal. Whitehead explicitly concluded that continuity belongs to the possible but atomicity to the actual—that is, to those acts of becoming that constitute actual entities.[2] In whatever way we look at it, then, the question of the continuous or the epochal nature of time confronts us exactly with an inquiry into the metaphysics of immediate experience.

Before developing the viewpoint that I shall propose, it will be useful to attain further clarity concerning the philosophic controversy mentioned above. With that in mind I first briefly sketch Bergson's and Whitehead's respective conceptions of metaphysical method.

Bergson distinguished between two extreme ways in which we can use our minds. The more familiar is what he called *intelligence,* though one might also call it conceptualization. In it our mind approaches the real by means of concepts, intellectual snapshots that freeze for thought the intelligible patterns of reality. This is what we do when we form those abstractions from the particularities of the flow of experience that enable us to develop sciences or even just to get along successfully in the world.[3]

The contrasting way of using the mind he called *intuition,* by which we enter directly into an object or a process by immediate, reflective insight. We grasp it for itself without the intervention of concepts or even of symbols. The primary object of intuition, he wrote, is "our own person in its flowing through time, the self which endures" (CM 162), and he took this intuitive reflection upon immediate experience to be the essence of metaphysics (ibid.). In its perfection, intuition achieves an identity with its object. "Metaphysics will then become experience itself; and duration will be revealed as it really is—unceasing creation, the uninterrupted upsurge of novelty" (CM 18). For Bergson metaphysics is above all an immediate grasping of the self in its flowing through time, the flowing that he called *duration*. The primary object of intuition is immediate experience itself, duration, and the primary characters of duration discoverable by intuition, but opaque to conceptualization, are its continuity of flow and its freedom.

Whitehead also meant to build his metaphysics on an insight into immediate human experience. He called his ultimate ontological units "actual occasions" (of experience), and he wrote that in describing the capacities, realized or unrealized, of an actual occasion he had, with Locke, tacitly taken human experience as the model upon which to found the generalized description required for metaphysics (PR 112).

Furthermore, Whitehead held that "the true method of philosophical construction is to frame a scheme of ideas, the best that one can, and unflinchingly to explore the interpretation of experience in terms of that scheme" (PR xiv). He also very significantly wrote: "The true method of discovery [in metaphysics] is like the flight of an aeroplane. It starts from the ground of particular observation; it makes a flight in the thin air of imaginative generalization; and it again lands for renewed observation rendered acute by rational interpretation" (PR 5).

For both thinkers, then, metaphysics is intimately linked with immediate experience. But how did they interpret that experience with respect to time and continuity?

Bergson insisted that continuity belongs to the essence of duration, that inner process of becoming that is both the core of all our experience and our primary analogue for world-process and time. This internal duration, he held, is "succession which is not juxtaposition, a growth from within, the uninterrupted prolongation of the past into a present which is already blending into the future" (CM 32). And if we sometimes think of our inner states as if they were a multiplicity of items placed end to end, this stems in part from the diverse psychological acts by which we take note of the character of our inner life. "The apparent discontinuity of the psychical life is then due to our attention being fixed on it by a series of separate acts: actually there is only a gentle slope."[4]

The substantiality of the ego, he said, as also its duration, is "an indivisible and indestructible continuity of a melody where the past enters into the present and forms with it an undivided whole which remains undivided and even indivisible in spite of what is added at every instant, or rather, thanks to what is added" (CM 71). The heterogeneous moments of the succeeding states of the self permeate one another, so that for states to succeed one another means for them to melt into one another and form an organic whole.[5]

Whitehead, however, held that "if we admit that 'something becomes,' it is easy, by employing Zeno's method, to prove that there can be no continuity of becoming" (PR 35). He made much—arguably too much—of William James's assertion that reality grows literally by "buds or drops of perception."[6] Whitehead concluded that the only way to make rational sense of becoming is to hold that although instances of becoming succeed one another in time and are temporally thick, they are nevertheless not temporally divisible within themselves.

Whitehead's contention that becoming is thus atomic or epochal is most convincingly seen, I think, in the context of trying to make intellectual sense of human freedom.[7] John B. Cobb, Jr., has framed this argument with exceptional clarity and I paraphrase it here.[8] He takes for granted that each event or occurrence (and every aspect of it) is either caused or uncaused. If uncaused, then it simply happens, for no reason, and hence cannot be an act of moral agency. Human acts must be caused if we are to make sense of their ethical dimension. Further, they must be caused from within, for if they are caused by outside agents they are once again deprived of the ethical dimension of responsibility. The concern therefore centers neither on indetermination, nor on determination from without, but on self-determination.

But even self-determination is not compatible with freedom so long as we retain the usual assumption that the cause must temporally precede its effect. For on that assumption self-determination reduces to a succession of inner states and we are faced once again with the same dilemma as before: if each state is caused by a preceding state, there is no locus for a free state; if on the other hand the determination or decision in question is simply *un*caused we are in the arena of chance not freedom. Clearly the kind of "causation" that takes place in free self-determination must be such that the "cause" (the agent or agency) is somehow simultaneous with its "effect" (the decision), not antecedent to it.

Now this moment of deciding must either be instantaneous or occupy some finite interval of time. But it cannot be the former, says Cobb, for no action can occur in a timeless instant.[9] But neither can it be the latter so long as we continue to view process as continuous, for we could not then justify supposing that the free act occurs during an extended temporal interval. For if we continue to suppose that becoming is continuous, not only is the length of the assumed interval essentially arbitrary, its unity becomes ultimately illusory. Just as the temporal flow is infinitely divisible, so also is the act of deciding. Zeno's argument shivers the act into an infinite succession of instantaneous states, in which, presumably, there can be no process.

Only two routes of escape seem to lie open. One route is to suppose that although freedom makes no sense within the causal fabric of human experience, it yet makes intelligible sense within a realm transcending that experience. This is the route taken by Kant. The other is to suppose that process or becoming is *dis*continuous; that although acts of becoming succeed one another in such a way as to "take time," they are not themselves temporally divisible but are in some sense all-at-once, thus forming atomic yet temporally thick units of becoming. This is the route taken by Whitehead. He wrote:

> The conclusion is that in every act of becoming there is the becoming of something with temporal extension; but that the act itself is not extensive, in the sense that it is divisible into earlier and later acts of becoming which correspond to the extensive divisibility of what has become. (PR 69)

And in another place he wrote:

> Temporalisation is not another continuous process. It is an atomic succession. Thus time is atomic (*i.e.* epochal), though what is temporalised is divisible.[10]

But what is divisible is not yet divided. Thus Whitehead places continuity on the side of potentiality, whereas the actual, he says, is "incurably atomic" (PR 61, 67).

The consequences of this view for Whitehead's whole metaphysics are considerable. Since time is derivative from the very activity of becoming, Whitehead was adopting an epochal theory of all becoming—a kind of event-atomism.[11] The most radical consequence of this appears to be his "societal" theory of the make-up of the human person. In virtue of the above sort of reasoning, he cannot regard the person as enduring self-identically through a significant span of time—certainly not through a lifetime—but must think of the person as a temporally ordered succession of extremely brief occasions of experience all of which are ontically distinct from one another.

For some of us this atomistic conception of the human person seems unbelievable. Certainly it seems to contradict the evident character of that immediate experience on which Whitehead wished to model his own metaphysics. As Sandra Rosenthal has put it:

> Whitehead holds the view that the continuity of the stream of experience is a surface feature prominent for consciousness, but the underlying reality is a succession of atomic experiences. . . . Hence our lived sense of time, time consciousness, is in some way subjective, set over against an alien objective reality of successive temporal atoms. The lived sense of time and the objective reality of time are incompatible, and the gulf between them is ultimately unbridgeable.
>
> . . . The temporal continuity of the flow of time consciousness is the most fundamental and pervasive feature of human experience, yet its nature as seemingly continuous closes us off from the cosmic reality of time as constituted by discrete temporal units.[12]

Besides appearing contrary to experience, the epochal view of becoming has its own intrinsic difficulties. A number of Whiteheadian scholars have wrestled, without general agreement, over the meaning to be assigned to the notions of the "earlier" and "later" phases of becoming that are essential to the Whiteheadian analysis. The predominant view has been that the phases cannot be said to take place earlier or later in time, yet it is difficult to see any other meaning that can be attached to this priority.[13]

This apparently anomalous character of the actual occasion, and the counter-experiential conception of human consciousness as a succession of discrete units, have long been taken for granted by Whiteheadian scholars, swallowed whole, as it were, in lieu of any alternative that seems acceptable. One simply gets used to ideas that at first seem outlandish. I wonder whether one of Whitehead's own remarks might not apply to this, his theory of epochal becoming. For he once wrote: "Of course it is always possible to work oneself into a state of complete contentment with an ultimate irrationality."[14]

II

I wish now briefly to suggest a simple theory of how metaphysics may be thought to relate to immediate experience. The theory will, I believe, illuminate what is going on in the divergent views we have just reviewed and will in a certain sense reconcile them. First I propose some theses about knowledge in general, theses that I expect the reader will find familiar and, as I hope, acceptable.

The first thesis is simply this: *All knowledge is relational.* That is, in knowing we never attain a thing-in-itself, an object just as it exists independently of its being known. Rather, we attain a thing precisely as it stands related to us in the act of knowing, and this holds whether we consider knowing in the narrow sense, or knowing in the broader sense that includes sense perception. I already noted that I am proposing a theory of epistemological realism; I maintain that we do attain real extramental objects in sensing and knowing. Yet these attained objects are of their very nature *relational* objects, objects precisely as they stand related to us in the act of knowing them and thus as embodying all the elements entering into that cognitive act. This thesis contrasts with a pure idealism on the one hand and with a naive realism on the other, as well as with any representational interpretation of perception, such as that of Locke.

The second thesis is this: *All knowledge, as relational, is also perspectival.* By that I mean, with the phenomenologists, that there is an

inevitable *polarity* between the heuristic perspective that we bring to
knowledge, however implicit or subconscious it be, and the horizon for
a possible world attainable in virtue of that perspective. In a profound
sense the world that we encounter can only be a world that falls within
the horizon already delimited by our heuristic perspective.

This polarity of all knowledge between perspective and horizon is
simply one particular specification of the relationality of knowledge. If
the world we encounter in knowing is inevitably relational to that act
of knowing, then the perspective—that is, the structured heuristic
anticipations that we bring to the act of knowing defines an essential
part of that relationship.

An analogue of this is afforded, I think, even by classical, Newto-
nian physics. If, for instance, one considers a satellite orbiting the earth
and asks why it orbits at a constant distance from the earth, the positing of a single force suffices to render the situation intelligible, namely
the centripetal force of gravity attracting the satellite toward the center
of gravity of the earth and thus constantly causing it to deviate from a
straight path in space. But suppose we place ourselves inside the satellite. Gravity is attracting us toward the earth yet we approach no closer
to it, so in order to understand the situation precisely from this perspective we must posit another force, centrifugal force, acting just opposite
to the force of gravity and exactly equaling it.

Now if we ask which of these two scenarios is correct, we must
reply "both," but each is a matter of heuristic standpoint or perspective. Centrifugal force is undoubtedly "real" for the person in the satellite (the non-inertial observer), but not real for the observer on earth
(who approximates an inertial observer). The reality of centrifugal force
depends on the perspective one adopts in viewing the situation. In an
analogous way, our metaphysical perspective or set of heuristic and
methodic presuppositions determines the sort of world that we shall
metaphysically encounter. The polar relationship between heuristic
standpoint and its corresponding horizon of reality is inescapable.

Combining the two theses proposed above, we can formulate a
third thesis: *Metaphysical knowledge of reality is both relational and perspectival.* Though it seems obviously true, the importance of this thesis
can scarcely be exaggerated. The old persuasion, so often since criticized, that metaphysics opens to our minds a sort of God's-eye view of

reality is patently false. If there be a God's-eye view of the world, we haven't got it and we can't possibly have it.

If, however, we are to assess the plausibility of a metaphysics of reality, we must attend to the perspective or set of presuppositions that is entailed in its analysis. These presuppositions are arbitrary in the sense that, as the foundation of all other thinking, they cannot be the outcome of any demonstrations. As Whitehead noted, one picks them "the best that one can" (PR xiv). Perhaps of even greater moment are the presuppositions that one does not deliberately pick but implicitly and subconsciously entertains. All these initial presuppositions will determine the whole outcome of the metaphysical analysis. As Gilson put it: "Philosophers are free to lay down their own sets of principles, but once this is done, they no longer think as they wish—they think as they can."[15] I believe that the choice of metaphysical views on the nature of time or becoming exactly demonstrates this inevitability.

Paramount among the presuppositions we bring to this analysis is the method we select in attempting to grasp the intelligibility of immediate experience. If Bergson is right, the ways in which we can use the mind range between the extremes of immediate intuition on the one hand and of conceptualization on the other. He recognized a legitimate place for both activities but considered that the true method of metaphysics is essentially intuitive rather than conceptual.

Whitehead also recognized both activities. He wished to ground his metaphysics on the immediacy of human experience, and he recognized the dual role of insight on the one hand and of conceptual abstraction on the other. Recall his airplane analogy in which metaphysics both begins and ends in direct insight into experience, but meanwhile ascends to high, conceptual abstraction, such as is monumentally embodied in his Categoreal Scheme, which nonetheless is meant to render that experience intellectually explicable. Sensitive to the loss of concreteness involved in abstract analysis, Whitehead himself repeated Wordsworth's phrase, "we murder to dissect" (PR 140).

What then was the upshot of the Bergsonian and Whiteheadian analyses of immediate experience when brought to bear on the question of time? Bergson pointed out that conceptual, rather than intuitive, analysis of immediate experience naturally leads to a *spacelike* conception of time (TFW 120). This is readily seen in Augustine's well-known perplexity about the length of the present. As he first analyzed it in its relation to a conceived past and future, he found the present shrink by a kind of Zenonian disintegration into an ultimate instant in which there was literally no time for time (*Confessions* XI, 15). He thus implicitly attributed to time a spacelike continuity inasmuch as he thereby thought of the present as indefinitely divisible in the same way as is a geometric line. To conceive space as if it were fundamentally like time is not only natural to us, it has been accentuated by the Einsteinian conception of time as a kind of fourth dimension of space. Thus the parts of time—the minutes and the days—are thought of as indefinitely subdivisible and so as *homogeneous*—one minute exactly like another— and also *mutually exclusive* of one another just as each part of space excludes every other.

But is this the sort of continuity that we actually encounter in immediate experience, not as we abstractly conceive it but as we live it? Augustine himself thought not, at least implicitly, for only a page or two after his above considerations about the seeming timelessness of the present, he went on to surmise, in a passage too little noted, "Perhaps it would be exact to say: there are three times, a present of things past, a present of things present, a present of things to come. In the soul there are these three aspects of time, and I do not see them anywhere else."[16]

Now when past, present, and future are thought of as laid out against one another like parts of a geometric line, there cannot possibly be a present of the past, for each part excludes every other. A present of the past would be a contradiction in terms. So if we in fact *experience* a present of the past, it follows that the time of immediate experience cannot be spacelike. And after all, why should we expect that? Spacelike time is exactly suited to the measurement of the motion of bodies in space, as Aristotle pointed out, and is it likely that this describes the activity of our psychic life?

In fact there are excellent reasons for thinking otherwise. Two of our most ordinary experiences show this. One is the familiar experience of hearing a melody, another is communication through speech. A melody is not simply a succession of different notes, it is those different notes as forming a unity, the past notes with the present together with a certain anticipation of the future ones. But where is this unity of different successive notes, where does the melody, as such, exist except in consciousness or, as Augustine put it, in the soul? In our experience of hearing a melody the present does indeed include the past rather than exclude it. So too, if you do not retain within your conscious awareness the earlier words of my sentence, you cannot draw meaning from it at the end. In immediate experience the past is included rather than excluded from the present.[17]

I now propose that we can shed light on the diverse views we have seen concerning the nature of time by considering them from the perspective of the respective *conceptions of continuity,* implicit or explicit, that are taken for granted in the two analyses. If Bergson is right, the conception of continuity that fits conceptual analysis, such as Augustine's reduction of the present to a timeless instant or Whitehead's conclusion that becoming must be epochal, is one wherein the parts of time or becoming are thought of as homogeneous, differing from other parts only in their position within the continuity. Each second necessarily *excludes* every other second just in being itself. Thus we have conceived a *continuity of exclusive, quantitative homogeneity.* But such a continuity is immediately prey to Zeno's endless and paradoxical subdivision, as Augustine demonstrated.

Direct attunement to immediate experience, however, reveals a very different sort of continuity, a continuity that somehow *includes* its parts within a single whole and whose parts differ qualitatively, not quantitatively, from one another since, unlike miles or minutes, no conscious state is qualitatively just like any other. The continuity proper to immediate experience is, therefore, a *continuity of inclusive, qualitative heterogeneity* quite unlike the other *continuity of exclusive, quantitative homogeneity* that is the natural result of conceptualization. How can two such radically different sorts of continuity have been confused?

Now the conception of a particular sort of continuity—a conception that is all the more influential if it is merely implicit and therefore unrecognized—forms an essential part of the heuristic structure of any metaphysical analysis of immediate experience. It constitutes a particular perspective that antecedently determines the sort of reality that can be acknowledged.

But since the continuity of the time that is thought of as necessarily epochal is patently spacelike, and the continuity of the time of immediate experience is quite the opposite, it follows that epochal time and epochal becoming constitute derivative, conceptual abstractions drawn from experience rather than a metaphysical description of direct experiencing itself. Epochal time, as for instance in Cobb's argument above, is a necessary interpretation of the nature of intelligible experience but only on condition that that interpretation is conceptual rather than intuitive, and that it presupposes a spacelike notion of continuity. That last condition inevitably defines a horizon of reality into which immediate experience simply does not fit. It is the horizon of reality that Whitehead calls "the thin air of imaginative generalization." The same must be said, I think, of Whitehead's consequent theory of the human person as a socially ordered series of discrete occasions.

I repeat: Whitehead's theory of epochal becoming is a necessary conclusion of metaphysical analysis if, but only if, one remains on the plane of conceptual abstraction and presupposes, as he did, a conception of continuity that is essentially spacelike. But that method and that presupposition are neither necessary nor sound. One arrives at a quite different world when one denies them. Whitehead himself realized that there was a mismatch between his theory of epochal time and the immediacy of experience that was supposed to be the model for his occasions of experience. Thus he found himself constrained to distinguish between what he calls a "coordinate," quasi-quantitative analysis of the actual occasion taken as a whole, and a "genetic," nonquantitative analysis of it when it is regarded in its interior becoming. Coordinate analysis, taken from the outside, supposes a time occupied by the occasion that is indefinitely divisible just as is its space. But genetic analysis, viewing the occasion on the inside, must deny such divisibility even though the occasion is temporally thick. Whitehead is doubtless right in feeling the need for this distinction, but the paradoxical nature of his conclusion arises in part because in his analysis of experience he is employing, though not recognizing, two different and mutually incompatible conceptions of continuity.

III

In this brief look at the relation of metaphysics to immediate experience and at the old controversy about epochal time I have advanced

two central considerations about metaphysical method. One, following
Bergson, is that intuitive insight into immediate experience is essential
to metaphysical analysis, and that this nonconceptual, immediate insight describes experience more concretely than abstract conceptualization. The other consideration, borrowed from the phenomenologists,
is that metaphysical knowledge, like all forms of knowledge, is un-
avoidably perspectival, so that the reality we encounter and endeavor
to render intelligible is inescapably a function of the heuristic perspective that we bring to the analysis. Different perspectives define different world-horizons.

I propose that if we grant these two suppositions, as well as recognize the radical difference between the two kinds of continuity I have
distinguished above, we can suggest a satisfactory reply to the question
whether time and becoming are epochal or continuous, and whether
the human person need be conceived as an historical succession of minute, successive though interrelated occasions of experience.

Bergson contended that immediate experience as we actually find
it is in fact continuous, not successive, and for Bergson this contention
was not only phenomenological, it was metaphysical, inasmuch as his
method of introspective intuition claims to be the metaphysical method
par excellence. Bergson of course was not so naive as to suppose that we
find no succession of qualitative divergences in our experience, but he
held that these recognizable changes melt into one another so as to
form a continuous unity that he compares to a melody (CM 127). Is
Bergson right about this, or is Whitehead?

In facing this question directly, I find it illuminating first to notice
a special difficulty that might be advanced against Whitehead's epochal
theory of time. If one supposes that ongoing experience seems, phe-
nomenologically, to be continuous, then the question naturally arises
why one does not notice the repeated succession of occasions that are
demanded by Whitehead's analysis. Now it would be pointless for a
Whiteheadian to reply that the succession is simply too rapid to be
observed, as in a motion picture, because that reply overlooks a contradiction already contained within the difficulty itself. The only way to
notice the successiveness of the series would be to view it from the outside, as one views cars on a passing train, and such an external view
seems to be the habitual standpoint for Whiteheadian discussions of

personal identity. Yet the objection also points out that the successiveness is not noticed, that is, not immediately experienced. But noticing
takes place only within the interior of an actual occasion; it belongs to
its subjective immediacy. Thus the objection is intrinsically inconsistent in demanding that one simultaneously stand both within and without the series. It does, however, illustrate that the conception of the
person as a rapid succession of occasions must belong to the horizon of
conceptual abstraction rather than to that of subjective immediacy.

IV

It is now possible, I think, to give a direct reply to the question whether
time and becoming are epochal as Whitehead thought, or continuous as
Bergson thought. I say that if becoming is analyzed from a perspective
of conceptual abstraction, which, Bergson maintained, entails the tacit
supposition that the form of continuity in question is spacelike, then
the Whiteheadian conclusion that becoming is epochal or atomic is
probably unavoidable, as Cobb's form of the argument shows. But the
horizon of reality that is thereby described lies within the realm of conceptual abstraction. That is, in concluding that time is epochal Whitehead is still flying in what he himself called "the thin air of imaginative generalization." He has not yet returned to direct observation of
immediate experience. For the sort of continuity that he rightly denies
to genetic or subjective immediacy is clearly spacelike, a continuity of
exclusive quantitative homogeneity, quite unlike the continuity that
actually characterizes immediate experience. But when he concludes
that becoming must be epochal, Whitehead seems to conceive of no
form of continuity other than the spacelike, no continuity of inclusive,
qualitative heterogeneity, and so when he describes becoming and time
as necessarily noncontinuous or epochal, Whitehead is not in fact describing immediate experience but rather an abstract, conceptual surro-
gate artificially derived from it. He is describing a different world from
that of immediate experience. The same conclusion, I would argue,
holds for his description of the human person as a serial succession of
atomic units of becoming. Such a "person" exists only as a kind of conceptual virtual image substituted for the concrete person who grasps

him- or herself as enjoying an unbroken continuity of experiencing over time.

I know of no better way of finally driving home this point than by recalling a famous passage from the English physicist, Sir Arthur Eddington. At the beginning of his Gifford Lectures he wrote:

> I have settled down to the task of writing these lectures and have drawn up my chairs to my two tables. Two tables! Yes; there are duplicates of every object about me—two tables, two chairs, two pens. . . .
>
> One of them has been familiar to me from earliest years. It is a commonplace object of that environment which I call the world. How shall I describe it? It has extension; it is comparatively permanent; it is coloured; above all it is *substantial.* . . .
>
> Table No. 2 is my scientific table. It is a more recent acquaintance and I do not feel so familiar with it. It does not belong to the world previously mentioned—that world which spontaneously appears around me when I open my eyes. . . . My scientific table is mostly emptiness. Sparsely scattered in that emptiness are numerous electric charges rushing about with great speed. . . .
>
> I need not tell you that modern physics has by delicate test and remorseless logic assured me that my second scientific table is the only one that is really there.[18]

Is Eddington's conclusion not correct? Is the logic of science not remorseless? Of course we might point out to Eddington that it is inappropriate to speak of a scientific table, inasmuch as "table" is not a term that belongs to the horizon of science. But that aside, does not science describe reality more authentically than our senses do?

No it doesn't. It describes a *different* horizon of reality, not a more real one. The sensible table is, in fact, the only table that is really there, and it belongs to the commonsense horizon attainable though the use of our senses. That is as real a table as you could have or want. Eddington's perceived table really *was* smooth and hard and brown.

Of course if we take certain sophisticated scientific instruments and involve a sensible table, or some part of it, in an interaction with those instruments, scientific theory will interpret that interaction, which we cannot ourselves sensibly experience, as indicative of an array of molecules moving in a kind of empty space, and so forth. But the horizon of reality to which that scientific entity belongs is very different from that of direct perception. It is narrower in its scope and it essentially involves an instrumental interaction that is not, and cannot be, part of immediate human experience. What science's remorseless logic concludes to is an abstract conceptualization drawn from concrete human experience only through highly indirect theoretical means. The scientific table, if you can call it that, belongs to that abstract, conceptualized world, and our affirming it does not acknowledge it to have a more authentic reality than that of the table we sense. In fact, even affirming that the scientific table exists depends upon the use of our senses, at least in the perception of the instrument's reactions.

I grant that the parallel between Eddington's so-called scientific table and Whitehead's conception of time as epochal or of the human person as a successive society of minute occasions is not indeed perfect because, as I said, science deliberately narrows its field of interest to only certain factors given in immediate experience and it needs to utilize indirect, instrumental reactions. Nevertheless the similarity between the two conceptions—and they are conceptions—remains striking. Whitehead's conclusion that time is epochal and that the human person is a succession of actual occasions plausibly resembles Eddington's conviction that the table must be mostly empty space because science presumably assured him that this was so. For if one remains within the horizon defined by the perspective of conceptual abstraction rather than of an intuitive grasp of immediate experience, and if one also conceives the continuity of experience as fundamentally spacelike, then it might indeed follow that time or becoming, so conceived, is epochal and the human person, so conceived, is an atomic succession of discrete occasions. But that is a metaphysical description not of the time of immediate experience or of a living person but of their virtual images projected into the thin air of conceptual generalization. To confuse such an image with the concrete person seems, ironically, to commit the very error that Whitehead tried to avoid, "the fallacy of misplaced concreteness." In fact, does not applying spacelike time to immediate experiencing, and confusing the two horizons of intuitive insight and of conceptual generalizations, amount to a kind of "ultimate irrationality"? Yet most Whiteheadian philosophers have long since worked themselves into a state of complete contentment with it.

What Whiteheadians could learn from Bergson is to take seriously Whitehead's own requirement that in metaphysics one return from the realm of abstraction to the immediacy of experience from which one started. Process philosophy sometimes seems less like the flight of an airplane than that of a balloon which need not, in principle, come back down again. To allow discussion of immediate experience or of the human person to terminate at the level of conceptual abstraction rather than of intuitive awareness is not, I am afraid, to return to that concrete experience from which the philosophic enterprise took off.

If we accept, with Bergson, an intuited continuity of time and becoming, as well as an ontological identity of the self through a span of time, we do not directly contradict Whitehead's theory of epochal time, or of the successive multiplicity of the person, because Whitehead is not thereby describing either the time or the person that are found in immediate experience but rather their conceptual surrogates within the horizon of abstraction. Bergson, however, points us back to immediate experience itself. He calls on us, not only as phenomenologists but as metaphysicians, finally to land the plane.

I dare to think that what I have here said crudely fits what T. S. Eliot said with unforgettable power:

> We shall not cease from exploration
> And the end of all our exploring
> Will be to arrive where we started
> And know the place for the first time.[19]

SEVENTEEN

"Know Yourself!"

(2007)

I close this volume with excerpts from the last chapter of my book Aims: A Brief Metaphysics for Today, *which constitutes my best development to date of the melding of the metaphysics of Thomas Aquinas and of Whitehead that I invited in essay 2 of this volume. I hope it would be fair to say that it amounts to an enriching or modernizing of Thomas's metaphysics in terms of more contemporary insights. I began* Aims *with the challenge of the Delphic Oracle: "Know yourself!" In the course of my trying to develop a revised metaphysics by appealing to direct experience as well as to the thought of Thomas and of Whitehead there emerged a basic if skeletal metaphysics that is, as I think, coherent and most certainly teleological. Analogously to Plotinus's insight into being's "return," this metaphysics, like those of Thomas and of Whitehead, pivots around final causality, goal-directedness. The reader will understand, I am sure, that in* Aims *the following lines presupposed all the chapters that preceded them, and here they cannot con-*

Originally published in *Aims: A Brief Metaphysics for Today* (Notre Dame, IN: University of Notre Dame Press, 2007), 118–25.

*vey the same clarity of meaning. Yet they seem worth repro-
ducing here as suggesting the present end point of the above
explorations in unfashionable metaphysics.*

A SHORT PHENOMENOLOGICAL DESCRIPTION
OF IMMEDIATE EXPERIENCE

What I first notice in my experiencing are *objects* in a world. These objects confront me sensibly as making a difference to me, for better or for worse. I may choose to ignore them but I always do so at my own peril, for they give themselves to me as enjoying a certain autonomy of existence and activity. Taken together they make up a *world* that I feel myself part of and that, in another sense, is a part of me.

Furthermore in finding myself confronted with these objects I also sense a dimension of *value* that belongs to them as I experience them. This sense of value, good or bad, attractive or harmful, is an ineluctable aspect of my experience of them.

I also find that I directly experience a sense of *derivation* of the present from the past, and of the present as issuing into a future. This is a feeling not only of subjective continuity but a feeling of the continuity through time of the experienced world itself.

Always present in my experiencing is a sense of my own unity: that although my body and my psyche are doubtless complex, yet they constitute a single, unitary me.

Another aspect of my experiencing might be called its stimulus-response dynamic. I literally feel the causal impact of the things that make up my world. They impose themselves upon me willy-nilly, and they call for a response on my part. In fact that seems to be the basic character of all my ordinary experience: an interactive, causal commerce with things in the world.

There is one such interaction, however, that is for me paramount: my relations with other human beings. There is no more concrete or valuable aspect of my experiencing than interpersonal relationships.

I also notice that all my deliberate acts are *aimed* acts: they are performed with the intention of achieving some as yet nonexistent value. And such value is not peripheral to me like clothing, but it is value-for-myself. Better: it is a kind of self-ideal, a new and better me that is aimed at in my every intentional action. Most importantly, underlying every such action is the lure of that central aim toward which all my particular aims focus, what I have called my essential aim. The trouble is, it is not immediately clear just what that aim is. As E. B. White wrote in a short story: "My heart has followed all my days something I cannot name."[1] Aristotle identified this ultimate aim as "happiness," by which he meant an activity of soul according to what is best in the soul, and that, he said, is intellectual contemplation.[2] That may at first sound too abstract, yet it does say something important.

PRELIMINARY PHILOSOPHICAL INTERPRETATION OF EXPERIENCING

My experiencing involves both the experienced objects and me the experiencer. I have satisfied myself that what I directly experience in sense perception is extramental objects themselves, not just my own sense data. Yet I do not experience objects as they are in themselves but as they stand related to me in my act of perceiving them. What I perceive are real but relational objects. Yet, precisely because they do act on me in my perception of them, I am entitled to attribute to them an existence in their own right. I thus have solid metaphysical grounds underlying my immediate feeling of being in a world of objects.

Also, my every act of experiencing is an activity in existence. I accept Aquinas's insight that the act of existing is the act of acts and is the root of all value. I take it that all my natural activities are a manifestation of the tendency of existing to overflow or communicate itself. The apex of such activity is found in interpersonal relationships.

As for myself, I take myself to be a primary being in the sense worked out earlier. I am individuated from other primary beings by my body. At the same time I am a highly complex being, containing within myself a myriad of subordinate entities. How then do I explain my sense of personal unity?[3] In terms of my overarching *essential aim.*

Though my subordinate entities have particular aims of their own, yet, as part of me, their aims participate in my essential aim, so that my unity is dynamic and goal-aimed. I am one primary being because all of my parts share in my single essential aim.

I cannot myself have contrived or even chosen my essential aim, that of a human being; it must have been given to me from without. I have philosophically satisfied myself that just as my ongoing act of existing must continually be furnished to me, and kept in actual existence, by the Source of all existing that I call Alpha, so must my essential aim have been furnished to me, and kept in existence, by Alpha.[4] Also, the aim must have been precisely chosen so as to be conducive, in the fabric of things, to the realization of greater value.

It follows that the nature of my essential aim sets natural parameters for my life span. It must be at least theoretically possible for me to satisfy that essential aim through the particular activities that I engage in. My metaphysics, like Aquinas's but unlike Whitehead's, allows me to enjoy a real self-identity as a single primary being during all that time.

IN SEARCH OF ONE'S ESSENTIAL AIM

Again and again, then, I find that the central answer to the question, "What am I?" lies exactly in the nature of my essential aim.

I earlier distinguished my essential aim from what I call immediate aims, those particular, limited aims that I am constantly and explicitly adopting from moment to moment of my life. But they are all chosen only insofar as they are felt to conduce to my essential aim. One thinks of Aristotle who said that the ultimate aim underlying all other aims is happiness itself, so that particular aims are adopted just insofar as they are thought to contribute to happiness.

But, as I noticed earlier, my essential aim is too large, or rather too fundamental, to have been chosen by me. Even now, though it is the attractive force behind all my immediate aims, my essential aim is hard to describe precisely because I live it rather than choose it. Yet if all my immediate aims are chosen in view of my essential aim, should they not in some way point to it? Can they not tell me about my essential aim itself, about what it is that my heart has followed all my days but cannot name?

Perhaps it is easier to begin by considering what my essential aim is not. Thinking back to Aristotle again, I have to agree with him that it cannot consist in material pleasures. For however intense they might be, they are ultimately unsatisfying if for no other reason than that they are passing, fleeting, like water running through my fingers. Yet what I really desire is to lay hold of value that I can keep without losing it.

Aristotle says the same thing about reputation and a sense of power. They too are ephemeral. What better examples of this than Alcibiades, or the young man Aristotle is reputed to have tutored in his youth? Alexander did live a dazzling life but for how long?

Well, what about interpersonal relationships? Do they not constitute the best sort of experience? Yes, this seems highly probable, though I also note sadly that even those whom I love do die and are taken out of my life. Interpersonal relationships themselves are haunted by fragility and incompleteness.

I try another tack. The Oracle's admonition is directed toward knowing, understanding. Do I not have a natural appetite for that? And would not knowing myself include knowing my relationships both to the world around me and to the people I encounter?

I do in fact find that my thirst for knowledge is open-ended. Of course the limitations of my own personality place unfortunate limits on my interests, yet in general I find that I would like to know not only about this or that sort of being, but about beings of all sorts, or even the understructure of being—which is to say, metaphysical philosophy. There is more I desire to know than I shall ever have time to learn.

With these initial observations I can focus more exactly on the problem of knowing myself.

. . .

I find myself lured not just to particular goods but, somehow, to the Good. Everything I desire has the aspect of good—and that means richer existing—yet no good that I have ever experienced adequately satisfies this desire. There is always a sense of incompleteness.

In particular, my desire transcends anything material, it goes beyond space and time. Physical enjoyment breeds its own weariness, and in any case it cannot last. Yet the good that I ultimately desire is a good that in some way I would possess and possess permanently. Only a good that I could never lose would ultimately satisfy my drive.

But no matter what such a possessing might consist of, I do not see how it could be permanent. Indeed, any possessing that is permanent seems simply incompatible with human mortality. As Heidegger pointed out, we humans, precisely as such, carry in our psyches the specter of possible non-existence.

Perhaps Aquinas is right, however, in identifying this possessing with an activity of my intellect by which I grasp the Good Itself insofar as it is given to me.[5]

That my desire transcends materiality, however, is not surprising since my thought clearly does that. Signs of that are: the self-reflexivity of knowing (knowing that I know), and the human ability to grasp universal concepts both as such (even to understanding whole logical or mathematical systems of them) and as instantiated in particular bodies though not *as* universals. I grant that there is an undeniable dependence of my thinking on my brain states, yet it does not follow that thinking is nothing other than brain processes. Logically it may just as well be that the right brain processes are a necessary condition for thinking, not thinking itself, and there are strong reasons for thinking that that is exactly the case.[6]

I have argued above that Alpha adjusts each immediate aim exactly to the situation of the nascent primary being and to what is best possible for it in view of Alpha's knowledge of the universal order of possibility. It would therefore appear paradoxical, if not contradictory, that Alpha should furnish any primary being with an essential aim that is in principle impossible of fulfillment.

CONCLUSIONS AND LIMIT QUESTIONS

In the end, then, I seem to have achieved some better knowledge of myself. I understand what makes me one even though I am also complex. My unity lies in my directedness toward my essential aim, an aim

that all my parts share in. All my immediate aims and their corresponding activities arise from a drive toward my own self-fulfillment, and
this drive is an instance of the universal thrust of the act of existing
back toward its source, which is Existing Itself under the aspect of the
Good.[7] I also understand better how I relate to the world and the world
to me in causal interactivity. My perceived world is the real world,
though not the world in itself, and my perception of it and reaction to
it is part of what I am. The most meaningful aspect of such interactivity
occurs in interpersonal relationships.

Yet I am left with limit questions that philosophy seems unable to
answer. On the one hand I find myself drawn to the Good as such, but I
never encounter it. I long to possess it, but I don't even know what that
would mean, and certainly I haven't possessed it yet. And though such
possession would be incomplete if it were to be ultimately erased by
time, yet my death is inevitable. Death eventually puts an effective end
even to interpersonal relationships.

So it seems that my essential aim, which attracts me to the Good,
must necessarily be frustrated even though it is given me by Alpha
who, to speak humanly, should know better. But perhaps there is some
way in which I am to transcend even death itself and possess the Good
in a way that I cannot now imagine or conceive. Ideally I should expect
this possessing to be some form of interpersonal relationship, if that is
conceivable, with Alpha itself. How could this be possible?

Thus I find myself at the farthest boundary of philosophy, asking
questions that philosophy itself, so far as I can see, cannot answer. If
there is another horizon beyond where I have gone it does not belong to
philosophy, it belongs to religion and theology. And if that is the case,
then perhaps that itself is the most important thing about myself that I
have discovered in trying to respond to the challenge of the Oracle.

Notes

ONE.   On Being Yourself
(2008)

1. Hermann Hesse, *Demian* (New York: Bantam, 1970), 107–8.
2. Henri Bergson, *The Creative Mind* (Totowa, NJ: Littlefield, Adams, 1965), 93.

TWO.   Invitation to a Philosophic Revolution
(1971)

1. Charles Hartshorne, *The Divine Relativity: A Social Conception of God* (hereafter DR; New Haven: Yale University Press, 1948).
2. From Whitehead's letter to Schilpp in *The Philosophy of Alfred North Whitehead,* ed. Paul Arthur Schilpp, 2nd ed. (New York: Library of Living Philosophers, 1951), 664.
3. Kelvin made his celebrated observation in a lecture at the Royal Institution on April 27, 1900, published as "Nineteenth Century Clouds over the Dynamical Theory of Heat and Light," *Philosophical Magazine* 2 (1901): 1–40. A modern writer observes: "Looking back at Kelvin's comment, it is not easy to decide which is the more surprising—his honesty in his belief of the completeness of science, or the insight which enabled him to pinpoint the origin of the trouble even though he did not believe in it." And in a remark singularly appropriate to the theme of this article the author of the above statement goes on to

say: "In its decline, classical physics provides the ultimate lesson that even the greatest of scientific doctrines can eventually reach the end of its concepts and experiments, so that it must be replaced by a new doctrine" (J. Andrade e Silva and G. Lochak, *Quanta* [New York: McGraw Hill, 1969], 14–15).

4. Thomas S. Kuhn, *The Structure of Scientific Revolutions* (Chicago: University of Chicago Press, 1962).

5. Whitehead points out these two forms of progress in his *Adventures of Ideas* (hereafter AI; New York: Macmillan, 1933), 286.

6. Here I do not point to the familiar distinction between beings and principles of beings; I refer rather to the sense in which we take these principles to be "real." The will, for instance, does not belong to the commonsense horizon of knowledge, hence does not enjoy the same *sort* of reality as the piece of bread. I believe, therefore, that one would be making a category-mistake if one spoke of the will as if it were real in the same sense as an eye or an ear.

7. Compare in Whitehead: "The history of European thought, even to the present day, has been tainted by a fatal misunderstanding. It may be termed the Dogmatic Fallacy. The error consists in the persuasion that we are capable of producing notions which are adequately defined in respect to the complexity of relationship required for their illustration in the real world. Canst thou by searching describe the Universe?" (AI 185).

8. Where these problems concern the experience we call "revelation" it is also possible to throw in our philosophic hand altogether on the plea of "mystery." But mystery, like sleeping pills, is addictive and should be resorted to as seldom as possible.

9. "The chief danger in philosophy is that the dialectic deductions from inadequate formulae should exclude direct intuitions from explicit attentions" (AI 177–78).

10. AI 185–86.

11. In making these criticisms I shall freely adapt some of the criticisms of traditional scholastic philosophy made by Whitehead and also by Charles Hartshorne, particularly in DR. For the limited purposes of this article I shall confine myself to the problem of giving a philosophic account of some of the facts accepted in the Judaeo-Christian tradition. In general these are described as a variety of ways in which God has related Himself to us.

12. This of course does not contradict the traditional Franciscan view that the Incarnation would have taken place even if man had not sinned.

13. Here I readily acknowledge that the late Walter E. Stokes, S.J., has made a significant advance beyond traditional Thomism by showing how it is possible, by enlarging its principles, to posit real rather than merely rational relations of God to creatures. He does this by considering God as "person" rather than as

"nature." (See his paper, "Is God Really Related to this World?" *Proceedings of the American Catholic Philosophical Association* 39 [1965]: 135–51.) As a result of his analysis he concludes: "Between a philosophy of creative act which excludes the possibility of the real relation of God to the world and a modal philosophy which demands reciprocal relations between God and the world, it is possible to posit a 'third position': a philosophy of creative act with real but asymmetrical relations between God and the world" (151); see also his reformulation of this argument in "God for Today and Tomorrow," *The New Scholasticism* 43 (1969): 351–78.

Stokes's discovery of a way to give the notion of person an enlarged and crucial status within Thomism constitutes genuine philosophic progress. But since it is uncertain how widely his view has been accepted by Thomists, and since it falls short of that enlarged viewpoint that would conceivably reconcile process with substance philosophy, I shall confine my succeeding remarks to the more usual understanding of Thomism.

14. The classical loci in Thomas for this point are *Summa Theol.*, I, 13, 7; *Sum. cont. Gent.*, I 12; *De Pot.*, 7, 10. In the first of his articles cited above Stokes gives an excellent summary of Thomas's position (see "Is God Really Related to this World?" 147).

15. W. L. Lacy maintains that the God proved by the Five Ways need not be immutable in a sense that precludes that potentiality requisite for knowledge in conforming the knower to the known. See his "Aquinas and God's Knowledge of the Creature," *The Southern Journal of Philosophy* 2 (Summer 1964): 43–48. It seems doubtful, however, whether his view is acceptable to most Thomists.

16. Note also Hartshorne's remark: "All the time that men were being told that their 'end' was God, they were also being told, in effect, that it was of no importance to God that they attain this end, but only important to *them.* Thus essentially the end was humanly self-regarding—and in my opinion blasphemous. It made man, what he can never be, something ultimate" (DR 130–31).

17. Proslogium, chap. 8, trans. S. N. Deane, *Saint Anselm: Basic Writings* (La Salle, IL: Open Court, 1962), 13–14.

18. DR 54–55. It should be noted in passing that there is no escape from Anselm's appalling conclusion by an appeal to the humanity of Christ as the locus of a divine compassion that God could not otherwise experience. For it is not a nature that suffers but a person, one who can say "I." One notes, too, that the traditional view seems to entail that it made no difference to the Second Person, as a person, that He became incarnate.

19. *Summa Theol.*, I, 14, 5; I, 14, 6 ad 1; I, 14, 8 ad 1.

20. Indeed, how on this view are we to avoid the consequence that God does not really know me but only His own *idea* of me! On this general point see also Hartshorne, DR 118.

21. See Hartshorne, DR 11; also DR 75: "It is sheer contradiction to say that the knowledge that P is true is the *same* as the knowledge that P is not true. He who infallibly knows P is true cannot be concretely and in all respects the same subject as he who infallibly knows P is false; indeed the existence of either subject excludes the existence of the other. Thus an actual divine knowing cannot be exclusive of relations, cannot be wholly absolute."

22. Henri Bergson, *The Creative Mind,* trans. Mabelle L. Andison (Totowa, NJ: Littlefield, Adams, 1974), 110.

23. For an illuminating first introduction to Whitehead's metaphysics I commend to the reader Thomas E. Hosinski, *Stubborn Fact and Creative Advance* (Lanham, MD: Rowman & Littlefield, 1993). It is to be noted that Charles Hartshorne, whose *Divine Relativity* so much inspired this essay , differs from Whitehead in several significant respects, especially with regard to the concept of God.

24. The following essay (3) of this collection is designed to overcome, at least in part, this difficulty from within Whitehead's own metaphysical perspective.

25. In this regard Hartshorne writes: "Medieval and modern realists are right . . . in positing a one-sided relativity of subject to object; but the medieval reversal of this relativity in the case of the divine knower is unnecessary and untenable. What is necessary is that, as subject knowing all things, and as immutable absolute, God should not, in every sense, be identically the same entity. Rather, in conceiving God as absolute, we must recognize that we are abstracting from his actual subjectivity or knowing. The Absolute is God with something left out of account. God is more than his absolute character" (DR 83).

26. This is not to say that in Whitehead's view God changes. The distinction between "process" and "change" is crucial in Whitehead's philosophy, but it cannot be elaborated here. For Whitehead, God never changes as do the enduring objects of our experience (shoes, ships, and sealing wax). Hence it should not be thought that Whitehead's God is in this respect on a par with other entities. One should note, though, that in some respects Hartshorne disagrees with Whitehead on this point.

27. Hartshorne writes: "All our experience supports the view that cognitive relativity is a merit and possession, not a weakness or defect. Why should we refuse to attribute an eminent form of this relativity to God? There is but one reason: the prejudice that God must be absolute, not simply in some intelligible sense, but in every sense, intelligible or otherwise" (DR 123). The reader of this collected volume should know that W. Norris Clarke, S.J., has beautifully responded to this legitimate criticism and did it by an extrapolation of St. Thomas's own principles. See Clarke's *Person and Being* (Milwaukee: Marquette University Press, 1993).

28. Alfred North Whitehead, *Process and Reality,* corrected ed. (hereafter PR; New York: Free Press, 1978), 342.

29. And since there is no coercion, there is always the possibility of failure of the finite entity to respond adequately. God does not then choose sin, not even by way of permitting it in order to achieve a greater good. We alone choose it. From a Christian viewpoint we may say that in choosing to create free beings, God knew that the possibility of sin was thus opened up. Love is not love unless it is given freely; but then we can also freely refuse to give it. But this refusal of love, this sin, I would argue, is "foreseen" not as a concrete fact but as an abstract possibility. In any case, God's power, given the creation, does not include an absolute ability to prevent sin. This note partially anticipates essay 8, "God's Choice."

THREE.   The Temporality of Divine Freedom
(1974)

1. Lewis S. Ford, "The Non-Temporality of Whitehead's God," *International Philosophical Quarterly* 13, no. 3 (September, 1973): 347–76; hereafter "Non-Temporality."

2. Delwin Brown, "Freedom and Faithfulness in Whitehead's God," *Process Studies* 2, no. 2 (1972): 137–48, at 145; hereafter PS.

3. This is equally true for Brown, who shares this view, though he does not notice its pinch with regard to divine faithfulness, since in his societal view God's primordial nature continually reconstitutes itself in time.

4. Alfred North Whitehead, *Process and Reality,* corrected ed. (hereafter PR; New York: Free Press, 1978), 346, 351.

5. John B. Cobb, Jr., *A Christian Natural Theology* (Philadelphia: Westminster Press, 1965), 155ff.

6. Alfred North Whitehead, "Immortality," in *The Philosophy of Alfred North Whitehead,* ed. Paul Arthur Schilpp, 2nd ed. (New York: Library of Living Philosophers, 1951), 686.

7. Alfred North Whitehead, *Adventures of Ideas* (hereafter AI; New York: Macmillan, 1933).

8. Alfred North Whitehead, *Modes of Thought* (New York: Free Press, 1966), 161; 149–50; 159.

9. Henri Bergson, *Time and Free Will,* trans. F. L. Pogson (hereafter TFW; New York: Harper & Row, 1960).

10. This view resembles that of Leibniz insofar as Leibniz's God was, as Ford put it, "programmed to choose the best of all possible worlds," even down to the last detail. This is in virtue of the Principle of Sufficient Reason, of a

divine vision of all conceivable world orders hierarchically valuated, and of the tacit but essential rationalistic presupposition that abstract patterns adequately describe the concrete. Thus for Leibniz, too, there can be no significant sense to a temporality of divine freedom.

FOUR.   Philosophic Understanding and the Continuity of Becoming (1978)

I am in the debt of Andrew G. Bjelland, Lewis S. Ford, George L. Kline, and Mary Christine Morkovsky for valuable suggestions toward revising earlier versions of this paper.

1. Bertrand Russell, *A History of Western Philosophy* (New York: Simon & Schuster, 1945), 793.

2. Alfred North Whitehead, *Process and Reality,* corrected ed. (hereafter PR; New York: Free Press, 1978), vii.

3. Henri Bergson, *The Creative Mind,* trans. Mabelle L. Andison (hereafter CM; Totowa, NJ: Littlefield, Adams, 1946), 32.

4. Henri Bergson, *Creative Evolution,* trans. Arthur Mitchell (hereafter CE; New York: Modern Library, 1944), 5.

5. Henri Bergson, *Time and Free Will: An Essay on the Immediate Data of Consciousness,* trans. F. L. Pogson (hereafter TFW; New York: Harper & Row, 1960), 221.

6. Quoted in William Ernest Hocking, "Whitehead as I Knew Him," in *Alfred North Whitehead: Essays on His Philosophy,* ed. George L. Kline (Englewood Cliffs, NJ: Prentice-Hall, 1963), 8.

7. Milič Čapek, *Bergson and Modern Physics,* Boston Studies in the Philosophy of Science 7 (Dordrecht-Holland: D. Reidel, 1971), 91. Compare Whitehead's PR 35; also a parallel sentence in his essay "Time," in *Alfred North Whitehead: The Interpretation of Science,* ed. A. H. Johnson (Indianapolis: Bobbs-Merrill, 1961), 246.

8. That a general analysis of becoming may legitimately be framed within the more limited context of human freedom calls for justification. Whitehead did in fact regard the structure of immediate human experience as essentially typical of all events. (See his *Adventures of Ideas* [New York: Macmillan, 1933], 237.) This view becomes plausible if, firstly, we accept Whitehead's contention that the concrete real is wholly constituted by instances of experience ("apart from the experiences of subjects there is nothing, nothing, nothing, bare nothingness" (PR 167), and if, secondly, we agree with him that human experience lies within nature, not outside it. It is then both an instance and an outcome of the evolution-

ary process of the cosmos, and conscious experience is that cosmic process come to self-awareness. Hence we should expect, through consciousness, to discover within the process that is experience the basic structure of all process. Partly for this reason Whitehead supposes some degree of freedom in all actual entities, however primitive. This is also consistent with his teleological view of the nature of all becoming.

9. John B. Cobb, Jr., "Freedom in Whitehead's Philosophy: A Reply to Edward Pols," *The Southern Journal of Philosophy* 7 (1969–70): 409–13.

10. I must now, in this collected volume, confess that I am no longer persuaded that Cobb is right in ruling out an instantaneous event. Naturally that will depend on how you choose to define "event," but the event par excellence for these considerations is the *act of deciding* on one particular possibility for action rather than another. All the preceding acts of considering the weights of different motives, etc., will of course take time, but must the free act of deciding *itself* take time? If the free act in its essence belongs to subjective becoming, as it must, then it does not take place in abstract time ("clock time," as described in the following essays 10 and 11) but in "lived time," which is not extended or divisible in clock time. If the act of deciding is in that sense *non*-temporal, then perhaps it may as well be "instantaneous" from the temporal perspective.

11. *Science and the Modern World* (hereafter SMW; New York: Macmillan, 1953), 126. Just how Whitehead's "phases of concrescence" succeed one another without themselves being temporally divisible has been a matter of some perplexity. For present purposes I shall assume that Whitehead's position is consistent but direct the dissatisfied reader to the following discussions: William A. Christian, *An Interpretation of Whitehead's Metaphysics* (New Haven: Yale University Press, 1959), 80–81; in *The Southern Journal of Philosophy* 7 (1969–70): John B. Cobb, Jr., "Freedom in Whitehead's Philosophy," 409–13, Edward Pols, "Freedom and Agency: A Reply," 415–19, and Lewis S. Ford, "On Genetic Successiveness: A Third Alternative," 421–25; Lewis S. Ford, "Can Whitehead Provide for Real Subjective Agency? A Reply to Edward Pols's Critique," *The Modern Schoolman* 47 (1970): 209–25; in *The Modern Schoolman* 49 (1972): Edward Pols, "Whitehead on Subjective Agency: A Reply to Lewis S. Ford," 144–50, and Ford's reply to Pols, 151–52; also Ford's "Genetic and Coordinate Division Correlated," *Process Studies* 1 (Fall 1971): 199–209.

12. John B. Cobb, Jr., *A Christian Natural Theology* (hereafter CNT; Philadelphia: Westminster, 1965), 71–72.

13. Alfred North Whitehead, "Immortality," in *The Philosophy of Alfred North Whitehead,* ed. Paul Arthur Schilpp (New York: Tudor. 1951), 688–91.

14. See for instance Charles Hartshorne, "Personal Identity from A to Z," *Process Studies* 2 (1973): 209–15; Donald W. Sherburne, "Responsibility,

Punishment, and Whitehead's Theory of the Self," in Kline, *Alfred North White-head: Essays on His Philosophy,* 179–88; William S. Hamrick, "Whitehead and Merleau-Ponty: Some Moral Implications," *Process Studies* 4 (1974): 235–51.

15. The absence, in fact, of an ontological identity corresponding to the experience of identity seems to underlie the difficulties that Cobb frankly acknowledges to remain with his own view (CNT 78–79).

16. David A. Sipfle, "Henri Bergson and the Epochal Theory of Time," in *Bergson and the Evolution of Physics,* ed. P. A. Y. Gunter, 275–94 (Knoxville: University of Tennessee Press, 1969).

17. That of Vere Chapell, "Time and Zeno's Arrow," in Gunter, *Bergson and the Evolution of Physics,* 253–74.

18. Henri Bergson, *Matter and Memory,* trans. Nancy Margaret Paul and W. Scott Palmer (hereafter MM; New York: Humanities Press, 1970).

19. Henri Bergson, *Time and Free Will,* trans. F. L. Pogson (hereafter TFW; New York: Harper & Row, 1960).

20. Whitehead, "Time," 246; my emphasis.

21. "If there exists a means of possessing a reality absolutely, instead of knowing it relatively, of placing oneself within it instead of adopting points of view toward it, of having the intuition of it instead of making the analysis of it, in short, of grasping it over and above all expression, translation or symbolical representation, metaphysics is that very means. *Metaphysics is therefore the science which claims to dispense with symbols*" (CM 191; Bergson's emphasis).

22. This was suggested to me by Professor Andrew G. Bjelland.

23. In this connection it is instructive to read Bergson's own account of how he came to use the word "intuition" and with what intent: "I hesitated for a long time before using the term 'intuition'; and when I finally decided to do so I designated by this word the metaphysical function of thought: principally the intimate knowledge of the mind by the mind, secondarily the knowledge by the mind of what there is essential in matter, intelligence being, no doubt, made above all to manipulate matter and consequently to know it, but not having as its especial destiny to touch the bottom of it. . . . By an increasing care for precision I was later [after 1902] led to distinguish more clearly between intelligence and intuition, as well as between science and metaphysics" (CM 306, n. 26; see also CM 33–35, 153–59).

24. In his *Two Sources of Morality and Religion* (trans. R. Ashley Audra and Coudesley Brereton; New York: Holt, 1935), 212, Bergson refers to a kind of "fringe" or "halo" of instinct around intelligence.

25. In the same place Bergson asserts that supra- or ultra-intellectual intuition is likely to be in continuity with sensuous intuition. For Whitehead this

would directly apply to our reflective (non-intellectual, intuitive) awareness of what he calls perception in the mode of causal efficacy.

26. This use of the word "perspective" is, I think, consonant (though perhaps not identical) with Whitehead's, in which the perspective of an actual occasion lies in its prehension as objective rather than initial datum. (See PR 231, 236.)

27. Whitehead tentatively identified Bergson's "intuition" with "physical purposes" within his own scheme, and thought that it abstracts from the subjective quality of emotion and purpose (PR 33, 280). This seems to me inaccurate, but this is not the place to argue the matter.

28. Alfred North Whitehead, *Modes of Thought* (hereafter MT; New York: Free Press, 1968), 110, 116, 118.

29. I am using "complementary" in the ordinary sense, not in the technical sense of modern physics. Robert Blanché has already used the notion of complementarity to overcome some of the sharp dualisms characteristic of Bergson. But Blanché's complementarity balanced Bergson's intuition of psychological continuity with an argued "intuition of the instant." I am concerned, rather, with a certain complementarity of philosophic *methods,* intellectual and intuitive, and a correlative complementarity of conclusions as to the nature of becoming. Furthermore, Blanché appears to use the notion of complementarity in just the sense developed by Niels Bohr. This seems risky. The complementarity of macroscopic models, waves and particles, in giving us a better insight into the microworld, which is neither waves nor particles, seems ill suited for discussing Bergsonian intuition by which, if Bergson is right, we attain the real itself. See Robert Blanché, "The Psychology of Duration and the Physics of Fields," in Gunter, *Bergson and the Evolution of Physics,* 105-20.

30. Čapek, *Bergson and Modern Physics,* 170.

FIVE. Transmutation and Whitehead's Elephant
(1981)

1. Alfred North Whitehead, *Process and Reality,* corrected ed. (hereafter PR; New York: Free Press, 1978), 4.

2. Alfred North Whitehead, *Adventures of Ideas* (hereafter AI; New York: Macmillan, 1933), 321.

3. PR 251; my emphasis. I have of course given merely a sketch. I have not considered the possibility of conceptual reversion, nor have I linked this account specifically with Whitehead's general theory of perception in the mode of presentational immediacy. All that is required for my present purpose is that the account

I have given be accurate as far as it goes, not that it be exhaustive. Some principal *loci* in which Whitehead describes transmutation are PR 27, 251–54, and AI 314–16, 322–23.

4. See Galileo, "The Assayer," in *Discoveries and Opinions of Galileo,* ed. Stillman Drake (Garden City, NY: Doubleday Anchor, 1957), 274–75; and Isaac Newton, *Opticks* (New York: Dover Publications, 1952), 124–25.

5. I must in this collected volume acknowledge that my above description of Whitehead's account of sense perception is too simple. Michael Hauskeller, in his book, *Alfred North Whitehead: zur Einführung* (Hamburg: Junius, 1994), replies to my above criticism with some justice, though hardly with grace, in section 9, "Einwände gegen die Kategorie der Umwandlung," 68–75. He mentions my first difficulty, about the impossibility of microentities being colored, and passes it off as somehow not applicable to Whiteheadian perception in the mode of causal efficacy. He mainly focuses, however, on my complaint that Whitehead's theory of perception seems to exemplify a kind of naive realism inasmuch as it assumes that the brown of the elephant, for instance, is already in the elephant's hide before my perception of it, and in the same sense. He stresses, and I think rightly, that Whitehead puts perception in the mode of causal efficacy as underlying that of presentational immediacy. I should not, therefore, have given the impression that "brown," as a particular quality, lay within the actual entities of the elephant's hide in the manner conceived by naive realism. The brown was ingredient within the mutual *perceptions* of the actual entities of the hide; it pertained to their mode of experiencing. But I did in fact say that it was the (physical and conceptual) "feelings" that uniformly exhibit the eternal object in question (here: brown).

Yet Hauskeller goes on to say that my critique is "clearly unable or unwilling" to recognize that Whitehead distinguished the two modes of perception mentioned above, so that my critique acknowledges only perception in the mode of presentational immediacy (69). I am in fact quite willing to distinguish the two modes of perception, and I regret it if I gave the impression that I wasn't. Hauskeller then goes on at some length developing texts from Whitehead's *Adventures of Ideas* that are supposed to refute my critique, though, with the exception of my concession above, I fail to see how they meet the difficulty arising from *Process and Reality*. In fact, Hauskeller's development of some of those texts appears to me to be self-refuting as a response to my difficulty. Thus he invokes a passage from *Adventures of Ideas* in which Whitehead writes: "The emotional moods of the mother nursing the infant, moods of love, or gaiety, or depression, or irritation, are directly perceived on the mother's face by the infant. . . . The infant feels its mother's cheerfulness as a datum, and feels it conformally, with that affective tone. It is precipitated upon that present region occupied by the nexus of occasions which constitute the complex fact of the mother's existence, body and soul. For the infant, the Appearance includes the qualification of cheerfulness" (AI 316).

Who would contest the accuracy of Whitehead's experiential observation? But can we believe—if Whitehead stands by the passages in *Process and Reality*—that the innumerable actual entities making up the mother's face *individually experience cheerfulness,* and that the infant, feeling those innumerable, distinct micro-experiences of cheerfulness, then applies that felt cheerfulness to the face or to the mother as a whole? O fortunate world, full of tiny, cheerful actual entities!

6. I elaborate more fully on this interpretation of perceiving in "Relational Realism and the Great Deception of Sense," essay 13 of this volume, and even more fully in *Human Knowing: A Prelude to Metaphysics* (Notre Dame, IN: University of Notre Dame Press, 2005).

7. Elizabeth Kraus, *The Metaphysics of Experience* (New York: Fordham University Press 1979), 82–83.

8. Henri Bergson, *Matter and Memory,* trans. Nancy Margaret Paul and W. Scott Palmer (hereafter MM; New York: Humanities Press, 1970), 24.

9. MM 25, 276; and see 268.

10. Ivor Leclerc "The Problem of the Physical Existent," *The International Philosophical Quarterly* 9 (1969), 55; also his *The Nature of Physical Existence* (New York: Humanities Press, 1972), chaps. 23–27.

11. Edward Pols, *Meditation on a Prisoner* (Carbondale: Southern Illinois University Press, 1975), passim.

12. Paul Weiss, "Nature, God, and Man," a paper delivered at the Hartshorne Conference at the University of Chicago, November 2, 1981.

13. See F. Bradford Wallack, *The Epochal Nature of Process in Whitehead's Metaphysics* (Albany: State University of New York Press, 1980), chap. 1.

SIX.   Coming Around Again in Philosophy
(1982)

1. Proslogium, chap. 8, trans. S. N. Deane, *Saint Anselm: Basic Writings* (La Salle, IL: Open Court, 1962), 13.

2. Charles Hartshorne, *The Divine Relativity* (New Haven: Yale University Press, 1948), 55.

3. This Principle of Creative Synthesis, whose name and formulation are, as far as I remember, original, is perhaps my first written expression of the more detailed three principles and two corollaries that I develop in essay 7 and use in several later essays.

4. Alfred North Whitehead, *Modes of Thought* (New York: Free Press, 1968), 116.

5. Ibid., 110.

6. Robert Pirsig, *Zen and the Art of Motorcycle Maintenance* (New York: Bantam, 1980), 215.

7. W. Norris Clarke, S.J., *The Philosophical Approach to God: A Contemporary Neo-Thomist Perspective* (Winston-Salem, NC: Wake Forest University, 1979).

8. John Stacer, S.J., "Integrating Thomistic and Whiteheadian Perspectives on God," *International Philosophical Quarterly* 21, no. 4 (December 1981), 366.

9. I developed this point at some length five years later in "Intuition, Event-Atomism, and the Self," essay 10 of this volume.

SEVEN.   Impossible Worlds
(1983)

1. See for instance Bruce R. Reichenbach, "Must God Create the Best Possible World?" *International Philosophical Quarterly* 19 (1979): 203–12. And St. Thomas Aquinas affirms that God could always make better things than He did: *Summa Theologiae,* I, 25, 6.

2. David K. Lewis, *Counterfactuals* (Cambridge, MA: Harvard University Press, 1973), 84.

3. Ibid., 84–85.

4. Nicholas Rescher, "The Ontology of the Possible," in *Logic and Ontology,* ed. Milton Munitz (New York: New York University Press, 1973), 213. That essay is also reprinted as chap. 8 of Michael I. Loux, ed., *The Possible and the Actual* (Ithaca: Cornell University Press, 1979).

5. I should like to make my own the words of Bishop Berkeley in the Preface to the first edition of his *Treatise Concerning the Principles of Human Knowledge:* "What I here make public has, after a long and scrupulous inquiry, seemed to me evidently true and not unuseful to be known. . . . Whether it be so or no, I am content the reader should impartially examine, since I do not think myself any further concerned for the success of what I have written than as it is agreeable to truth. But to the end this may not suffer I make it my request that the reader suspend his judgment till he has once at least read the whole through with that degree of attention and thought which the subject matter shall seem to deserve" (New York: Liberal Arts Press, 1957), 4.

6. Alfred North Whitehead, *Process and Reality,* corrected ed. (hereafter PR; New York: Free Press, 1978), 3.

7. Lewis, *Counterfactuals,* 88.

8. As I mentioned in the introduction to this essay, the formulation of these principles is, as far as I now recall, my own.

9. To preclude sophisticated difficulties possibly arising from the principle of quantum indeterminacy, I provisionally, for the sake of this study, restrict discussion to the realm of ordinary perception.

10. I have added the final statement, "This is the precise location of the free act," to this collected volume.

11. In that theory, of course, in animal generation a specifically similar form is in the agents (parents); so also, in the case of artifacts, in the intention of the agent.

12. Charles Hartshorne, *Creative Synthesis and Scientific Method* (LaSalle, IL: Open Court, 1970), 64, 225.

13. Robert C. Stalnaker, "Possible Worlds," *Nous* 10 (1976): 65–75; reprinted as chap. 12 of Loux, *The Possible and the Actual.*

14. Ibid., 227.

15. Ibid., 229.

16. Phil Weiss, "Possibility: Three Recent Ontologies," *International Philosophical Quarterly* 20 (1980), 201–2.

17. Rescher, "The Ontology of the Possible," in Munitz, *Logic and Ontology,* 214.

18. Ibid., 213.

19. Ibid., 216–17.

20. Ibid., 214, 218, 220.

21. Ibid., 216, 220.

22. Ibid., 219.

23. Charles Hartshorne, *Anselm's Discovery* (LaSalle, IL: Open Court, 1964), 189–90.

24. For a summary of Molina's doctrine see the articles "Molinism" and "Futuribles" in *The New Catholic Encyclopedia* (New York: McGraw-Hill, 1967).

25. In C. I. Gerhardt, ed., *Die philosophischen Schriften von Gottfried Wilhelm Leibniz* (Hildesheim: Georg Olms, 1978), VI. Band, pp. 124–25.

26. Ibid., par. 42; my emphasis and translation.

27. As for instance in *Summa Theologiae,* I, 14, 9, c. In Thomas's language, that which is purely possible is a *ratio* or pattern for God's *scientia simplicis intelligentiae,* not an *exemplar* for God's mind. See also *Summa Theologiae,* I, 15, 3, ad 2.

28. Difficult, but not impossible. Leibniz thought God simply must not have had a better choice, and Alvin Plantinga has recently tried to show that this might indeed be the case. In *The Nature of Necessity* (Oxford: Clarendon Press, 1974, esp. chap. 9), he ingeniously argues that the existence of God is logically compatible with that of moral evil in the world since it is at least *possible* that the

only possible worlds available for God's choice are worlds that contain moral evil. Unfortunately for the (literally) triumphant view he takes of this argument, his demonstration hinges on the assumption that it is possible that God knows that *every* free agent would commit some moral misdeed in any possible world whatsoever. But it *cannot* be possible that God knows this, since there is just no such thing as what a purely hypothetical free agent *would* definitively do. Plantinga freely grants that to suppose that there is something specific that a hypothetical agent *would* do in a particular situation is to make an assumption, an assumption he confesses himself unable to prove (p. 180). But that assumption is just Molinism all over again and must be ruled out. This affinity between Molina and Plantinga has been pointed out by Robert Merrihew Adams in "Middle Knowledge and the Problem of Evil," *American Philosophical Quarterly* 14 (1977): 109–17.

29. Stalnaker, "Possible Worlds," in Loux, *The Possible and the Actual,* 229.

30. I am in the debt of several philosopher friends for helpful criticisms of earlier versions of this essay, especially to Richard J. Blackwell, Daniel O. Dahlstrom, Vincent G. Potter, S.J., and Youree Watson, S.J.

EIGHT.   God's Choice: Reflections on Evil in a Created World
(1984)

1. I say that the choice was "essentially" one of creating or not creating, rather than of picking out an exact scenario of human history. This does not preclude God's setting whatever conditions He likes on the environment or on the initial situation of that history.

2. The Third Principle is reminiscent of Whitehead's "ontological principle." At the same time it rules out Whitehead's supposition of an autonomously existent and inexplicable multiplicity of discrete, though interrelated, atemporal patterns of existence (his "eternal objects").

3. See especially Bergson's essay "The Possible and the Real," chap. 3 of *The Creative Mind,* trans. Mabelle L. Andison (Totowa, NJ: Littlefield, Adams, 1965).

4. The reader will notice that the principles developed here flatly contradict not only Leibniz's presupposition of possible worlds available for creation, but also Molina's positing of conditional futures (or "futuribles") open to divine inspection.

5. The majority of modern process philosophers deny any such transcendent divine knowledge, at least of what is to us future, but they do so because in

one way or another they put God into time, a move I am unwilling to make and see no adequate reason for making.

6. Romans 8:21–23.

7. "Neque enim deus omnipotens . . . cum summe bonus sit, ullo modo sineret mali esse aliquid in operibus suis nisi usque adeo esset omnipotens et bonus ut bene faceret et de malo"; *Enchiridion,* III, par. 11; quoted by Aquinas in *Summa Theologiae,* I, 2, 3 ad 1.

NINE.   Whitehead's Misconception of "Substance" in Aristotle (1985)

1. Aristotle, *Metaphysics,* trans. W. D. Ross, in *Basic Works of Aristotle,* ed. Richard McKeon (New York: Random House, 1941), Zeta, chap. 1, 1028b2–4.

2. Leonard J. Eslick, "Substance, Change, and Causality in Whitehead," *Philosophy and Phenomenological Research* 18 (June 1958): 503–13, at 504.

3. Charles Hartshorne, "Whitehead on Process: A Reply to Professor Eslick," *Philosophy and Phenomenological Research* 18 (June 1958): 514–20.

4. The other principal factors, as far as I can judge, are Zeno's arguments (see Alfred North Whitehead, *Process and Reality,* corrected ed. [hereafter PR; New York: Free Press, 1978], 68–70, 106–8) and the tendency in modern science to view nature in terms of quanta (see Alfred North Whitehead, *Science and the Modern World* [New York: Macmillan, 1953], chap. 8). If, as I think can be argued, neither of these considerations is a cogent argument against the possibility of any sort of metaphysics of Entity, then the question of the validity of Whitehead's rejection of Aristotle's notion of substance takes on special importance. It may be the last substantial foundation, so to speak, of the modern antisubstance bias.

5. Henri Bergson, *The Creative Mind,* trans. Mabelle L. Andison (Totowa, NJ: Littlefield, Adams, 1974), 110.

6. PR 49–50.

7. Hartshorne, "Whitehead on Process: A Reply to Professor Eslick," 514.

8. Charles Hartshorne, "Recollections of Famous Philosophers—and Other Important Persons," *Southern Journal of Philosophy* 8 (Spring 1970): 67–82, at 72.

9. Eslick points out that at the crucial passage in *Process and Reality* in which Whitehead says Descartes' concept of substance is a true derivative from Aristotle's (PR 50, Whitehead's note 14), Whitehead refers the reader not to Aristotle's *Categories* but to W. D. Ross's book *about* Aristotle (Eslick, "Substance," 504).

10. PR 77–78. Leclerc points out that the notion of substance that White-head was most concerned to attack was that of Locke. It is also clear that White-head saw in Aristotle's notion the clear forerunner of that of Locke, as well as that of Descartes. Leclerc in effect grants as much in his subsequent explana-tions. See Ivor Leclerc, "Whitehead's Transformation of the Notion of Substance," *Philosophical Quarterly* 3 (July 1953): 225–43, esp. 225–26 and n. 6.

11. Joseph Owens, *The Doctrine of Being in the Aristotelian Metaphysics* (Toronto: Pontifical Institute of Mediaeval Studies, 1951), 72.

12. *Categories,* trans. E. M. Edghill, in Ross, *Basic Works of Aristotle,* chap. 5, 2a11–2b6, with substitution, here and henceforth, of "Entity" or "entity" for "sub-stance."

13. W. D. Ross, *Aristotle* (New York: Routledge, 1995), 22.

14. Aristotle, *Categories,* chap. 2, 1a17–23. Confusion readily arises from this passage inasmuch as Aristotle here intermixes a linguistic relation ("predicable of" a subject) with an ontological relation ("present in" a subject).

15. This relation to Plato was called to my attention by Professor Richard J. Blackwell of Saint Louis University. I am also indebted to him for other sugges-tions concerning an earlier version of this essay.

16. Aristotle, *Categories,* chap. 5, 4a10–21; my emphasis.

17. Ibid., 4a30–4b3, emphasis added.

18. Ivor Leclerc, *The Nature of Physical Existence* (New York: Humanities Press, 1972), 257–58.

19. Ross, *Aristotle,* 171; Ross's emphasis.

TEN.   Intuition, Event-Atomism, and the Self
(1987)

1. Etienne Gilson, *The Unity of Philosophical Experience* (San Francisco: Ignatius Press, 1999), 246.

2. See Henri Bergson, *Creative Evolution* (Lanham, MD: University Press of America, 1984), "Editor's Introduction," xvii.

3. Henri Bergson, *The Creative Mind,* trans. Mabelle L. Andison (hereafter CM; Totowa, NJ: Littlefield, Adams, 1946), 109–10.

4. A few examples: Ivor Leclerc and his theory of compound substances, in *The Nature of Physical Existence* (London: Humanities Press, 1972), esp. chap. 24; Edward Pols's criticism of Whitehead's theory of the person, as in *Whitehead's Metaphysics* (1967) and his theory of "act-temporality" in *Meditation on a Prisoner* (1975), esp. chap. 4 (both pub. Carbondale: Southern University of Illinois Press); Paul Weiss, *Reality* (New York: P. Smith, 1949), 207–8, and *Modes of Being* (Car-

bondale: Southern University of Illinois Press, 1958), 30–34, 242; F. Bradford Wallack, *The Epochal Nature of Process in Whitehead's Metaphysics* (Albany: State University of New York, 1980), passim.

5. Henri Bergson, *An Introduction to Metaphysics,* trans. T. E. Hulme (hereafter IM; Indianapolis: Bobbs-Merrill, 1955), 24.

6. For a challenge to this antithesis, see David A. Sipfle, "Henri Bergson and the Epochal Theory of Time," in *Bergson and the Evolution of Physics,* ed. P. A. Y. Gunter, 275–94 (Knoxville: University of Tennessee Press, 1969); also my reply to the challenge, "Philosophic Understanding and the Continuity of Becoming," essay 4 of this volume.

7. Alfred North Whitehead, *Process and Reality,* corrected ed. (hereafter PR; New York: Free Press, 1978), 35.

8. PR 69. Another strong reason for Whitehead's adopting a corpuscular or epochal theory of reality was the increasing awareness among physicists of the importance of describing nature in terms of quanta. See, for instance, his *Science and the Modern World* (New York: Macmillan, 1967), chap. 8; also PR 78, 239.

9. Henri Bergson, *Time and Free Will,* trans. F. L. Pogson (hereafter TFW; New York: Harper & Row, 1960), 128; Bergson's emphasis. On the very next page Bergson goes on to elaborate this idea in a way curiously like the distinction Whitehead makes between perception in the mode of presentational immediacy and that in the mode of causal efficacy: "Our perceptions, sensations, emotions and ideas occur under two aspects: the one clear and precise, but impersonal; the other confused, ever changing, and inexpressible, because language cannot get hold of it without arresting its mobility or fit it into its common-place forms without making it public property."

10. Henri Bergson, *Matter and Memory,* trans. N. M. Paul and W. S. Palmer (New York: Humanities Press, 1970), 243–44; Bergson's emphasis.

11. Bergson writes: "Freedom is therefore a fact, and among the facts which we observe there is none clearer. All the difficulties of the problem, and the problem itself, arise from the desire to endow duration with the same attributes as extensity, to interpret a succession by a simultaneity, and to express the idea of freedom in a language into which it is obviously untranslatable" (TFW 227).

12. It is an old Aristotelian principle that powers are distinguished by their activities and by their objects. I suspect that we might say here that diverse conclusions concerning personal identity are a natural function of different mental activities applied to different aspects of reality.

13. Alfred North Whitehead, *Modes of Thought* (New York: Free Press, 1968), 110.

14. P. A. Y. Gunter, "Bergson's Philosophical Method and Its Application to the Sciences," *Southern Journal of Philosophy* 16, no. 3 (1978): 167–81, at 175.

15. See for instance William A. Christian, *An Interpretation of Whitehead's Metaphysics* (New Haven: Yale University Press, 1967), 80–82; also Donald W. Sherburne, *A Key to Whitehead's Process and Reality* (New York: Macmillan, 1966), 38–40. The seemingly paradoxical nature of Whitehead's doctrine is heightened by a very natural tendency to try, as Sherburne does, to schematize the relations of the phases by means of a visual diagram. Of its very nature such a schematization implicitly attributes to the successiveness of the phases the continuity appropriate to space, not that appropriate to subjectivity, and hence exacerbates rather than relieves the difficulty.

16. This is what I proceeded to do in essay 9 of this volume.

ELEVEN   Faces of Time
(1987)

1. Aristotle, *Physics,* trans. R. P. Haride and R. K. Gaye, in *Basic Works of Aristotle,* ed. Richard McKeon (New York: Random House, 1941), 219b2.

2. Sir Isaac Newton, *Principia Mathematica,* trans. A Motte and F. Cajori (Berkeley: University of California Press, 1962), 6.

3. William Wordsworth, "*Ode:* Intimations of Immortality from Recollections of Early Childhood," in *Immortal Poems of the English Language,* ed. Oscar Williams (New York: Washington Square, 1964), 260.

4. On this ontic unity of human actions, see Edward Pols, *Meditation on a Prisoner* (Carbondale: Southern Illinois University Press, 1975), passim. Alfred North Whitehead, also realizing that human actions cannot be thus indefinitely subdivided, tried to escape Zeno's disintegrating argument by regarding all activity, including human actions, as basically quantized, made up of societies of inheriting, ontic microevents. Pols argues in several places, including *Whitehead's Metaphysics* (Carbondale: Southern Illinois University Press,1967) and *The Acts of Our Being* (Amherst: University of Amherst Press, 1982), that this kind of atomic metaphysics is neither necessary nor satisfactory.

5. Saint Augustine, *Confessions,* trans. Rex Warner (New York: Mentor, 1963), XI, 20.

6. Augustine wrote, for instance: "The mind is moved through time when it recalls what had been forgotten, or learns what it did not know, or wills what it had rejected—but the body is moved through place. . . . The created spirit moves itself through time and its body through time and place." Quoted in Vernon Bourke, ed., *The Essential Augustine* (Indianapolis: Hackett, 1978), 64.

7. T. S. Eliot, *Four Quartets* (New York: Harcourt, 1971), lines 137–40.

8. This is the way, I suspect, that brute animals live—in conditioned responses to a world that is felt simply as present, never as past or future, a world, in short, without any time at all.

9. Henri Bergson, *An Introduction to Metaphysics,* trans. T. E. Hulme (Indianapolis: Bobbs, 1955), 162. It is, I believe, Bergsonian intuition that Whitehead in effect appealed to in pointing to our immediate awareness of "perception in the mode of causal efficacy." By opening our inner eye to what gives itself in perception, we are, he thought (Hume—and especially Hume—notwithstanding), aware of the continuity of the present with the immediate past, aware of the influence of the past (and in its own way, of the future) on the present, and aware of the value-weight of experience.

10. In "The Feeling for the Future," *Process Studies* 3, no. 2 (1973): 100–103.

TWELVE.   Fatalism and Truth about the Future
(1992)

1. Whether it makes any sense to speak of a proposition as true "now" or at any other time will be considered below.

2. Aristotle, *De Interpetatione,* trans. J. L. Ackrill (Oxford: Oxford University Press, 1963), chap. 9, 18b9–16.

3. Steven M. Cahn, *Fate, Logic, and Time* (New Haven: Yale University Press, 1967), 8.

4. This sense focuses on the comparative "taller than" as requiring both *relata* if it is to be affirmable or deniable at all. There is another sense, utilized by Aristotle in *Categories,* chap. 10, in which Mary's assertion would be regarded as false. In that sense Aristotle appears to understand Mary's statement as asserting that her own state of being has the character of being taller than her sister, but, since she has no sister, it obviously doesn't. In that same sense Aristotle would grant that if Mary made the contradictory statement, "I am not taller than my sister," her new statement would be true. This again focuses not on the other *relatum* but on Mary's state of being that is *not* characterized by her being taller than a non-existent sister. In the first sense, however, the sense I am using, it makes no sense to say that it is true or that it is false that Mary exceeds in height a person who does not exist at all.

5. This definition of fatalism leaves unspecified the reasons one might have for asserting fatalism. Taken with Thesis 2, the definition amounts to rejecting any definition of fatalism that implies that the laws of logic alone suffice to prove that the future is fixed, given any present.

6. This is only another way of saying that *esse* enjoys an ontological priority to its forms. That metaphysics enjoys precedence over logic is also an essential presupposition in making metaphysical sense of the popular notion of "possible worlds." One may note here my essay, "Impossible Worlds," essay 7 in this volume, in which I argue that most of these "possible worlds" aren't in fact possible since they are metaphysically incoherent. See also essay 14.

THIRTEEN.   Relational Realism and the Great Deception of Sense
(1994)

1. Thomas Hobbes, *Human Nature,* in *The English Works of Thomas Hobbes,* vol. 4, ed. W. Molesworth (London: Scientia, 1966), chap. 2, 8–9, italics in the original.

2. Bertrand Russell, *The Problems of Philosophy* (Oxford: Oxford University Press, 1912).

3. Galileo Galilei, *The Assayer,* ed. Stillman Drake (Garden City, NY: Doubleday Anchor, 1957), 274.

4. Isaac Newton, *Opticks* (New York: Dover, 1952), 124–25.

5. John Locke, *An Essay Concerning Human Understanding,* ed. P. H. Nidditch (Oxford: Clarendon Press, 1975), book 4, chap. 4, 563. Hume agrees as well: "The slightest philosophy," he says, "teaches us, that nothing can ever be present to the mind but an image or perception, and that the senses are only the inlets, through which these images are conveyed, without being able to produce any immediate intercourse between the mind and the object"; David Hume, *An Enquiry Concerning Human Understanding,* ed. P. H. Nidditch (Oxford: Clarendon Press, 1975), sect. 12, par. 118, p. 152.

6. This holds even though they might also grant that they could not see a red light unless at the same time they had an *impression* of a red light—which impression, of course, is not an impression of *seeing* a red light.

7. Plato, *Republic,* book 7.

8. It is an historical irony that Galileo and Newton, the great founders of classical modern science with its aim at a purely objective, quantitative description of the world itself apart from the subjective perspective of observers, should at the same time have numbered themselves among the philosophers who affirmed that we never sensibly encounter the objective world itself but only our own private sense impressions provoked by it.

9. This is entirely in agreement with the epistemology of St. Thomas Aquinas and of Aristotle, particularly as found in the latter's *De Anima,* book 3, so that I make no claim that the view I here develop is entirely novel. If Aristotle was

basically right—that the act of perception is the actualizing of both the perceiver (as such) and the perceived (as such) in their mutual relationship—he still is.

10. The ontological and epistemological status of the relational table will be considered in some detail below.

11. Hume, *Enquiry,* sect. 4, part 1, p. 29.

12. Hume, *Enquiry,* sect. 5, part 1, p. 41.

13. Aristotle, *Physics,* trans. W. D. Ross, in *Basic Works of Aristotle,* ed. Richard McKeon (New York: Random House, 1941), book 3, chap. 3, 202a18–22. And a few lines later he added: "It is *not* absurd that the actualization of one thing should be in another. Teaching is the activity of a person who can teach, yet the operation is performed *on* some patient—it is not cut adrift from a subject, but is of *A* on *B*" (202b5–7).

14. Hume, *Enquiry,* sect. 4, part 1, p. 29; sect. 7, part 1, p. 63.

15. Alfred North Whitehead, *Process and Reality,* corrected ed. (New York: Free Press, 1978), 175.

16. The phrase "relational realism" is exactly apt but not novel. It was already used, for instance, by W. Norris Clarke, S.J., in his essay, "Action as the Self-Revelation of Being: A Central Theme in the Thought of St. Thomas" in *History of Philosophy in the Making,* ed. Linus J. Thro, S.J., 63–80 (Washington DC: University Press of America, 1982), 76.

17. Bertrand Russell, *Portraits from Memory and Other Essays* (New York: Simon and Schuster, 1956), 39.

18. Immanuel Kant, *Critique of Pure Reason,* trans. Norman Kemp Smith (New York: St. Martin's Press, 1965), A30, pp. 73–74.

19. See especially Whitehead's *Process and Reality,* part 2, chap. 8, and also his *Symbolism* (New York: Capricorn Books, 1959), chap. 2. We have already noted Whitehead's example of the man in the dark room who claims that the sudden light made him blink, and that he knows this because he felt it. Besides this feeling of the causal impact of the world upon us, and inextricably connected with it, there are two other chief dimensions of experience that Whitehead thinks are immediately given in this mode of perception. One is the feeling of the ongoing *derivation* of the present from the immediate past. The other is the value dimension of experience, its worth. In the remarkable sixth lecture of *Modes of Thought* (New York: Free Press, 1968), Whitehead repeatedly juxtaposes these latter two aspects of perception.

20. John R. Searle, *Intentionality: An Essay in the Philosophy of Mind* (Cambridge: Cambridge University Press, 1983), 74.

21. In Whitehead's metaphysics, one actual entity is not only felt by another as causally influential upon it, it is an intrinsic constituent of the very identity of the entity feeling it.

FOURTEEN.   Why Possible Worlds Aren't
(1996)

1. David Lewis, *On the Plurality of Worlds* (hereafter OPW; New York: Basil Blackwell, 1986), 207.

2. OPW 141.

3. Etienne Gilson, *The Unity of Philosophical Experience* (Westminster, MD: Christian Classics, 1982), 302–3.

4. Alfred North Whitehead, *Process and Reality,* corrected ed. (hereafter PR; New York: Free Press, 1978), 6.

5. The reader will by now recognize these principles from earlier essays in this volume, as well as in my *Making Sense of Your Freedom* (Ithaca, NY: Cornell University Press; repr. Notre Dame, IN: University of Notre Dame Press, 2005). They amount to my reformulation of a fundamental conceptuality of Henri Bergson.

6. Here I am using "actual" and "actuality" in a broader sense than does Lewis, but the difference is irrelevant to this principle.

7. Principle (C) bears an obvious resemblance to Whitehead's "ontological principle" as described in his eighteenth Category of Explanation: "That every condition to which the process of becoming conforms in any particular instance has its reason *either* in the character of some actual entity in the actual world of that concrescence, *or* in the character of the subject which is in the process of concrescence. This category of explanation is termed the 'ontological principle.' It could also be termed the 'principle of efficient, and final, causation.' This ontological principle means that actual entities are the only *reasons;* so that to search for a *reason* is to search for one or more actual entities" (PR 24).

8. Henri Bergson, "The Possible and the Real," in *The Creative Mind* (Totowa, NJ: Littlefield, Adams, 1975), 101; my bracketed elucidations.

9. If it is true that a Mozart can conceive in his mind an entire symphony, and perhaps all at once, then I would grant that that conception constitutes the definiteness of the symphony even prior to its being written down or performed. The point is that the form of definiteness had no existence prior to Mozart's creative activity, whether that was purely mental or also physical.

10. Willard Van Orman Quine, *From a Logical Point of View* (Cambridge, MA: Harvard University Press, 1953), 4.

11. Throughout this essay I use the term "agent" broadly to refer to any originative cause, regardless of whether it is conscious or not.

12. This is not to say that they are omni-temporal, as if they existed at all times, but rather that, precisely as patterns, they contain no reference to temporal realization at all.

13. In a manner analogous to that of this essay, Lewis S. Ford has called attention to the difficulty of reconciling Whitehead's theory of eternal objects with Whitehead's "ontological principle." Ford elaborates this difficulty and suggests an emendation of Whitehead's metaphysics to circumvent it. See Lewis S. Ford, "The Creation of Eternal Objects," *The Modern Schoolman* 71 (1994): 191–222.

14. David Lewis, *Counterfactuals* (Cambridge, MA: Harvard University Press 1973), 84.

15. OPW viii.

16. Here I have avoided using the word "actual," to which Lewis has attributed a special meaning. As the reader probably knows, Lewis takes "actual" to be an indexical term, like "here" or "now"—that is, as bearing an implicit reference to the world of the speaker. Thus "actual" refers exclusively to events taking place in the speaker's own world. This allows Lewis to deny any special priority to the world that we inhabit since, as he says, inhabitants of other possible worlds have as much right to refer to their own worlds as actual as we do to our own. (Lewis, *Counterfactuals,* 85–86.)

17. I have sketched what I take to be some features of an appropriate theory of agency in chap. 7 of *Making Sense of Your Freedom.*

18. OPW 2.

19. Here and hereafter I decline to restrict the word "actual" to Lewis's indexical sense.

20. Thomas Aquinas, *Commentary on Aristotle's De Interpretatione,* in *Aquinas: Selected Philosophical Writings,* trans. Timothy McDermott (Oxford: Oxford University Press, 1993), 1.9 (18b26–19a22), p. 277.

21. Nicholas Rescher comes close to this view when he insists that the human mind plays an essential role in establishing possibilities. He writes: "It is my central thesis that by the very nature of hypothetical possibilities they cannot exist as such, but must be thought of: They must by hypothesized, or imagined, or assumed, or something of this sort." In "The Ontology of the Possible," reprinted in *The Possible and the Actual,* ed. Michael Loux (Ithaca, NY: Cornell University Press, 1979), 167. Yet he seems not to go far enough, for he goes on to say that such a state of affairs need not *actually* be conceived but must be conceiv*able* (169). This appears to assume an intrinsic definiteness of these possible objects of the mind apart from their being actually conceived. If so, it violates the above principles since it renders inexplicable the assumed definiteness of these unconceived but conceivable states of affairs.

22. Robert Merrihew Adams "Theories of Actuality," *Nous* 8 (1974): 211–31; reprinted in Loux, *The Possible and the Actual,* chap. 10.

23. Alvin Plantinga, *The Nature of Necessity* (Oxford: Clarendon Press, 1974), 45.

24. If one chose to introduce God for this purpose, as Leibniz seems to have done, it would make God not only an agent but the sole agent. If it is God who from eternity decides the definiteness of all actual events, then there is no deciding left over for temporal agents. But that is just to deny, it seems to me, that there are any temporal agents at all. The above principles presuppose creative, decision-making activity on the part of temporal agents.

25. OPW 3.

26. See Pegis's introduction in Anton C. Pegis, ed., *Introduction to Saint Thomas Aquinas* (New York: Modern Library, 1948), xviii.

27. Charles Hartshorne, *Anselm's Discovery* (LaSalle, IL: Open Court, 1965), 189–90.

28. OPW 23.

29. L. Frank Baum, *The Wizard of Oz* (Indianapolis: Bobbs-Merrill, 1903), 152.

FIFTEEN.   Proposal for a Thomistic-Whiteheadian
Metaphysics of Becoming
(2000)

1. Alfred North Whitehead, *Process and Reality,* corrected ed. (hereafter PR; New York: Free Press, 1978), 6.

2. Thomas S. Kuhn, *The Structure of Scientific Revolutions,* 3rd ed. (Chicago: University of Chicago Press, 1996), 77.

3. Etienne Gilson, *The Unity of Philosophical Experience* (Westminster, MD: Christian Classics, 1982), 307.

4. That these criticisms were not always on the mark may well have been due in part to the fluidity of the understanding of the Thomistic position even among Thomists. Thomas has probably never been understood so well as during the Thomistic renaissance during the first third of the twentieth century, but that new understanding entailed a kind of evolutionary reconstruction of Thomas's thought by such thinkers as Gilson, Maritain, Sertillanges, Geiger, Garrigou-Lagrange, and others, including, most lately, W. Norris Clarke, S.J.

5. See particularly Charles Hartshorne, *The Divine Relativity* (New Haven: Yale University Press, 1964).

6. Terence L. Nichols, "Aquinas's Concept of Substantial Form and Modern Science," *International Philosophical Quarterly* 36 (1996): 303–18.

7. Nichols, "Aquinas's Concept," 313; and see Thomas's *Summa Theologiae* (hereafter ST) I, 76, 4 ad 4.

8. Huston Smith, "Has Process Theology Dismantled Classical Theism?" *Theology Digest* 35 (1988): 303–18.

9. On this latter point, see PR 112, and Reto Luzius Fetz, "In Critique of Whitehead," *Process Studies* 20 (1991): 1–9; also Rem B. Edwards, "The Human Self: An Actual Entity or a Society?" *Process Studies* 5 (1975): 195–203.

10. See particularly W. Norris Clarke, S.J., *Person and Being* (Milwaukee: Marquette University Press, 1993).

11. In essay 9 of this volume.

12. Whitehead himself writes: "The factor of temporal endurance selected for any one actuality will depend upon its initial 'subjective aim.'" (PR 128). Yet for Whitehead, because of his option for an event-microatomism, such an entity cannot be anything like a human being.

13. For a strong development of this argument see J. P. Moreland, "An Enduring Self: The Achilles' Heel of Process Philosophy," *Process Studies* 17 (1988): 193–99. The structure of Moreland's argument is related to Kant's First Analogy and his Third Paralogism, and it has also been exploited by H. D. Lewis and A. C. Ewing. It begins with the felt character of connected experience itself: "In successive moments of experience, I not only have an awareness of those successive experiences, but I also am aware of an I which is identical in each moment and which is identical to my current self" (Moreland, "Enduring Self," 193).

14. This muddling of the unity and the individuation of a primary being is a blunder that I unfortunately repeated in my *Coming To Be* (Albany: State University of New York Press, 2001), 84–88, but that I have tried to correct in my *Aims: A Brief Metaphysics for Today* (Notre Dame, IN: University of Notre Dame Press, 2007), section 5.4, "Individuation," and that I want now to acknowledge in this volume. The correct view is that the root principle of numerical individuation from other entities of the same species cannot be qualitative, hence cannot lie in the subjective aim, but depends on the particularity of the entity's bodily, space-time location. Thomas and Aristotle are right about that. But the intrinsic *unity* of the entity within itself is indeed furnished by its subjective aim, just as it is for Thomas by the substantial form.

15. For some of these suggestions one may see the following: Fetz, "In Critique of Whitehead"; Lewis S. Ford, "Inclusive Occasions," in *Process in Context: Essays in Post-Whiteheadian Perspectives,* ed. Ernest Wolf-Gazo, 107–36 (Bern: Peter Lang, 1988); Ivor Leclerc on the "compound individual" in *The Nature of Physical Existence* (New York: Humanities Press, 1972), chap. 24; and John B. Cobb, Jr.'s suggestion of "overlapping occasions" in his *A Christian Natural Theology* (Philadelphia: The Westminster Press, 1965), 82–87.

16. In thus accepting Whitehead's hypothesis of the divine origin of all subjective aims, I reject the obvious complaint that this smacks of introducing a *deus
ex machina* arbitrarily invoked to get ourselves out of a metaphysical pickle. Here
is a clear point of intersection between the Thomistic theory of participation in
esse and the Whiteheadian analysis of temporal becoming. Why should it not be
expected that the universal source of existence is also the universal source of both
the order and the novelty found in the fabric of existence?

17. I have later attempted this in my two books mentioned above, *Coming To
Be* and *Aims.*

SIXTEEN.   Epochal Time and the Continuity of Experience
(2003)

1. One is liable, for instance, to find in the local Yellow Pages a heading
such as the following: "Metaphysics: See Astrologers, Psychic Consulting &
Healing Services, Spiritual Consultants, Yoga Instruction. . . ."

2. Alfred North Whitehead, *Process and Reality,* corrected ed. (hereafter
PR; New York: Free Press, 1978), 61, 67.

3. See for instance Bergson's "Introduction to Metaphysics," which is
chap. 6 of his *Creative Mind,* trans. Mabelle L. Andison (hereafter CM; Totowa,
NJ: Littlefield, Adams, 1974).

4. Henri Bergson, *Creative Evolution,* trans. Arthur Mitchell (New York:
Modern Library, 1944), 2–3.

5. Henri Bergson, *Time and Free Will* (hereafter TFW; New York: Harper
and Row, 1960), 128.

6. William James, *Some Problems of Philosophy* (Cambridge, MA: Harvard
University Press, 1979), 80. Sandra Rosenthal has argued in *Time, Continuity, and
Indeterminacy* (Albany: State University of New York Press, 2000), 123, that in the
context James likely had something rather different in mind than the interpretation Whitehead gave to the passage.

7. That a general analysis of becoming may legitimately be framed within
the more limited context of human freedom calls for justification. Whitehead did
in fact regard the structure of immediate human experience as essentially typical
of all events. (See again PR 112, and his *Adventures of Ideas* [New York: Macmillan: 1933], 237). This view becomes plausible if, first, we accept Whitehead's
contention that the concrete real is wholly constituted by instances of experience
("apart from the experiences of subjects there is nothing, nothing, bare nothingness" [PR 167]) and if, second, we agree with him that human experience lies

within nature, not outside it. It is then both an instance and an outcome of the evolutionary process of the cosmos, and conscious experience is that cosmic process come to self-awareness. Hence we should expect, through consciousness, to discover within the process that is experience the basic structure of all process. Partly for this reason Whitehead supposes some degree of freedom in all actual entities, however primitive. This is also consistent with his teleological view of the nature of all becoming.

8. John B. Cobb, Jr., "Freedom in Whitehead's Philosophy: A Reply to Edward Pols," *The Southern Journal of Philosophy* 7 (1969–70): 409–13. I am no longer entirely persuaded by Cobb's argument, but this is not the place to disagree with it and it still seems to me the clearest form of Whitehead's position.

9. But see the remarks toward the end of the introduction (above) to this essay.

10. Alfred North Whitehead, *Science and the Modern World* (New York: Free Press, 1967), 126.

11. In Lewis S. Ford, *The Emergence of Whitehead's Metaphysics* (Albany: State University of New York Press, 1984), 51–65 and 247, Ford speculates on how Whitehead came to adopt this theory.

12. Rosenthal, *Time, Continuity, and Indeterminacy,* 29.

13. See, for instance, William A. Christian, *An Interpretation of Whitehead's Metaphysics* (New Haven: Yale University Press, 1959), 80-81; Lewis S. Ford, "On Genetic Successiveness: A Third Alternative," *The Southern Journal of Philosophy* 7 (1969–70): 421–25; Lewis S. Ford, "Can Whitehead Provide for Real Subjective Agency? A Reply to Edward Pols' Critique," *The Modern Schoolman* 47 (1970): 209–25; in *The Modern Schoolman* 49 (1972): Edward Pols, "Whitehead on Subjective Agency: A Reply to Lewis S. Ford," 144–50, and Ford's reply to Pols, 151–52. Also see Lewis S. Ford, "Genetic and Coordinate Division Correlated," *Process Studies* 1 (1971): 199–209; and John W. Lango, "The Time of Whitehead's Concrescence," *Process Studies* 30 (2001): 3–21.

14. Alfred North Whitehead, *Modes of Thought* (New York: Free Press, 1968), 148.

15. Etienne Gilson, *The Unity of Philosophical Experience* (San Francisco: Ignatius Press, 1999), 243.

16. Saint Augustine, *Confessions,* trans. Henry Chadwick (Oxford: Oxford University Press, 1992), XI, 20, p. 235.

17. See TFW 128, 226.

18. Sir Arthur Eddington, *The Nature of the Physical World* (Ann Arbor: The University of Michigan Press, 1963), xi–xiv.

19. T. S. Eliot, *Four Quartets,* "Little Gidding" (San Diego: Harcourt Brace Jovanovich, 1971), 59.

SEVENTEEN.   "Know Yourself!"
(2007)

1. E. B. White, "The Door," in *50 Great Short Stories,* ed. Milton Crane (New York: Bantam Books, 1971), 288.

2. Aristotle, *Nicomachean Ethics,* book 10, chap. 7.

3. Notice that this is a distinct question from asking the source of my individuation. I did not keep this distinction sufficiently in mind in my book *Coming To Be* (Albany: State University of New York Press, 2001).

4. "Alpha" in *Aims* is a purely philosophical concept considered apart from any religious or historical considerations.

5. See Thomas Aquinas, *Summa Theologiae* I-II, 2, 8.

6. I have given a cumulative argument for this conclusion in *Human Knowing: A Prelude to Metaphysics* (Notre Dame, IN: University of Notre Dame Press, 2005).

7. This drive toward the Good would naturally ground an ontology-based ethics.

Index

act and potency, 15

"actual," meaning of, for David Lewis,
    261n16

Adams, Robert Merrihew: on Alvin
    Plantinga and Molinism, 252n28;
    on possible worlds, 79, 185,
    193–94

aims: initial (Whiteheadian),
    particular, and subjective, 206–7;
    origin of subjective aims, 210,
    264n16

ancillarity of intelligence to intuition,
    51–52, 55

Anselm, Saint, 13, 70

appearance and reality, 170–73; a third
    possibility, 173–74, 180

Aquinas. *See* Thomas Aquinas, Saint

Aristotle: the causality of the cause is
    in the effect, 175; the effect of his
    logic on later metaphysics, 116;
    and Parmenides, 86; on
    potentiality, 78, 85; on "the sea
    battle tomorrow," 153, 158

Augustine, Saint: perplexity over the
    nature of time, 141, 224–25;
    recognition of two kinds of time,
    142, 146–47, 223–24

becoming: and being, principles of,
    186–90; difficulties with epochal
    view, 44–46; as epochal
    (Whitehead), 42–44, 138;
    proposed as both epochal and
    continuous (complementary), 55;
    and time, 39–41. *See also* essay 16
    of this volume

Bergson, Henri: the continuity of
    becoming, 39–42; "contraction"
    in sense perception, 66; criticism
    of Kant, 52; duration (*durée*), 39,
    132, 216; his eclipse as a
    philosopher, 129; on freedom and
    time, 40–41, 135; human freedom,
    30; the human person (*see* essay
    10 of this volume); intelligence
    and intuition, 38, 49–53, 57, 59,

JAMES W. FELT, S.J.,

is professor emeritus of Philosophy at Santa Clara University.

He has published a number of books, including

Human Knowing: A Prelude to Metaphysics

(University of Notre Dame Press, 2005) and

Aims: A Brief Metaphysics for Today

(University of Notre Dame Press, 2007).